Meer

VERMEER
PORTRAITS OF A LIFETIME

by

Lawrence R. Spencer

FIRST EDITION PUBLISHED 2009

ISBN: 978-0-557-04367-5

Meer

Vermeer:
Portraits of a Lifetime

Published by Lulu.com
USA

Books Published by Lawrence R. Spencer

∞ **The Oz Factors**

∞ **Pan, God of The Woods**

∞ **The Big Bleep: The Mystery of A Different Universe**

∞ **The Oracle of Pan**

∞ **Alien Interview** (Editor)

∞ **Vermeer: Portraits of A Lifetime**

Available at your favorite on-line bookstore.

For the best price and fastest shipping, order from the Publisher at:

http://www.lulu.com/pan

TABLE OF CONTENTS

Meer *Anthony, The Surveyor* (The Geographer)   (c. 1669)

Meer *Maria Vermeer Reading Mail* (Girl Reading a Letter)

Meer *The Faith of Maria Thins* (Allegory of Faith)

Meer *Holding Life In The Balance* (Woman Holding a Balance)

Meer *Mistress of The Light* (Young Woman with a Water Pitcher)

Meer *My Maria Mona Lisa* (The Milkmaid)

Meer *Elizabeth Vermeer: Turban and Kimono* (Girl with a Pearl Earring)

Meer *A Portrait of Beatrix Vermeer* (Study of a Young Woman)

Meer *Cornelia Vermeer Making Lace* (The Lacemaker)

Meer *Aleydis Vermeer Dressing Like Mother* (Woman with a Pearl Necklace)

Meer *Cornelia Vermeer, Musician* (Young Woman Seated at the Virginals)

Meer *Woman, Thou Art Beauty* (Woman in Blue Reading a Letter)

Meer *Elizabeth Vermeer: A China Hat* (Girl with a Flute)

Meer *Elizabeth Vermeer: A Fuzzy Red Hat* (Girl with a Red Hat)

Meer *Aleydis Vermeer, A Hidden Secret* (The Love Letter)

Meer *Maria Vermeer, Keeping Up Appearances* (Mistress and Maid)

Meer *Maria Vermeer Writing a Letter* (Lady Writing a Letter with her Maid)

Meer *Beatrix Vermeer Musing* (Woman with a Lute)

Meer *Cornelia Vermeer Playing Guitar* (The Guitar Player)

Meer *Aleydis & Cornelia Enjoying Music with A Friend* (The Concert)

Self-portraits of Johannes Vermeer
Many Faces Of Catharina Bolnes Vermeer
The Vermeer Daughters
Right Profiles of the Vermeer women
Left Profiles of the Vermeer women
Maria Thins: Grandmother and Patroness
Tanneke Everpoel, Live-In Servant
The Ability to Paint
Painting In One's Own Universe

APPENDIX:

A Lesson In Dutch Political / Economic History
The Guild of St. Luke: A Successful Education System
Contemporaries of Vermeer in the Guild of St. Luke
The Camera Obscura
Autopsy Of An Artist

FOOTNOTES

INTRODUCTION

Beauty and ugliness are an opinion of the observer. This book is dedicated to beings who think the paintings of Vermeer are beautiful.

My intention in writing this book is to help remove mysteries and misinformation about Vermeer. Our comprehension of his work, to be more complete, must be framed within the context of his life.

The greatest understandings in life come from assuming the point of view of that which on desires to know. To know cold is to be the cold, stop the cold and make it colder still. To know love is to love and be loved, at will. To know, one must occupy the identity of the thing, without becoming it. Make it breathe, walk, talk, think and sing!

Based on this premise, ***Vermeer: Portraits of a Lifetime*** is written from an empathetic point of view: I am pretending to be Vermeer. I invite you to be Vermeer with me. To know Vermeer, is to be Vermeer.

This book is dedicated to those who care to look and know for themselves, and not be told what to think by an "authority" or "critic". Art "critics" are notoriously unable to paint. They criticize paintings because they cannot be a painter or do what painters do. Painters do not criticize: they paint!

If one has not painted, one cannot possibly be able to confront or comprehend the nearly infinite number of technical and spiritual details required to create a painting. However, one can certainly admire it, or not. It is your opinion. But to say that the opinion of one person is more valid than the opinion of another person about whether or not beauty is beautiful to you, is the epitome of arrogance and stupidity.

There are no "reasons" for painting what one paints. To paint is to understand painting. There is no substitute. There is no "reason" for painting, other than to create an effect on oneself or an observer.

An artist emanates an aesthetic wave, from the spiritual essence of themselves, weather music, graphic, written, or performed: it is an inspiration, just as a god creates a universe. There is no reason. It is what it is. The technical quality of the creation, whether considered beautiful or not, is solely and only, the opinion of the observer.

I trust you will share being Vermeer with me: his joy, his grief, his loves, his agony, his family, his tragedy, his creations of beauty, his soul.

ABOUT THE BOOK COVER ART

The cover art for this book is an adaptation of paintings by Johannes Vermeer, designed and rendered artfully by Slavo Kotula. You can review his graphic designs, animations at http://www.slavoart.com, as well as his original music and guitar performances at http://www.slavomusic.com.

Images of Vermeer's wife and children from various of his paintings have been incorporated together to convey a more realistic likeness of Johannes and Catharina, who produced a total of 15 children together during their 22 years of marriage. All but 4 of the children survived to adulthood.

Catharina, and five of her daughters, Maria, Elizabeth, Cornelia, Alyedis and Beatrix, are the cast of players who posed in the artwork on the cover of this book. The devotion to his familial bevy of women, and the passionate affection with which he painted them, combined with his mythical technical skill, are the source of the light and life he endowed in his canvases.

We can not do him justice, but we can honor him, his family and his art.

-- Lawrence R. Spencer

DISCLAIMER

I am very sure that this book will be considered by many people to be delusional or heretical. Many will dismiss my observations and comments because they don't follow the dictates of "authoritative research" or the opinions of art "experts".

This book may threaten persons who have a financial vested interest in the Vermeer paintings that still exist today, as their livelihood or financial well-being depend to some degree on the value currently assigned to the paintings.

Although the monetary value of Vermeer's paintings have been vastly inflated, in part, due to the mystique created by authorities or speculators, it is not my intention to devaluate them. It is not my intention to invalidate property that was sold or bartered by Vermeer and his wife, Catharina, hundreds of years ago. Quite the contrary.

My intention is to honor the lives of Johannes, Catharina, their eleven surviving children and Maria Thins, his mother-in-law and patroness.

This book does not represent or endorse any financial, spiritual, religious, political organization or practice or philosophy of any kind. All personal observations and opinions offered by the author herein are purely and solely personal opinions, with no other source than those noted in the footnotes or appendix.

Any and all individuals or organizations from whom research and/or opinions have been borrowed or sited for referential purposes in this book are not affiliated with and do not in any way acknowledge the validity of or endorse the findings or assertions of the author or publisher of this book.

Finally, this book is not intended for people who have a vested interest, or who "know best". Personal observations, whether visual, empathetic or conjectural, of the author about the life and death of Vermeer, 300 years after the fact, are wholly subjective.

-- Lawrence R. Spencer, Author

ACKNOWLEDGEMENTS

One cannot offer sufficient praise to the *Essentialvermeer.com* which has become the internet's essential tool for exploring every facet of the life and work of the great 17th century Dutch painting master, Johannes Vermeer.

My most earnest thanks and appreciation for the tremendous labor of love provided to us by the author and webmaster Jonathan Janson.

If one were seeking to find Johannes Vermeer, reincarnated, in the present moment, one need not look any further. See for yourself at the website of his own paintings:

http://www.essentialvermeer.com/jonathan_janson/jonathan_janson.htm

Also my thanks to the very excellent research and writing about the life and times of Vermeer by Anthony Bailey, in his book: *A View of Delft, Vermeer Now and Then*, published in 2001.

A very conclusive study made by Philip Steadman, (*Vermeer's Camera: Uncovering the Truth Behind the Masterpieces*, Oxford, 2001) of paintings done by Vermeer using the *camera obscura* in his room at the house on *Oude Langendijk*, is indispensable to an understanding of technical qualities and perspectives achieved by Vermeer.

My thanks to many other persons, especially those who have done earlier studies of the life, times and works of Vermeer upon whom our current comprehension of him is built, which includes, most especially, the book by John Michael Montias, *Vermeer and His Milieu: A Web of Social History*.

Lawrence R. Spencer, Author

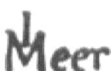

INSIGHTS INTO IMMORTALITY THROUGH THE MILLENNIA

Krishna - Bhagavad Gita (5th Century B.C.E. or earlier)

"Learn thou! the Life is, spreading life through all; It cannot anywhere, by any means, Be anywise diminished, stayed, or changed. But for these fleeting frames which it informs with spirit deathless, endless, infinite, They perish. Let them perish, Prince! and fight! He who shall say, "Lo! I have slain a man!" He who shall think, "Lo! I am slain!" Those both know naught! Life cannot slay. Life is not slain!"

Socrates

(469 BC–399 BC) Classical Greek philosopher.

"I am confident that there truly is such a thing as living again, that the living spring from the dead, and that the souls of the dead are in existence."

Origen (ca. 185–ca. 254) was an early Christian scholar, theologian, and one of the most distinguished of the early fathers of the Christian Church.)

"It can be shown that an incorporeal and reasonable being has life in itself independently of the body... then it is beyond a doubt bodies are only of secondary importance and arise from time to time to meet the varying conditions of reasonable creatures. Those who require bodies are clothed with them, and contrariwise, when fallen souls have lifted themselves up to better things their bodies are once more annihilated. They are ever vanishing and ever reappearing."

Voltaire
(21 November 1694 – 30 May 1778), Enlightenment writer and philosopher

"It is not more surprising to be born twice than once; everything in nature is resurrection."

Benjamin Franklin
(January 17, 1706 – April 17, 1790) was one of the Founding Fathers of the United States of America.

"I look upon death to be as necessary to the constitution as sleep. We shall rise refreshed in the morning." And, "Finding myself to exist in the world, I believe I shall, in some shape or other always exist."

Ralph Waldo Emerson
(May 25, 1803 – April 27, 1882) American essayist

"It is the secret of the world that all things subsist and do not die, but only retire a little from sight and afterwards return again. Nothing is dead; men feign themselves

dead, and endure mock funerals…and there they stand looking out of the window, sound and well, in some strange new disguise. The soul comes from without into the human body, as into a temporary abode, and it goes out of it anew it passes into other habitations, for the soul is immortal."

Walt Whitman

(May 31, 1819 – March 26, 1892) American poet

"I know I am deathless. No doubt I have died myself ten thousand times before. I laugh at what you call dissolution, and I know the amplitude of time."

Helena Blavatsky, Secret Doctrine, Vol. II, p. 424

(12 August 1831— May 8, 1891)

"That which is part of our souls is eternal. . . Those lives are countless, but the soul or spirit that animates us throughout these myriads of existences is the same; and though "the book and volume" of the physical brain may forget events within the scope of one terrestrial life, the bulk of collective recollections can never desert the divine soul within us. Its whispers may be too soft, the sound of its words too far off the plane perceived by our physical senses; yet the shadow of events that were, just as much as the shadow of the events that are to come, is within its perceptive powers, and is ever present before its mind's eye."

Herman Hesse

(2 July 1877—9 August 1962)

"He saw all these forms and faces in a thousand relationships become newly born. Each one was mortal, a passionate, painful example of all that is transitory. Yet none of them died, they only changed, were always reborn, continually had a new face: only time stood between one face and another."

Jack London, author, best known for book "Call of the Wild"

"I did not begin when I was born, nor when I was conceived. I have been growing, developing, through incalculable myriads of millenniums. All my previous selves have their voices, echoes, promptings in me. Oh, incalculable times again shall I be born."

Albert Schweitzer
(14 January, 1875 – 4 September, 1965) Alsatian theologian, who received the 1952 Nobel Peace Prize in 1953.

"Reincarnation contains a most comforting explanation of reality by means of which Indian thought surmounts difficulties which baffle the thinkers of Europe."

Mark Twain
(November 30, 1835 – April 21, 1910) American Author

"I have been born more times than anybody except Krishna."

Mahatma Gandhi
(2 October 1869 – 30 January 1948) leader of the Indian independence movement.

"I cannot think of permanent enmity between man and man, and believing as I do in the theory of reincarnation, I live in the hope that if not in this birth, in some other birth I shall be able to hug all of humanity in friendly embrace."

Henry Ford
(July 30, 1863 – April 7, 1947) Founder of the Ford Motor Company

"I adopted the theory of reincarnation when I was 26. Genius is experience. Some think to seem that it is a gift or talent, but it is the fruit of long experience in many lives. I am in exact accord with the belief of **Thomas Edison** *that spirit is immortal, that there is a continuing center of character in each personality. But I don't know what spirit is, nor matter either. I suspect they are forms of the same thing. I never could see anything in this reputed antagonism between spirit and matter. To me this is the most beautiful, the most satisfactory from a scientific standpoint, the most logical theory of life. For thirty years I have leaned toward the theory of Reincarnation. It seems a most reasonable philosophy and explains many things. No, I have no desire to know what, or who I was once; or what, or who, I shall be in the ages to come. This belief in immortality makes present living the more attractive. It gives you all the time there is. You will always be able to finish what you start. There is no fever or strain in such an outlook. We are here in life for one purpose—to get experience. We are all getting it, and we shall all use it somewhere."*

General George S. Patton
(November 11, 1885 – December 21, 1945) U.S. Army officer

"Through the travail of the ages,
Midst the pomp and toil of war,
Have I fought and strove and perished,
Countless times upon this star.

So as through a glass, and darkly
The age long strife I see
Where I fought in many guises,
Many names, - but always me."

PROLOGUE:

Recasting The Girl, Spray-Painting The Pearl

I will not soon forget seeing the horrendous Hollywood movie titled, *"The Girl With A Pearl Earring"* in 2004. It is a fictional depiction of a fictionalized relationship between Vermeer and an imagined *"...young peasant maid working in the house of painter Johannes Vermeer becomes his talented assistant and the model for one of his most famous works."* It was nominated for 3 Oscars by the Academy of Motion Picture "arts" and "sciences".

This tragically tacky spin on the life of Vermeer is classic Hollywood magic: take the true life story of a teen-age daughter of one of the finest painters in history, re-cast her as whore, and her father as an brutish ogre, spray-paint her naturally luminescent pearl earring with glitter glue and, presto! Nominate it for an Oscar!

Absurdly cliché characterizations contrived by the brain-dead writers invent a debased relationship between a fictional "peasant maid" and Vermeer that are typical of the money-motivated Hollywood swill fed to and gobbled up by an uneducated public. The socially redeeming value of this food for swine (to be polite) is a pile of steaming shit! Sexual intrigue may sell movie tickets, but pigs are stupid, and shit stinks.

The writers, producers and actors associated with this morose movie would have been more kind to Vermeer, his family and his artistic legacy if they had spent the budget for the film to visit the museums of the world, in which his priceless works hang, and spray them with graphic graffiti.

The film was written and directed without regard for historic fact or common sense. The preposterous personae of Vermeer was portrayed by the British actor, Colin Firth, with the charisma of a cardboard cereal box. Scarlett Johansson, who plays the role of the gawkish "girl", is garish at best.

The premise of the ludicrous book and movie script, entirely ignores and abuses the obvious, and thoroughly researched historical information about Vermeer and his life. A few of the grossest omissions are:

1) All of the women in the Vermeer paintings, with one or two minor exceptions, are his wife, and daughters. To postulate that he hired a "peasant maid", or that he had a painting assistant, much less that he had a sexual relationship with such an imaginary person, are sick, fictional contrivances.

2) That the Vermeers could afford to pay a servant, who could spare the time away from vitally needed chores, to become an artists assistant, is blatantly stupid. Household helpers were not something they could afford, except early in their marriage, at best. Some of the thoroughly researched facts about Vermeer were that he and his wife produced 15 children in 22 years! They lived in the small village of Delft, with his wife's very Catholic mother, in <u>her</u> small house, to help reduce expenses. He died from overwhelming depression due to his inability to support his wife and 11 surviving children, who were left in <u>extreme</u> <u>poverty</u> at his premature death at the age of 43.

In a plea to her creditors after her husband's death Catharina stated, in the public record, the final footnotes to Vermeer's brief life:

"during the ruinous war he not only was unable to sell any of his art but also, to his great detriment, was left sitting with the paintings of other masters that he was dealing in."

Catharina summarized the circumstances of his death: *"as a result and owing to the great burden of his children, having no means of his own, he had lapsed into such decay and decadence, which he had so taken to heart that, as if he had fallen into a frenzy, in a day or day and a half had gone from being healthy to being dead."*

Obviously, the man she describes is the antithesis of the man portrayed in the movie.

3) That a woman would be allowed to become an artists apprentice or assistant, is an absurd fantasy. It was forbidden by the Guild of St. Luke which maintained strict, Puritanical oversight of the activities of every member.

4) It is a documented fact that Maria Thins employed a live-in servant woman in her home in the later years of her life. *(Born ca. 1593 - died, December 27, 1680)* Maria was 82 years old when Vermeer died in 1675 at the age of 43. Her servant's name was Tanneke Everpoel. Maria bequeathed a small sum of money (20 guilders) to Tanneke upon her death. It is very likely that Tanneke is the servant shown in Vermeer's painting, " The Love Letter".

5) The girl in the legendary painting (as well as in several other of his paintings) is his second daughter, Elizabeth! Vermeer never hired models -- he painted only family and friends. It doesn't take a cosmetic surgeon to compare the features of the women in the majority of his paintings to observe that the same women are being painted in their own home, again and again in different poses, settings, lighting and clothing.

Most of his paintings feature his wife, Catharina, who was not only his constant accomplice in creating a family, she was his foremost ally in his life as an artist!

The paintings named (by others), "girl with a pearl earring", as well as "the girl with a red hat", and "the girl with a flute", and others, are all of his second daughter, Elizabeth, who was a teenager when they were painted. He used her as the model for a series of very small "tronie" or facial portraits, which were popular at the time.

These miniature "head shots" were especially well suited to the use of the camera obscura to create what we know now to have a photographic quality, rendering the light and perspective differently than the unaided lens of the human eye perceives it.

The women in his family, during his lifetime, enjoyed dressing in the finest clothes and jewelry available to them, as well as exotic costumes, imitating the apparel of mysterious lands. Many of the accessories included in these paintings were borrowed. Trading vessels often brought fascinated news and relics to Delft from around the world. He and his family rarely ventured more than a short walk or boat ride from home.

That Vermeer would have an elicit affair with a maid in his own home is an insult to common sense and decency. Anyone who looks at paintings of his wife and nine daughters can plainly see his obvious love and devotion -- if not obsession -- for the women in the small house they shared. Vermeer's family permeated every aspect of his life, and dominated his home.

His days were consumed with his work with the Guild of St. Luke, the militia of Delft, and interaction with other painters for whom, like his father before him, he sold their paintings to earn money to feed and clothe his 15 children. As his family grew, Vermeer barely had time work on his own paintings!

That there was ever any enmity or discord between Johannes and Catharina during their lives is a fantasy contrived by the Hollywood money machine that perverts reality to appeal to the lowest common denominator of prurient interest suitable only for soap operas, pornography, and girl-gossip magazines.

The self-proclaimed "artists" of Hollywood, driven by money mongers, like any mindless mercenary who act the part they're paid for, notoriously devoid of ethics or integrity, are akin to any common soldier who massacres innocent civilians, and justifies their crimes in the name of war.

Vermeer, in this movie, and in his own lifetime, was a victim of brainless brutality. The stupid soldiers of Louis XIV of France who invaded Holland, together with the bloody British aristocracy combined to murder peasants, and plunder goods to enrich and glorify themselves. The net result for Vermeer was attested, after his death, by his wife, Catharina Bolnes, *"during the ruinous war he not only was unable to sell any of his art but also, to his great detriment, was left sitting with the paintings of other masters that he was dealing in."* And further, *"as a result and owing to the great burden of his children, having no means of his own, he had lapsed into such decay and decadence, which he had so taken to heart that, as if he had fallen into a frenzy, in a day or day and a half had gone from being healthy to being dead."*

Let us hope, sincerely, that those unfortunates who saw this "ruinous movie" can assess for themselves the denigrating massacre of an artist by Hollywood, compared with his own biographical portraits of a lifetime and the family he adored, magnificently embodied in his paintings, to judge for themselves the aesthetic intention and ethical integrity of the man, Vermeer.

-- Lawrence R. Spencer

WHAT MAKES VERMEER PAINTINGS IMMORTAL?

W hy have the paintings of Johannes Vermeer intrigued, inspired and mystified so many for so long? It has been more than 300 years since the nearly anonymous "Sphinx of Delft" disappeared from the corporeal bond into the eternal ether of immortality.

There are several reasons for his lingering notoriety:

1) Timelessness

Only two of his surviving painting can be dated with certainty. Of the thirty-odd paintings that still exist, many are portraits of the women in his family. The women are primarily his own wife and daughters. On first inspection, this doesn't seem to be a problem. However, he and his wife, Catharina, gave life to 15 children in 22 years!

It is fairly certain, due to circumstantial documents, that his painting are made between 1653 and his death at age 43 in 1675. The family portraits, as it were, are spread over about 23 years, 11 surviving daughters, a wife, mother-in-law (with whom his family lived for at least 15 years) and miscellaneous, unidentifiable others.

The primary problem in identifying the women in the paintings is:

a) they look alike, because they're all related!

b) they all get a year older every year, so they never look exactly the same from one painting to the next! And, if this isn't complex enough, they are constantly changing poses, lighting, clothing, settings and hair styles.

Therefore, I have undertaken, in this book, to assign a sequence to the paintings of Vermeer **based on the appearance of the women** in them.

Using the known year of birth, of the eldest daughter (Maria) and subsequent sequence of births of the other Vermeer daughters who survived during the lifetime of the artist (till 1675), I have been able to divine a reasonable sequence for the Vermeer paintings. Extrapolating these dates is puzzle of appearances. How does a person look when they are 10 years old? How do they look 3 years later? What do they look like as an adult, compared to a childhood photo?

2) Unknown Origins

Like the Sphinx of Egypt, the paintings of Vermeer have very uncertain origins. Very little documentation exists concerning his life. A few signatures on public documents. A few signatures on paintings. Burial records. Membership in the Guild of St. Luke and the military. A few brief statements by his wife after his death. And, about 30 paintings, none of which was named or dated by the artist.

Like the Sphinx, no one knows for sure when it was built, who built it, or why it was built. Countless individuals have ventured endless assumptions, theories, opinions, arbitrary assessments, and educated guesses for thousands of years! The weight of all the books written about the Sphinx are greater than the weight of all it's sand stone blocks combined! Still, there is no agreement about any of the mysteries of the Sphinx.

Likewise, the life and paintings of Vermeer have too many unknowable, indefinable and undiscoverable aspects to enable any conclusive certainty to exist. In spite of the tomes written about him since his death in 1675, Vermeer remains essentially unknown after 334 years of study. This is one of the most important reasons for his lingering popularity!

3) Aesthetic: The Endowment of Life

Everyone loves a mystery. Everyone loves beauty. A mystery embodied in an aesthetic is irresistible. The women painted by Vermeer were not only beautiful, they are pristine, perfectly dressed and immaculate. The Vermeer women are endowed with, and embody the essence of the love that Vermeer felt for his own wife and children.

Passion quietly radiates from his pictures, not merely reflected light, canvas, layered varnish and pigments. Works of art, considered to be masterful; Michelangelo's statue of David, or the Mona Lisa, or Van Gogh's self portrait, are endowed with life by the artist!

The quality of aesthetics cannot be explained technically. Technical perfection can create an emotional impact on the viewer, but it is not aesthetic. It cannot be measured, tagged or catalogued. Beauty is beyond technique.

Aesthetics are the personal, subjective power to endow an essence of Life into objects. Art is the ability to bring life into being. It is an act of creating something from nothing. Aesthetics is the measurable, electronic wavelength that most closely approximates the immortal, spiritual essence of being. It is a quality, perceived by men, of the gods.

The dream of Mary Shelly's Doctor Frankenstein has been realized. The electric spark of life endowed and embodied in the faces of Vermeer paintings, continue to shine more than 300 years after their birth.

They're alive! They're alive! Their creator is Vermeer.

VERMEER'S STUDIO: A HOME FULL OF CHILDREN

Vermeer painted his pictures in his home. Before 1660 he lived with his wife in his father's home. Vermeer's 'The Little Street' shows the gable ends of two houses fronting onto a cobbled pavement and separated by two gateways. This shows a view at the rear of 'Mechelen', the inn on the Market Square owned by Vermeer's family. The evidence gathered by Dutch art historian, P.T.A. Swillens, (*Johannes Vermeer: Painter of Delft 1632-1675*, Utrecht, 1950), demonstrates that he painted the scene from a back window of the inn.

After 1660 he, his wife and 15 children (11 of whom survived infancy), lived in the home of his mother-in-law, Maria Thins, who had a large house on the *Oude Langendijk* in Delft.

Vermeer stayed at home most of his life. The longest journey he made away from Delft was a short trip to Amsterdam, only 60 kilometers away, near the end of his life.

You can view an excellent 3-dimensional model of the room Vermeer used to paint a great number of his paintings at the following website: *http://www.vermeerscamera.co.uk/3dhome.htm*

A very conclusive study made by Philip Steadman, (*Vermeer's Camera: Uncovering the Truth Behind the Masterpieces*, Oxford, 2001) of paintings done by Vermeer using the *camera obscura* in his room at the house on *Oude Langendijk*, shows the exact dimensions of the room and the position of his vantage point in each painting.   Example:

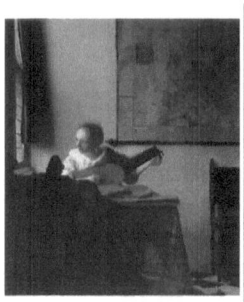

In "*Woman with a Lute*", the diagram at the right shows where Vermeer sat ("x") while painting, and the approximate scale of the room shown in this painting, i.e. "1 meter" measurement shown on the back wall.

1 metre

Exhaustive research conducted by a wide range of investigators during the 300 years since his death proves that Vermeer had no other studio outside of his home in which to paint.

The logical extension of this fact, inasmuch as Vermeer and his wife Catharina produced 15 children during his short life, what that he must have been constantly, and continually surrounded by his family in the house while he painted! By extrapolation, is it not obvious, even at the most casual investigation, that the most readily available models for his paintings would be his own family members?   This observation is compounded and ratified by the fact that nearly every one of his surviving paintings features young women as the principle model!

Therefore, it is reasonable to assume that Vermeer worked at home, and that he painted pictures of the women in his own family.

It is clearly documented that Vermeer had 5 daughters old enough to be the women shown in the paintings. Also, his wife and mother-in-law, are very likely candidates to be women shown in his paintings.

A very thorough comparison of the faces of each of the women shown in his paintings reveals the obvious observation that the same women are being painted again and again.

Further, Vermeer was relatively secure financially because of the support his was given by Maria Thins, his mother-in-law. His necessity for painting pictures for paying customers, most of his life, was relatively small when compared to the average Dutch portrait artists, like Rembrandt and many other who painted exclusively for clients.

Much speculation has been made as to why Vermeer seems to have painted relatively few pictures during his life (only 34 exist). Common sense dictates two fairly obvious answers to this question:

1) he didn't need to paint for a living, or so he thought, relative to other artists who painted hundreds of portraits for various patrons.

2) he painted at home, in a house FULL of children. If you have ever raised children of your own, you can easily imagine the constant cacophony of noise, the messes, the daily chores, childhood illnesses, household repairs, and demands for attention that 15 children can make on adults all living under one roof!

How could anyone get any work done under these circumstances? Much less painting, which is a very, very detail-oriented discipline requiring a lot of time, uninterrupted concentration and patience. Traditionally, men were not required to manage the affairs of the Dutch household, do laundry, cook, clean, mend and scrub. These were the duties of women. However, 15 children can disrupt and demand that the usual domestic division of labor be abandoned, for the sake of order, sanity and survival!

How much work do you image Vermeer would have been required to do around the house? How much of his time would his children consume?

How often would a sick child require his help? The pregnancy of his wife, which was almost <u>constant</u> during his life, must have made demands on him to help while she was indisposed with newborn babies. How could Vermeer possibly have had a good nights sleep on the average with restless, crying or sick children in the room? Who did the 2:00 o'clock feedings? What about family outings? Certainly the death of a one of his children, 4 of whom died as infants, would have been devastating to him and very disruptive to usual routines.

Nonetheless, I have assumed, because of the obvious technical mastery of Vermeer to observe and meticulously duplicate reality in his paintings, that the features of the persons he used as models are faithful to their actual appearance at the time each painting was done.

Apparently Vermeer was not a "portrait painter", as were many of his contemporaries in the Golden Age of Dutch art. There is no evidence that he ever painted a portrait of a paying customer, with the possible exception of Anthony van Leeuwenhoek. (*The Geographer* and *The Astronomer.*) Even here, there is no documentation that Vermeer was paid to paint these, or that the model is actually van Leeuwenhoek (in spite of all of the visual evidence and common sense to the contrary).

Therefore, one must also take into consideration the "artistic license", if any, of the artist in rendering a careful portrait of the model. Other important factors that influence the accuracy of each portrait are: the lighting of the painting, the age of the model, the position of the model relative to the light source and to the painter, the pose of the model, and the intended purpose of the painting.

A comparative analysis of the transitional appearance of persons shown in portraits, according to date of the painting, age of the model, the pose, clothing, and lighting of the model, can be seen in the following example:

WHO ARE THESE MEN?

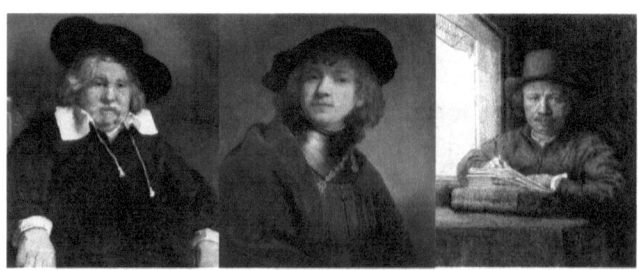

This book will examine the following questions:

1) Which members of Vermeer's family are shown in his paintings?

2) What are the names and ages of the models in his paintings?

3) Based on documented records of his life, and of his family members, what is the sequence in which the Vermeer paintings were produced?

The answer to the question above, "Who Are These Men?" becomes obvious when the portraits are arranged in the correct sequence.

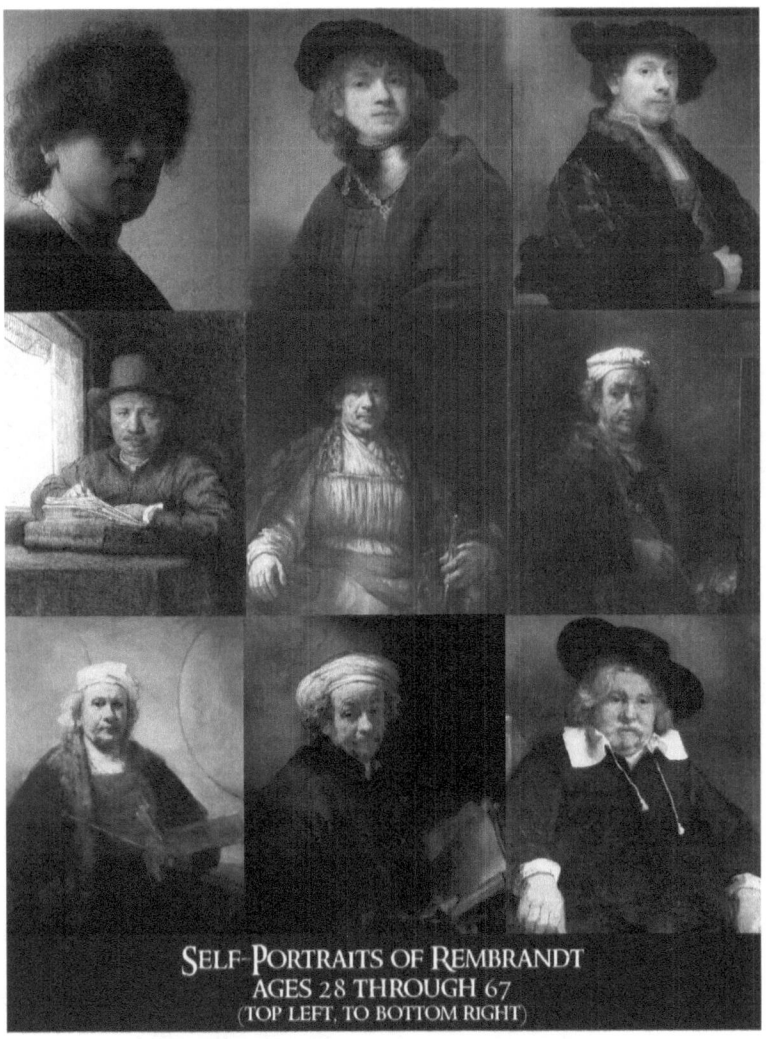

SELF-PORTRAITS OF REMBRANDT
AGES 28 THROUGH 67
(TOP LEFT, TO BOTTOM RIGHT)

**Rembrandt Harmensz van Rijn
Leiden 1606 - Amsterdam 1669**

A NOTE ABOUT TITLES and DATES ASSIGNED TO
PAINTING ATTRIBUTED TO VERMEER:

TITLES:

Over the years, scholars and museums have given a number of different titles to each of Vermeer's paintings. For the sake of uniformity, the titles which appear in Arthur K. Wheelock's catalogue on pages 169 to 186 of his book, "*Vermeer and the Art of Painting*", are sited as the "traditional titles" in this text.

No titles were assigned by Vermeer to any of his paintings.

DATING:

Only two of Vermeer's paintings were dated by his own hand.

The dates traditionally assigned to the paintings are a distillation of those estimated by Vermeer scholars. There is no signatures or documentation assigned by Vermeer himself, or any circumstantial documentation that affirms the actual date on any of Vermeer's paintings other than "The Procuress", and "The Astronomer".

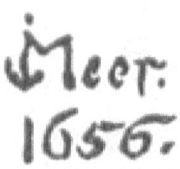

APPROXIMATE SEQUENCE OF PAINTINGS BY VERMEER BASED ON AGES OF FAMILY MEMBERS

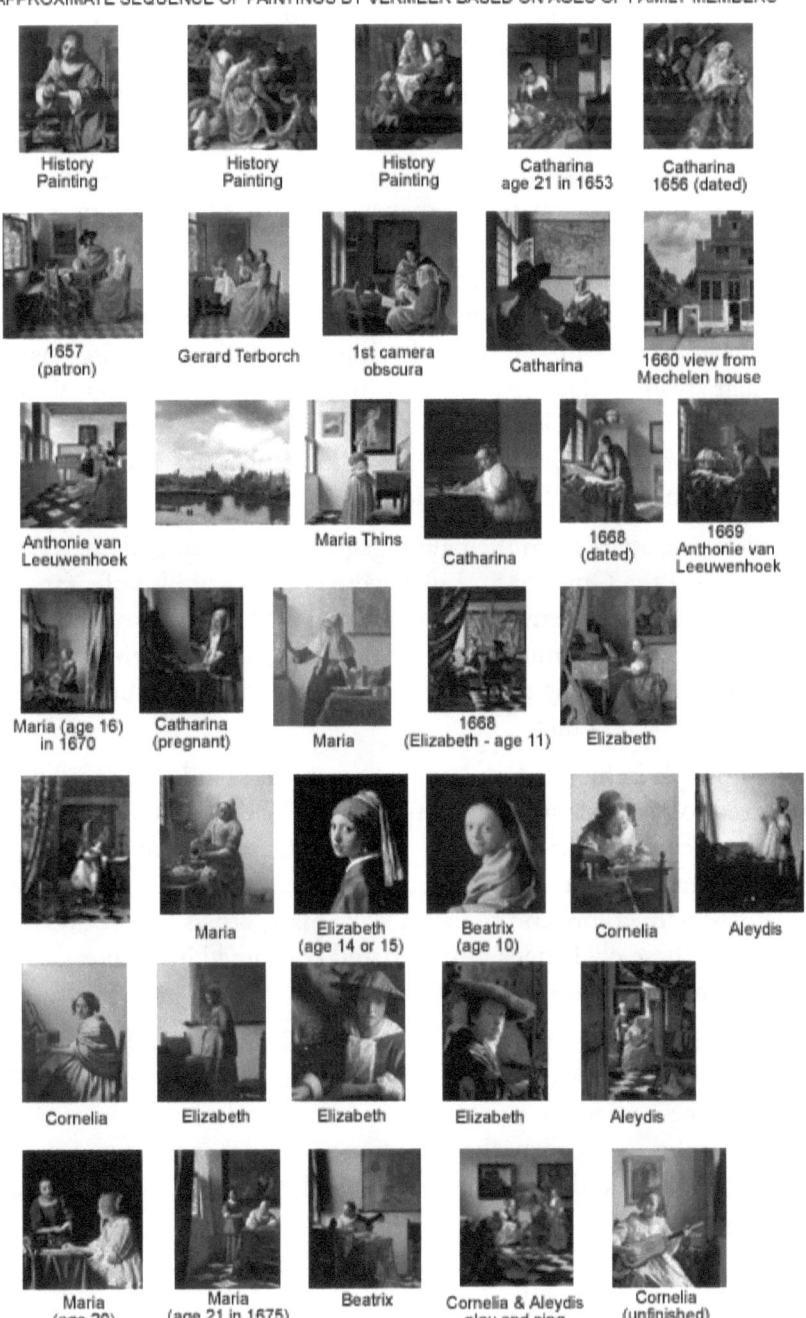

History Painting

History Painting

History Painting

Catharina age 21 in 1653

Catharina 1656 (dated)

1657 (patron)

Gerard Terborch

1st camera obscura

Catharina

1660 view from Mechelen house

Anthonie van Leeuwenhoek

Maria Thins

Catharina

1668 (dated)

1669 Anthonie van Leeuwenhoek

Maria (age 16) in 1670

Catharina (pregnant)

Maria

1668 (Elizabeth - age 11)

Elizabeth

Maria

Elizabeth (age 14 or 15)

Beatrix (age 10)

Cornelia

Aleydis

Cornelia

Elizabeth

Elizabeth

Elizabeth

Aleydis

Maria (age 20)

Maria (age 21 in 1675)

Beatrix

Cornelia & Aleydis play and sing

Cornelia (unfinished)

AN EMPATHETIC EXPLORATION OF VERMEER'S LIFE

Paintings of Johannes Vermeer exhort a mystic awe in the human soul. Aesthetics, women and mystery are each a glue that have baited many of the most powerful traps in history. Vermeer combines all three. Almost nothing factual is known about the painter personally, or the bevy of enchanting women he painted.

Compounding the mystery is the puzzle of identifying the people he painted so repetitively. Apparently, they were nearly all his wife or daughters! Moreover, they were portrayed at various ages in their lives, over a span of twenty-two years during which he and his wife produced an family of 15 children, 11 of whom survived! As a consequence of their common genetic similarities in their physical appearance, they also shared clothing, hair styles, and jewelry. Add to this monochromatic puzzle are identical rooms, windows, lighting, furniture, fixtures and the themes surrounding them. The resulting maelstrom of similarities make differentiating one person from another a near impossibility.

Most of his work, apart from the paintings produced during his six year apprenticeship at the Guild of St. Luke, were portraits of his wife, family and a few close friends. Vermeer never painted his family members, or his self-portrait, with the intention of selling them, any more than you and I would think of selling photographs or home videos of the members of our own family.

He painted people in his surroundings that were close at hand, familiar, and endeared to him. Mostly he painted for the love of aesthetics, and to innovate the technology of painting -- to discover new techniques to more exactly render the myriad subtleties of light, and to endow love, and life on canvas, with colors and brushes. Like many artists before and after Vermeer, these challenges intrigued and consumed his interest, intellect and spiritual passion.

Apparently, during his own life, it never occurred to him that anyone would be interested in paying money for many of his paintings. Most of his paintings were still in the possession of his wife when he died prematurely at the age of forty-three! Astoundingly, they were never sold, even though he and his family were literally starving from the want of money to buy food!

According to the research of Vermeer scholar, Anthony Bailey, the value of Dutch money was as follows: "...a Dutch cloth-worker in 1642 got eighteen **stuivers** a day; there were twenty stuivers to one **guilder**, and a 6-pound loaf of rye bread coast about four and a half stuivers...".

Imagine his shock and dismay to discover, 300 years later, that his paintings are worth many millions of dollars! Yet, during his own lifetime, he never earned enough from them to feed his family, and indeed, died from an overwhelming bought of depression because of it.

These facts confound comprehensive and compound the mystery of Vermeer.

In this book, I propose to travel this impossible labyrinth, to discover the long-hidden key to ancient riddles: Who were the people painted by Vermeer? Who was Vermeer, the artist and the man?

As though this were not daunting enough, I propose to do this, in part, by leaping the abyss of 300 years from the present year of 2008, returning through my own experience as an artist, a father, a husband and a man, through my own, personal life experiences, to re-experience the life of Vermeer, as though it were my own!

I do not claim that I am or was Vermeer. Such an assertion would be entirely subjective, impossible to prove, and irrelevant. As do myriad other people fascinated by his art and his life, I have a good deal of personal empathy and common life experiences that I share with this obscure man, as a father, as a parent, as an artist and as a spiritual being. I intend to employ this empathy as a tool of investigation and discovery: just as one might use a divining rod to seek out water in the desert.

As a lost dog uses native intuition to find it's way home, I am searching for a lost self. As a tourist in Italy feels a sense of *deja vu* when visiting the Coliseum in Rome: one can almost *smell* the roar of blood spattering on the sand, and *reel* at the lust for pain and death oozing from the crowd! And *thrill* as a blade slashes and vomits entrails to the ground. The spirit *writhing* to be free of a mangled corpse crumpled in the dust.

I yearn to recover a lost identity. Vermeer.

Does the intervening distance of time make a difference in this investigation? Let me propose that time is only an arbitrary measurement of the movement of objects through space that has no effect or relevance here.

Has time changed the emotions of love, lust or hatred in ten thousand years?

When struck in the heart by a spear, does a great-great grandson not bleed just as profusely now as when his ancestor was struck down on a ancient battlefield?

Were the tears shed and anguish suffered over the dead child of our mother's, mother's, mother any less real than our own in the eternal now?

If I experience what another man has experienced, am I not, to that degree, that man myself? If I am willing to invade, permeate and <u>be</u> that experience, and to assume responsibility for it, is it not my own?

My experiment is to <u>be</u> Vermeer. That is, to return to his life and time to experience <u>his</u> existence from the perspective of subjective emotional, artistic, and spiritual experience in present time. To this degree, ***I am Vermeer***.

To the degree that you re-experience his life with me, ***you are Vermeer***. In truth, Any Man who is willing to be Vermeer, is, to that degree, Every Man.

Therefore, to fully implement the effect of the experiment described herein, much of the text of this book, unless otherwise sited, is **written in the first person, subjective**: speaking <u>as</u> Vermeer, about myself.

EVERY PICTURE HAS A STORY

(NOTE: New Titles have been given to each painting by the Author to differentiate Models and Themes from the names assigned to the paintings in ages past by others.)

A History Painting of Saint Praxedis

oil on canvas (signed and dated 1655)
101.6 x 82.6 cm.(40 x 32 1/2 in.)

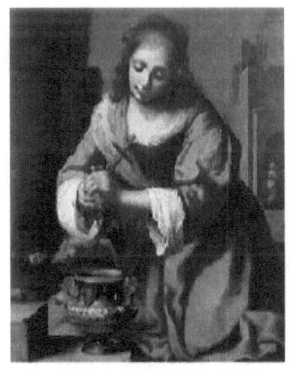

In order to complete an apprenticeship as a young artist, and gain the status of "master" painter, one must demonstrate virtuosity in the myriad, fundamental skills required of the trade. An artisan, worthy of a wage or commission, must demonstrate that he can paint as well, or better, than a forbearer who has already attained the status of master painter, even if only to copy the original work of another. Thus, the purpose of this painting, which has no particular aesthetic appeal, and is not a subject that one would choose to paint, if left to personal preferences. [1] (FOOTNOTE)

One might ask why a person from a Protestant family would copy a picture of such obvious Catholic content? Apart from the reason given above, there was another motivation: Love.

Growing up on the market place in Delft, I could scarcely avoid making the acquaintance of Catharina Bolnes. I was greatly enamored of her from the start. Her virginal and virtuous beauty, and my eagerness to marry made a volatile combination! She lived with her mother, a devote Catholic, across the market place, only a few paces from our house. My father, having recently passed away, left me with the responsibility of supporting myself and my mother, in his place, as an inn keeper and art dealer. Although reputable enough, it was antipathetic to my career aspirations as an artist, for which I had spent my formative years in preparation, and for which I had shown great promise.

Marriage to Catharina, with the attendant advantage of her higher social station, and the greater wealth of her mother, overshadowed my reluctance to avow myself to the Catholic faith, in order to win her hand. This painting was motivated, in part, as a demonstration to Maria Thins of my genuine intentions toward her daughter, and their faith.

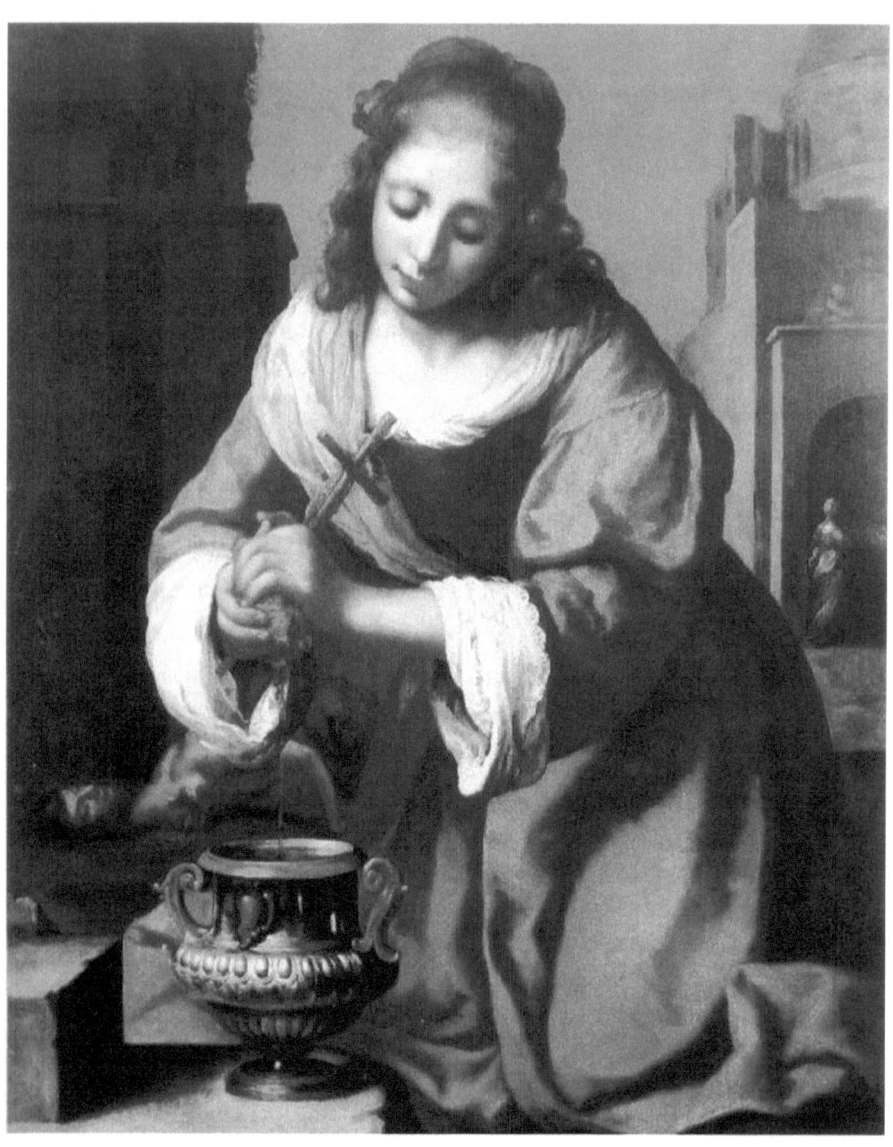

The Hunting Goddess

DIANA AND HER COMPANIONS
oil on canvas
38 1/4 x 41 3/8 in. (98.5 x 105 cm.)

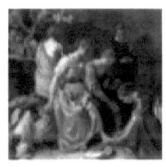

Diana and her ladies, or nymphs, are facially non-descript. The perspective of the footbath is incorrect. However, it is not a bad painting for a student artist, which was the case when I painted it. I was serving my apprenticeship at the [II] (FOOTNOTE) Guild of St. Luke when it was finished.

In many other paintings of Artemis, [III] (FOOTNOTE) she is portrayed as buxom, rotund and robust!   And, almost always naked. At the time I was a young groom. I thought that I dared not offend the tender sensibilities of my bride and her Catholic mother. Little did I know that Catharina was anything but shy. Quite to contrary, as the 15 children she bore are a testament! Further, nudity was not endorsed in polite Dutch society, principally by the wives of husbands who happily endorsed legal prostitution!

Diana is the Roman name for one of the panoply of gods stolen from the Greeks. In this case, Diana, or Artemis, is the Goddess of the hunt, Daughter of Zeus, supreme among the gods. In those days, mythology was actually read, by some, and suppressed heavily by the Roman Catholic Church.

The Church usurped their followers, burned their temples and destroyed the gods of what had been the state religion of Rome, until it became politically inconvenient for Emperor Justinian in the East, where the "pagan" gods were lesser known. He decreed that they were defunct! Justinian and his circus whore bride, were as debased a pair of degenerates as ever existed! They outlawed "pagan" mythology, the foundations of our world, which had existed for thousands of years, because it did not serve their own political and financial purposes.

This painting was an attempt a "history" painting, a popular genre at the time. However, this is not a good of example of that genre, or of painting, for that matter. The subjects, trees and background appear to be a copy of an classic Renaissance, the most obvious departure from which is the fact that the part of Diana, in the painting, is played by my pregnant wife!

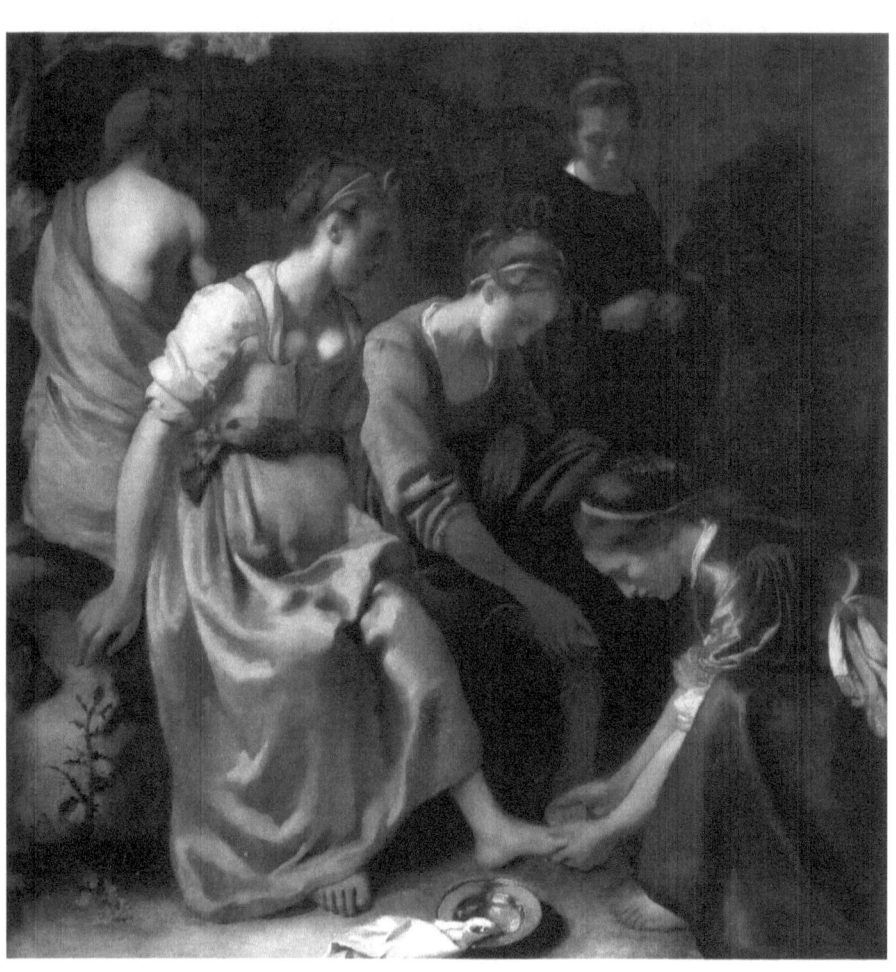

Jesus Served

CHRIST IN THE HOUSE OF MARTHA AND MARY
oil on canvas
63 x 53 7/8 in. (160 x 142 cm.)

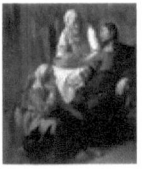

Another "apprentice painting", completed while I was being interned and educated in my craft. We were expected to paint pictures of classical themes, as one was expected to demonstrate the ability emulate earlier masters, as well as learning to paint pictures that would sell. The entire point of spending six years being tutored by master painters was to learn enough to earn a living as an artisan. Painters, in that day, were considered to be craftsman or artisans. Painting was not an craft that was elevated above other artisans who were members of the Guild of St. Luke.

Carl Fabritius
as Christ

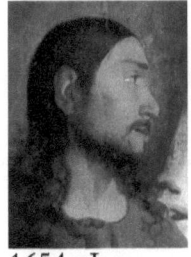

Carl Fabritius
Self-portrait

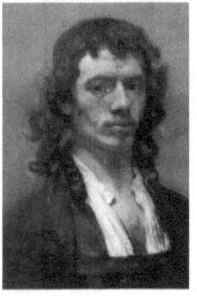

My friend, tutor and fellow artist, Carl Fabritius, IV (FOOTNOTE)

from whom I learned a great deal about painting, sat for me as a model for the part of Jesus. He was a scruffy fellow, in appearance, but, for me, no finer friend or artist existed. When he died in the explosion of the armory in Delft, near his house, in 1654, I was very much distressed and will always regret his loss at too early an age.

Carl worked in the studio of the great master, Rembrandt in Amsterdam before moving to Delft to be with his new wife, and had already been with the Guild of St. Luke for 4 years before his tragic death. I was my good luck to benefit from his friendship and knowledge of painting.

The painting itself, is a copy of an earlier master, I thought might influence Maria Thins to grant me permission to marry Catharina, as she was a strong Catholic. This theme features two ladies in an intimate dialogue with a man, who they trusted and revered above all others.

As a Protestant, I was forbidden by the laws of the Catholic Church to marry a Catholic person, unless I first converted to their faith. I did this gladly, as I had no pressing conviction or motivation to do otherwise. Marriage was a far more compelling justification for membership in a Church than ascribing to an organizational dogma, which to me were virtually the same, though not without political distinctions.

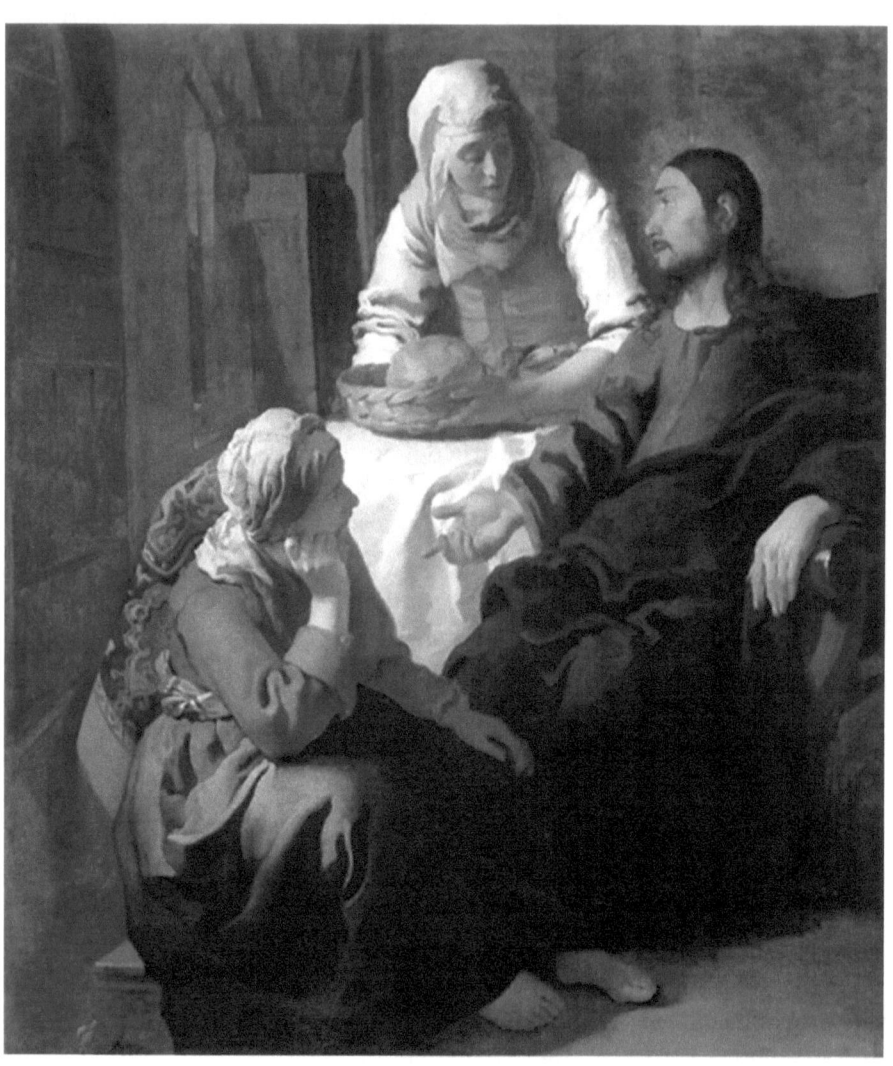

Catharina, Exhausted

A MAID ASLEEP
oil on canvas
34 1/2 x 30 1/8 in. (87.6 x 76.5 cm)

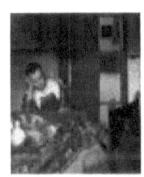

A new bride, Catharina Bolnes, exhausted by her daily chores, even in her youth, sleeps sitting at a table. The old saying, "a woman's work is never done" can not have been more accurate in 17th century Holland! Girls were raised by their mothers to become good wives, mothers and domestic laborers.

With none of the modern conveniences, taken from granted in the Western world in the 21st century -- especially everything that is driven by electricity -- manual labor was the only choice. Muscles, sweat, endurance and an indefatigable will to survive were to only tools available.

If one was wealthy enough to use the muscles of others, so much the better. This, however, was not the case with the Vermeer family. Even while they lived with Maria Thins, Catharina's mother, [V] (FOOTNOTE) whose cash reserve provided some convenience, their growing herd of children demanded and consumed every resource and effort they could provide.

Historically, marriage and motherhood have been the preeminent survival goal for females for millennia. This assumes that an honest, hardworking, loving, loyal man will defend her, care for her financial needs and that of her children. Usually, this exchange of "housekeeping services" for love, lodging and larder, completes the circle of survival wherein each new fledgling can be propagated, nurtured, educated and flung into the cold, cruel world, to begin this process anew, on their own.

In that age, as in any, for the working class, life is a desperate dash from day to day to conquer disease, starvation, weather and age. In a universe of energy and space only eternal time wins the race. All others keep pace as long as they can, only to finish last eventually. We are driven by a desire to enjoy some pleasant scenery and sensation along the way.

In this case I turned Catharina's sleep time into my painting time so that both interests could be served simultaneously. This was one of many modeling jobs she did with me during our marriage.

The hours we spent together as Catharina posed, were also the hours we afforded ourselves to share private conversation and personal confidences -- without the children! This arrangement enabled us to maximize our time, working and visiting simultaneously.

Maria Thins, and later, my older daughters, baby-sat the younger children on sunny days, while Catharina, and later, one of my older daughters, sat for a painting. She did not have much free time away from household duties. I also had my duties with the Guild, or with trading in the paintings of other artists to earn money for bread.

These painting sessions were done during pleasant weather to take advantage of the light, and the temperature in the room. It was almost always too cold to paint during the winter, as heating fuel was very expensive and primarily reserved for cooking.

These precious few painting sessions together with Catharina were a foundation of the communication, especially during the early years of our marriage. As I concentrated on rendering the tedious details of the painting, she would talk to me. She told me about the children, their activities, and anecdotes about them: comical things they did or said. She would discuss her concerns about each of them, and her dreams for them.

Catharina, whose universe was consumed by domestic details in our home, shared her world with me during our painting time together, including the gossip of women she heard in the market. A thousand minutia of domesticity droned from her during those hours. I listened with partial attention, but always with a bemused interest that made me feel as though I shared some responsibility for the household, at least to the degree that I was informed about them.

My actual participation in the daily chores was usually limited to heavy tasks of carrying or attending to affairs outside the home that required walking a great distance. More often my assistance was given to helping Maria Thins tend to the needs of the children while Catharina was ill or indisposed with child birth -- which was intermittent, but frequent, as we produced 15 children together during our 22 years of marriage.

VI (FOOTNOTE)

Unfortunately, as our family grew, the hours of free time Catharina could devote to serving as my model grew proportionately fewer. The demands of caring for a large, growing family, even with the help of Maria Thins, and our older daughters, were constant, to say the least!

As my daughters grew up, I used them more frequently as my models, as the demands on their time were less than that of their mother. My older daughters, -- Maria, Elizabeth, Cornelia, Aleydis and Beatrix -- all became accomplished models. Even Maria Thins sat for me on occasion.

The other children where too young to sit still patiently, so none of them were included. Ordinarily, I did not paint any of the girls until they were at least 12 years old or so, as my methods demanded long hours of patient posing. The pose must be very carefully duplicated from one day to the next or from one painting session to the next, in spite of an under drawing made on the canvas as seen through the lens of the camera obscura. [VII] (FOOTNOTE)

Painting sessions were not conducted on consecutive days, necessarily. Changes in the weather which affected the lighting in my atelier, the demands of the household, my duties at the Guild, my work at selling the paintings of others, social engagements, and any number of disruptions, prevented a rigid daily routine.

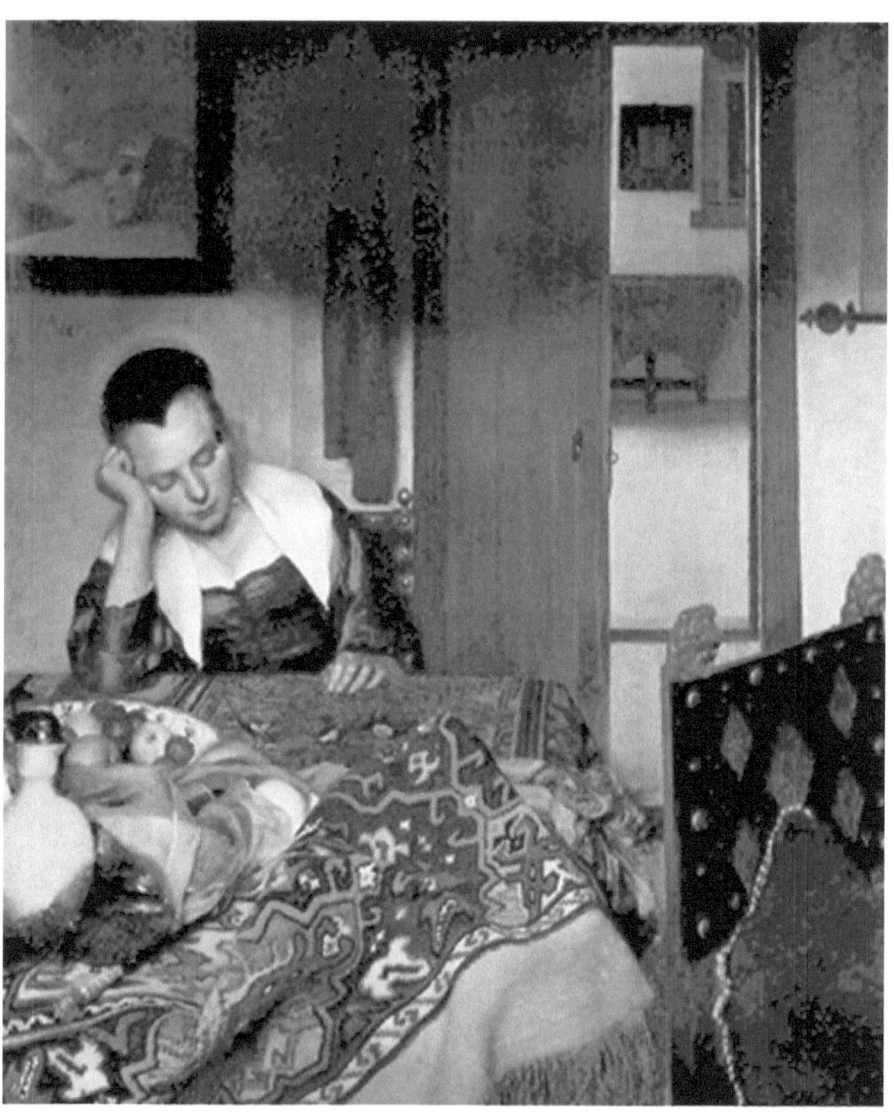

The Procurers of My Wife

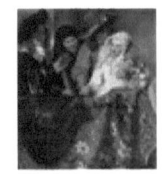

THE PROCURESS
oil on canvas (signed and dated 1656)
56 1/2 x 51 1/8 in. (143 x 130 cm.)

A scene commonly painted by Dutch artists during the 17th century, where prostitution was legal and sexual favors could be purchased forthrightly, without as much negative social stigma or modesty is may be required in the 21st Century, was that of a "procuress", and her whore, or escort.

The young lady in the painting, as with most of the paintings in which I feature a young woman, is the love of my life, my wife, and the mother of 15 children, Catharina Bolnes. When this was painted we had been married about 3 years, with one daughter, Maria. She was pregnant with our second daughter, Elizabeth, when this was painted.

Before our marriage, there had been considerable discussion between my representatives, myself, Catharina and her mother, Maria Thins, as to my true intentions toward her. I had no money or livelihood through which to support Catharina, except the promise of my good faith and potential as a young artist. Maria Thins was a woman of financial means, beyond my economic and social status.

At last, I won the begrudging permission of her mother to marry her oldest daughter. From that time forth, it was a joke between my wife and I as to whether I wanted her for love, or for money. This painting makes light of the question. In fact, I was love struck at first sight, and remained so all my life!

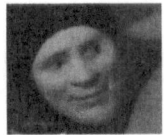

Two of my closest friends, and before me, friends of my father, served as emissaries on my behalf to seek the hand

Leonaert Bramer

Captain Bartolomeus Melling

of Catharina from her mother, Maria Thins. One, a fellow painter, Leonaert Bramer (left) from The Guild of St. Luke, [VIII] (FOOTNOTE) and the other, Captain Bartolomeus Melling, (right) a sea captain, were my servants on this merciful mission. In actual fact, they filled the role of "procurer" for me. I would not have stood the trial of gaining permission to marry Catharina on my own!

Leonaert was the best known painter in Delft. He was 34 years my senior. He had traveled extensively through Italy and France. He was my mentor, especially as regards my classical studies in painting, as well as friend, while I learned my trade. Leonaert, is shown in the painting, dressed in the garb of a madam, in an attempt to disguise his obviously masculine features.

My friend, Captain Melling, who is shown in this picture posing in military coat and sash, had sailed across half a world to far way Brazil, and became an officer and standard-bearer with the States-General, or militia.

Since they had both spoken so persuasively, as my ecumenical emissaries -- Captain Melling was a Protestant, and Leonaert was Catholic -- to Maria Thins, who better to pose for this painting than my actual champions?! Of course, I added myself to the festivities, toasting the acquisition of the Love of My Life. Thus, the painting is a playful, yet accurate, parody of actual events!

Both men were well traveled, tough and roughish fellows, who delighted in the joke. Catharina, the focus of the charade, was, as always, good humored. The least I could do to repay both men for their considerable efforts on my behalf was to immortalize them in paint.

I was careful to paint Catharina, as my model for the object of sexual desire, fully clothed, rather than with breasts revealed, as was usually done in other paintings of this theme. I don't like to exhibit myself in my own paintings as a rule, but since I was a principle player in this piece, I necessarily included myself.

I am dressed in my "Sunday Best" in the picture. Personally, I never had much money and didn't really desire a wardrobe of more than essential clothing, for the most part. This shirt, with the slitted sleeves, and the beret, looks artistic, although it was very much out of fashion at the time. I wore the same clothes in a later painting of myself seated at the easel painting a portrait of my daughter, Elizabeth.

As for the painting itself, the theme was chosen as an adaptation of a painting of the same title and subject matter owned by Maria Thins. She had a collection of paintings in her home that I often used as background content in many of my own. Moreover, at this stage of my painting career, I arranged the objects of the painting to provide myself with certain technical challenges that I did not enjoy during my years of apprenticeship.

The variety of objects, texture of fabrics, faces of live subjects, including myself, the lighting and the perspective were a wonderful combination of challenges to my ability to observe and faithfully render with my brushes and paints.

Observation the most fundamental skill of painting. One must force oneself to see what is there in the greatest detail. It is to easy to assume, or imagine, that one sees a thing. An object, when painted on a canvas, is proof of whether or not you have accurately observed.

In order to duplicate reality on a canvas, one must first and foremost, force oneself to see it! This patient discipline of observation is the foundation of painting. The artist may choose, for the sake of personal creativity, to alter an object once observed to suite a vision or communicate more effectively, but one must faithfully confront the thousand tiny details, in order to convey a concept effectively.

The technical ability of the artist, alone, can create a significant emotional impact on the observer. Conversely, the failure to confront what is, prevents technical accuracy. My fellow masters of Dutch art demonstrated the ability to convert a scene of dingy simplicity into glowing objects of art. Observation was the oyster shell they used to convert a gain of ordinary sand into priceless pearls of painting!

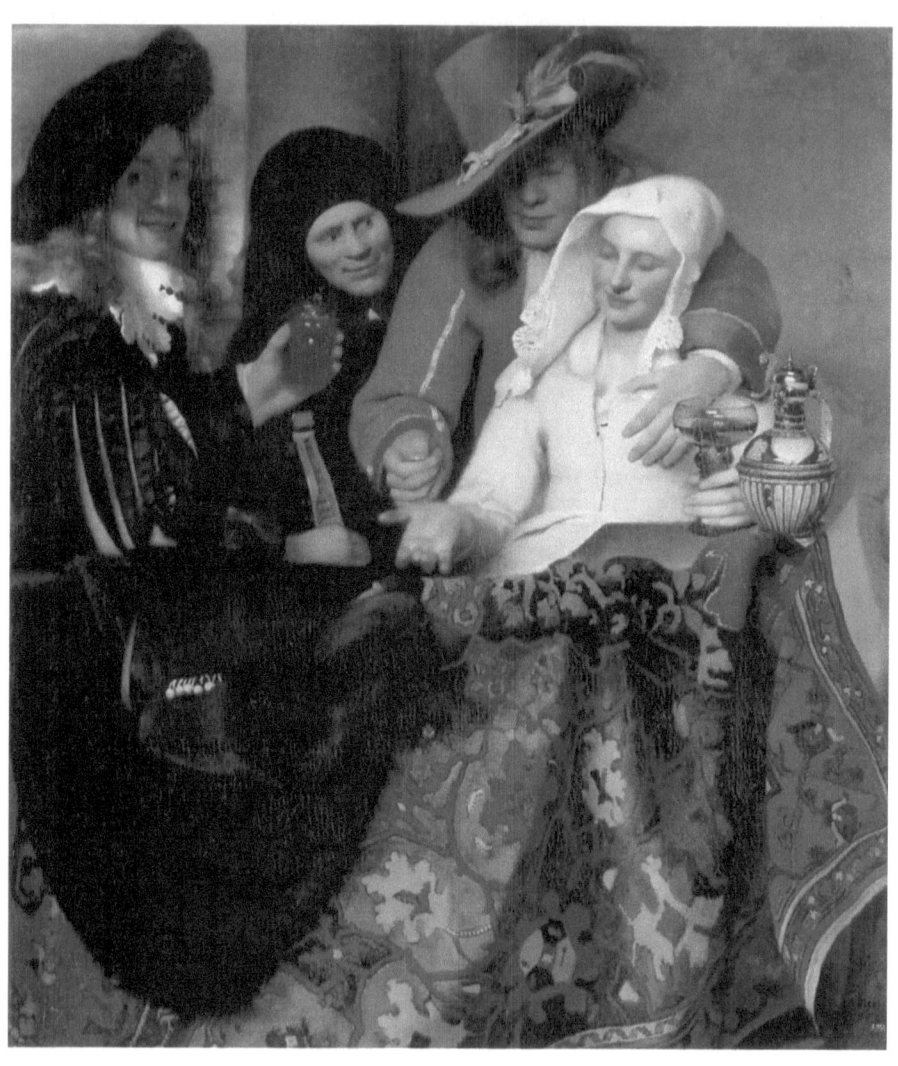

Portrait for A Patron

THE GLASS OF WINE
oil on canvas

25 1/8 x 30 1/4 in. (65 x 77 cm.)

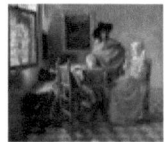

Symbolic significance has been assigned to the coat of arms in the window, I learned by reading the research of others. It is that of the female figure who personifies *Temperance*. She holds a level and bridle, bearing the admonition, *"The heart knows not how to observe moderation and applies reins to feelings when struck by desire."* This was painted at the request of my friend and patron, Pieter van Ruijven, to decorate his own home.

Pieter, and Catharina, posed for this very subdued version of another painting, titled by others, "The Girl With A Glass Of Wine." As you can see, he was a handsome, dashing fellow. His family brewery gave him the means to patronize my work. (Beer is good for more than drinking!) It was he who supplied the very fine dress Catharina wears in this piece. Of course he also loaned the glass window for the occasion, and the side-board underneath.

Since we had already hung the stained glass window, I used it for a second portrait: one that suited my own, less subdued, taste for artistic license and social blasphemy.

There is nothing especially striking or challenging in this painting. Although well done technically, it was done as a mercenary, rather than for love or for the sake of art. Painting for money, although often a necessity, was not an inspiration to me. Money is a base motivation. Aesthetics, love, honor and self-integrity are far more relevant to the soul of an artist, or any other being, for that matter.

Nonetheless, one must eat, if one insists on enjoying a body of flesh. So, most of the pictures I painted were intended for van Ruijven. He paid me well, while allowing the freedom to paint compositions of my own choice, provided they featured scenes of fashionable, contemporary life. He had no interest in history paintings, and as a protestant, was antipathetic to traditional religious themes. The support of my family by Maria Thins further enabled me the luxury to paint according to me will, rather than those dictated by the needs of a merchant or the whim of consumers.

In addition to which, I sold the paintings of other masters to supplement my own income, a trade I learned from my father. This I enjoyed greatly as I was thereby enabled to access the paintings of others. Everyone needed to sell their work, and a knowledgeable sales people were not commonly available for such work.

Both of inns my father owned and managed, wherein spent my formative years near the market square in Delft, were perfectly suited to learn the tricks and talk of the picture trade. The walls were continually covered with popular paintings of the day, affordable to the common class of men who frequented the inn for food and drink.

After my apprenticeship as an artist, having proven myself as a master in my own right, I had the great advantage of being able to demonstrate my knowledge of art to patricians and dealers alike. Further, I served several times in an official capacity at the Guild of St. Luke which secured and protected my rights from outside competitors, at least as an artist and dealer in the city of Delft, but not from those around and about.

As a young artist starting out, I imagined that I could have made a better arrangement for myself, which proved, for the most part of my life, to be true. Contentment, a condition though comfortable and calm, is not a permanent state, not even for a cow. Time changes the circumstances of one's life. All that lives will eventually be dead. It is our quest and reward to enjoy the intervening moments.

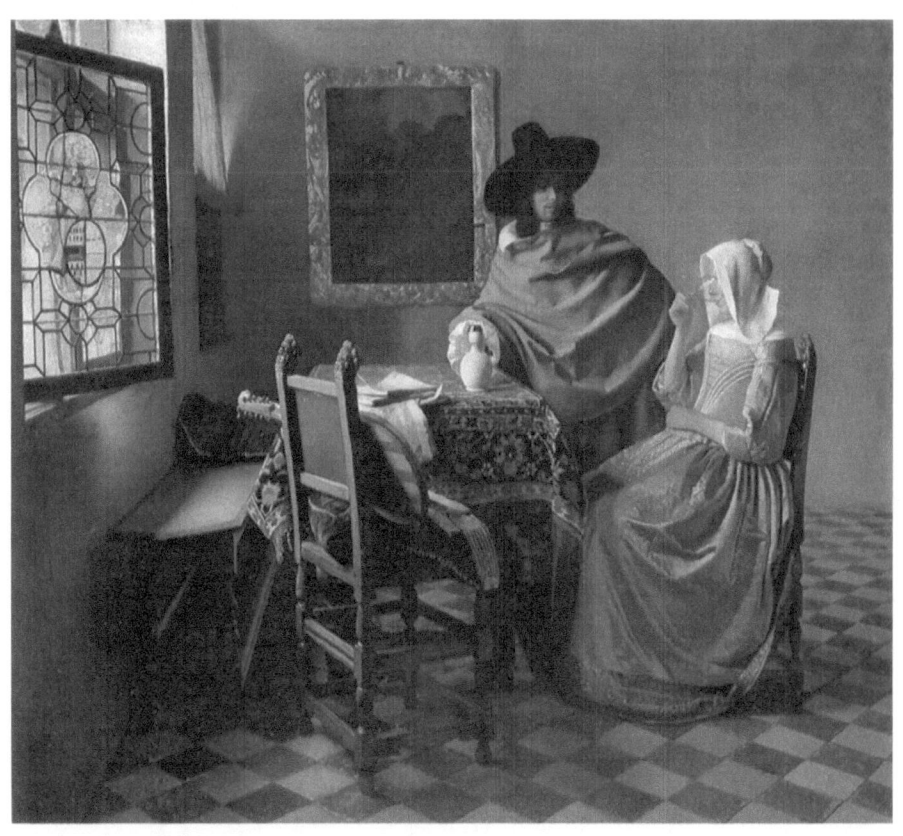

The Temptress (Another Self-portrait)

THE GIRL WITH A GLASS OF WINE
oil on canvas
30 3/4 x 26 1/8 in. (78 x 67 cm.

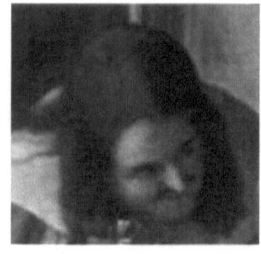

G erard ter Borch, [IX] (FOOTNOTE) my very good friend and master, fifteen years my senior, and a young lady, whose identity is that of Catharina's older sister, helped to inspire this picture. Gerard, who lived nearby in Haarlem, only a short distance from Delft, and later moved to Deventer, posed for this picture before 1668.

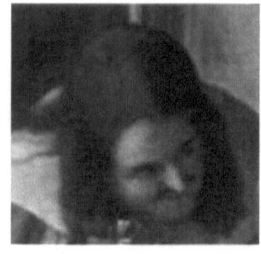

It includes myself seated, sleeping, in the background. This is one of only 3 pictures in which I used myself as a model.

Gerard ter Borch as a
model for Vermeer

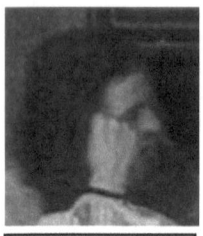

Vermeer in his
own painting

I don't think many people were interested in buying paintings of men, for decorative purposes. In this case, the window, featuring it's coat of arms, and illustrative seduction scene, are the featured attraction. My presence is only for compositional purposes, and for the vicarious indulgence of my own vanity. Had this picture not been painted for my good friend, Pieter van Ruijven, I would not have included myself.

I admired Gerard 's work very, very much, especially his magnificently lifelike rendering of silk cloth. His mastery of light, shade and texture in textiles inspired me to improve my own ability to observe and paint. He had a magical ability to breathe light and life into a canvas! We shared many long discourses together on this subject, comparing methods as to how to accomplish this.

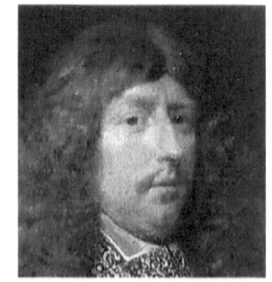

Gerard ter Borch.
1668, self-portrait

My own father had produced and traded in textiles, especially silk cloth, or *caffa*. My appreciation of fine fabrics was nurtured by his expertise when I was young.

The long hours required to plan and produce a painting were facilitated by sharing resources with other members of the Guild of St. Luke, of which were all required to become members before we could practice our craft and sell our wares in Delft, regardless of the art form. We assisted, yet competed with each other, to see which of us could conquer the unique technical challenges presented by painting the objects. I also posed for a painting by Gerard, featuring his mastery at painting fine fabrics. The fabrics, light, facial expressions, and the porcelain jug, an interesting household item we both owned and used in many pictures, were of interest as an object to be painted.

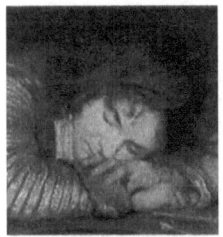

Gerard ter Borch painting with Vermeer as a model

This painting was my own practice in the experiment of making cloth appear supple and alive. I superimposed myself while looking in a mirror, pretending a state of repose, disinterested in the flirtatious intrigue a few feet from me -- an unlikely scenario, although morally

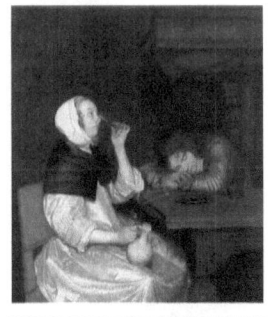

"Woman Drinking with a Sleeping Soldier" by Gerard ter Borch painted c. 1660-1669

allegorical. As before, the symbolic meaning of the coat of arms in the window is that of the female figure who personifies Temperance. She holds a level and bridle, bearing the admonition, "*The heart knows not how to observe moderation and applies reins to feelings when struck by desire.*" The level symbolizes good deeds and the bridle symbolizes emotional control. The irony of hypocrisy is self-evident in the painting.

This picture was also my attempt to capture an expression on her face: mirth at being flattered, although disinterested, by the attempted seduction by an amorous suitor. The scene is contrasted by a nonchalant companion, who takes for granted that the advances of his friend will be rejected, even though the wine is accepted. It is meant to be a comedy. Thus, the smile.

Nonetheless, the real stars of the show, as it was planned to be, are the fabrics of the gown and on the table, as well as the light through the ornate, stained glass of the window. This scene, as with others, was painted at the house of my father, before we moved to live the Maria Thins, Catharina's mother, though the window was a abstraction borrowed to add content not native to my own home at the request of those who commissioned it. After we moved to live with Maria Thins, I painted more for myself than for others.

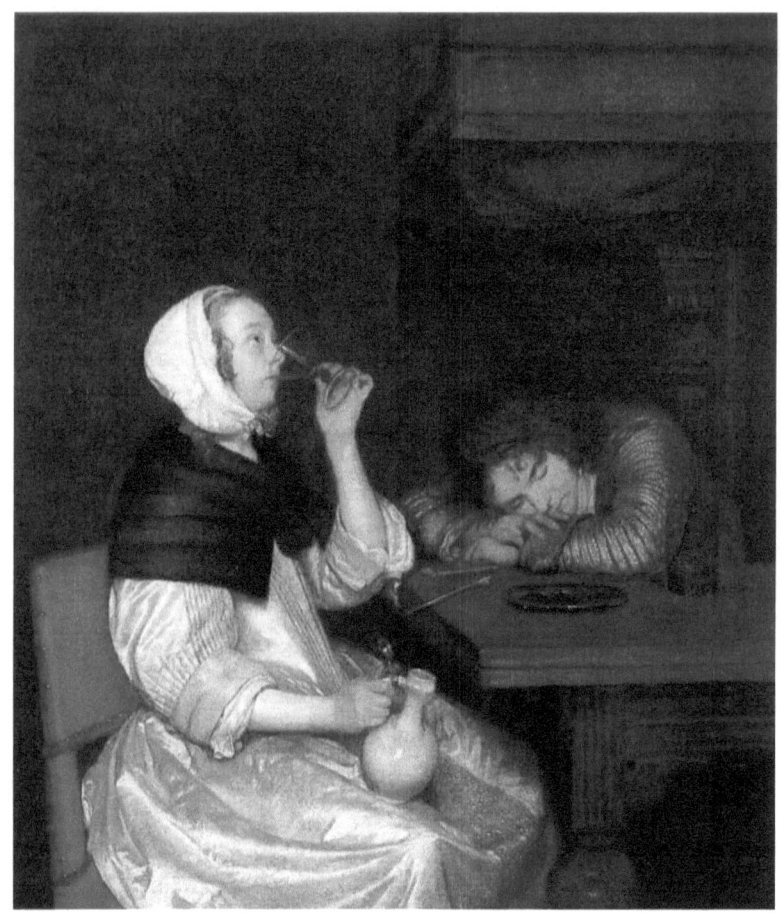

"Woman Drinking with a Sleeping Soldier"
by Gerard ter Borch painted c. 1660-1669

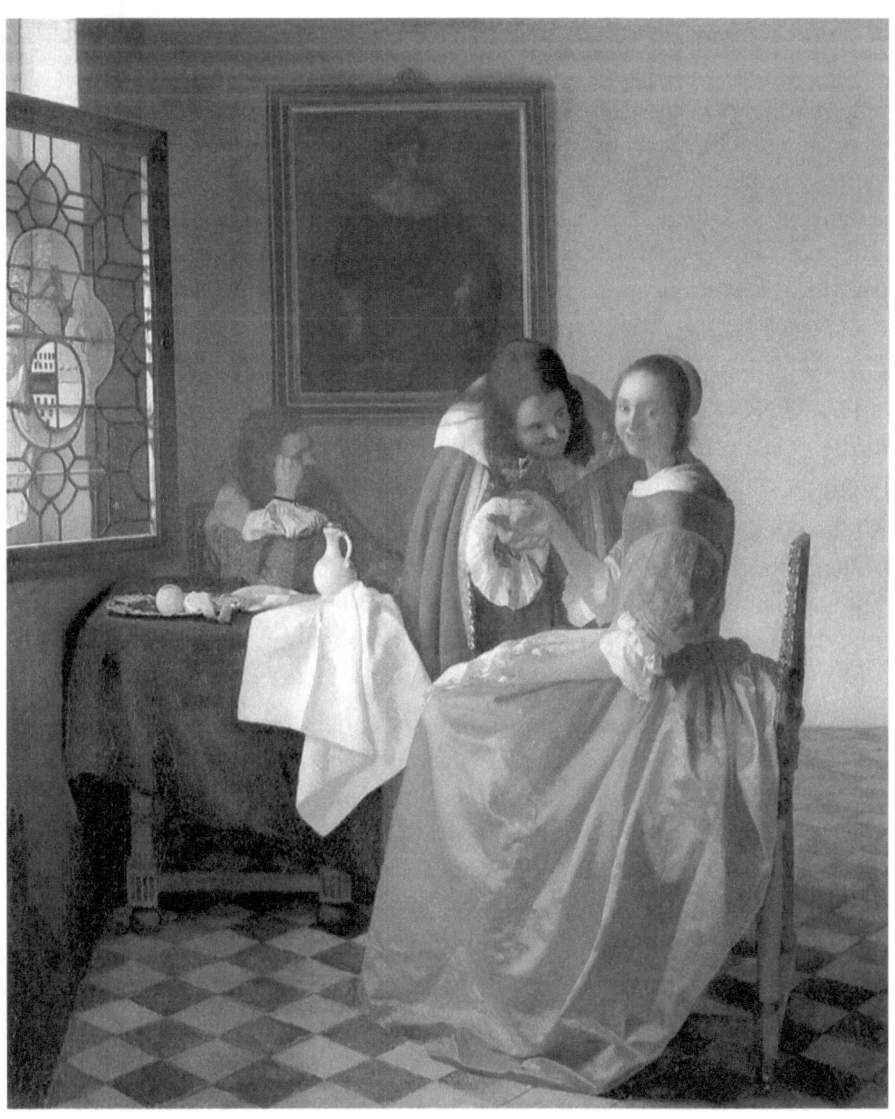

Impatient Student

GIRL INTERRUPTED IN HER MUSIC
oil on canvas
28 7/8 x 25 3/8 in. (73.3 x 44.4 cm.)

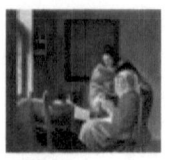

A young girl, my oldest daughter Maria, not more than 10 years old, in an accidental, spontaneous pose, which was originally meant to depict a mundane music lesson. She is very fortunate to have as her instructor, our dear friend, Constantijn Huygens, the music composer and poet. He also owned a unique virginal shown in several of my paintings, featuring on it's cover an inscription in Latin, "*music is the companion of joy, the balm of sorrow*".

Further, Constantijn introduced me to the use of the *camera obscura*, [X] (FOOTNOTE) as he owned one personally and was inspired advocate to the visual effects it produced. He allowed me to use his for this painting, even instructing me on the use of it.

While painting, she looked backed at me continually to ask a question, or because she was curious about how much longer she needed to pose. The inquisitive attention on me, rather than the object of the music lesson, was inspiration for a more appropriate, naturally intimate pose of a young, impatient girl, suffering the tedium of learning to read music.

Painting reality is primarily as discipline of looking, seeing, and duplicating the reflected light that is actually there, rather than that which one assumes, or imposes from one's own memory. Using living models, in ever-changing natural light to accomplish this task is a trial of patience, persistence and perseverance. Especially when using a young person as a model. Their nature energy and curiosity does not lend itself well this process. This is primarily the reason I waited for my girls to grow to adulthood before using them to pose as characters in my pictures.

Catharina, as I have mentioned, was a master model. I could not have hoped for a more patient and creative partner. Of course, being very much in love with her made it all the easier for me to look at the details of her for endless hours, when she could steal the time from the demands of her daily chores. And, she enjoyed being so thoroughly admired, even while fully clothed!

Most artists of the day did not share my fascination with and use of the camera obscura. To them it was an intriguing curiosity, but not a serious tool for the paintings they were paid to produce by patrons. Huygens was a rare exception to this, inasmuch as he had an intmate understanding and appreciation of it's uses.

For most, experiments, such at this, were not a luxury the average painter could afford to indulge. I had to advantage of support from Maria Thins, so I could dally with such contrivances as my daily bread was not at stake, for the most part. One could almost accuse me of being an artistic dilettante, if it were not for my obvious mastery, inasmuch that I wasn't forced to earn my daily bread by painting group portraits of old dressed in black suits and hats poised like marble waiting to be chiseled.

I did not have the wisdom, experience or willingness to suppress my whims for experimentation with the gadgetry that enabled me to observe and paint pictures using what now called "pointillism". This contributed to the financial demise of myself and my family. At that time, no "serious" painter departed from the standard portraits and genre paintings demanded of a paying client. I flaunted this fact in favor of indulging my own artistic fantasy so that I could improve upon methods for rendering light, for the benefit of posterity, and my own curiosity, rather than to be appreciated and compensated for it in my own lifetime.

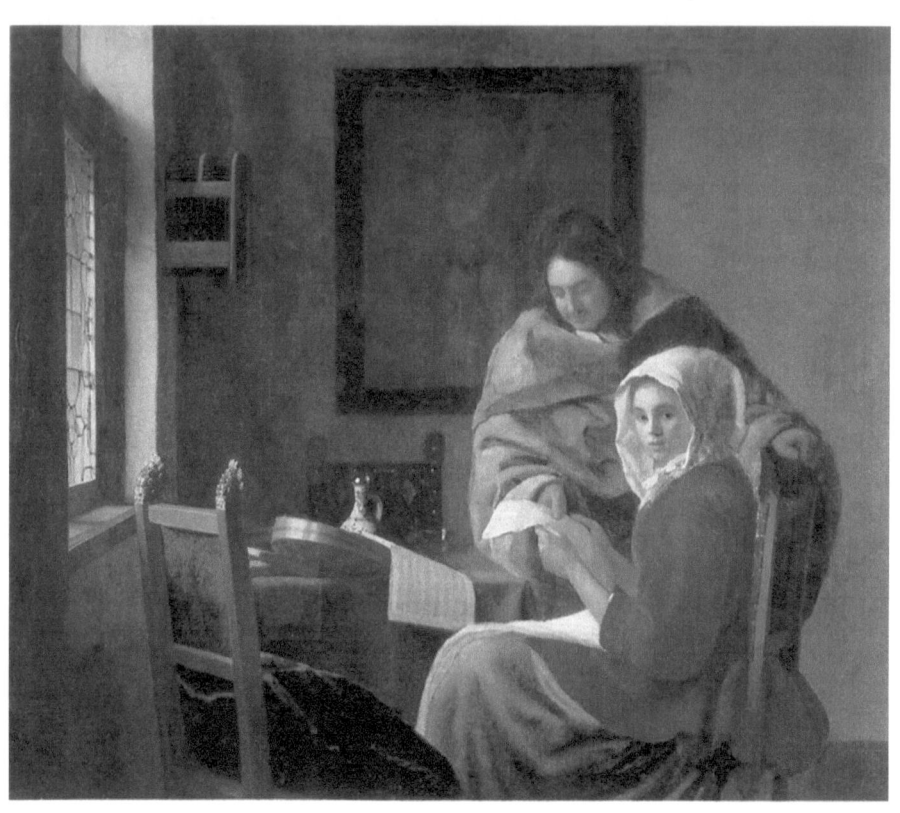

Catharina's Smile

OFFICER AND LAUGHING GIRL
oil on canvas
19 7/8 x 18 1/8 in. (50.5 x 46 cm.)

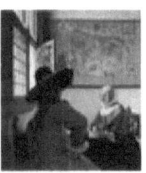

M y friend, Captain Melling, an army captain was a standard bearer in the forces of the States-General, sits across a table from Catharina. [XI] (FOOTNOTE) He, together with my artist friend, Leonaert Bramer, championed my proposal of marriage to Catharina to her mother, Maria Thins. Fortunately, in spite of her reluctance at giving up her youngest daughter to an lower-classed artisan, from a Protestant family, with no income and few prospects, accept those of an aspiring artist, they were able to persuade her to allow our marriage.

Catharina's smile is the reason for this painting. As usual, the painting has been misunderstood and misnamed, by others. Catharina does not laugh. She smiles at a trusted friend of our family and defender of the community.

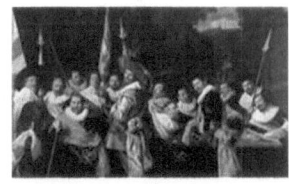

A Dutch Militia

Catharina had an endearing empathy and openness that welcomed everyone, whether man, woman or child. She never had a care for herself. Her life was lived in the service of others, most especially myself and our children, for which I am forever grateful!

Catharina wears a bodice also worn in many other paintings. It is a fine, expensive garment, and flattering to her features. Frankly, she looked good, to me, in any garment, or without!

His hat, military sash, coat and ruffled blouse create a swashbuckling air. His costume makes him a classic, dashing figure of a man, for which women swoon. In this picture Catharina is clearly endeared by his valor, and enamored by his military macho appeal. However, her forthright expression of interest in him, as a person, and her understanding smile, are the essence of what I intended to capture.

As you can see, I struggled somewhat with his right hand, to make it seem relaxed. Yet it seems a little awkward. He holds his elbow up as he leans forward, but his hand does not lay comfortably on the fabric of his coat.

The map is a favorite prop of mine, for it's complicated lines. Originally borrowed from the Guild of St. Luke, I used it many times before I gave it back. There were 51 painters, including myself, in the Guild during my prime, a goodly number of artisans with whom to share trade secrets, talk shop, fraternize and, also, compete for sales! As a part-time art dealer myself, this proved to be to my advantage, as their were always painters eager for someone to sell their wares at a fair rate.

The exaggerated perspective of the soldier, the size of his head in relation to that of Catharina, enhances the illusion that the viewer is an intimate participant in their conversation. We look directly over his shoulder. We share her warmth with him. We, too, are her friend. And so it was in life with her. Everyone was as welcomed by her, as she felt they might be by the Son of God himself!

Catharina was not a hypocrite. She lived what she read in the Christian scriptures. And, for her, wine was not just wine. It was the blood of Christ, as taught in the Catholic Church. She savored it as her beverage of choice. It was a sacramental rite and her duty to enjoy!

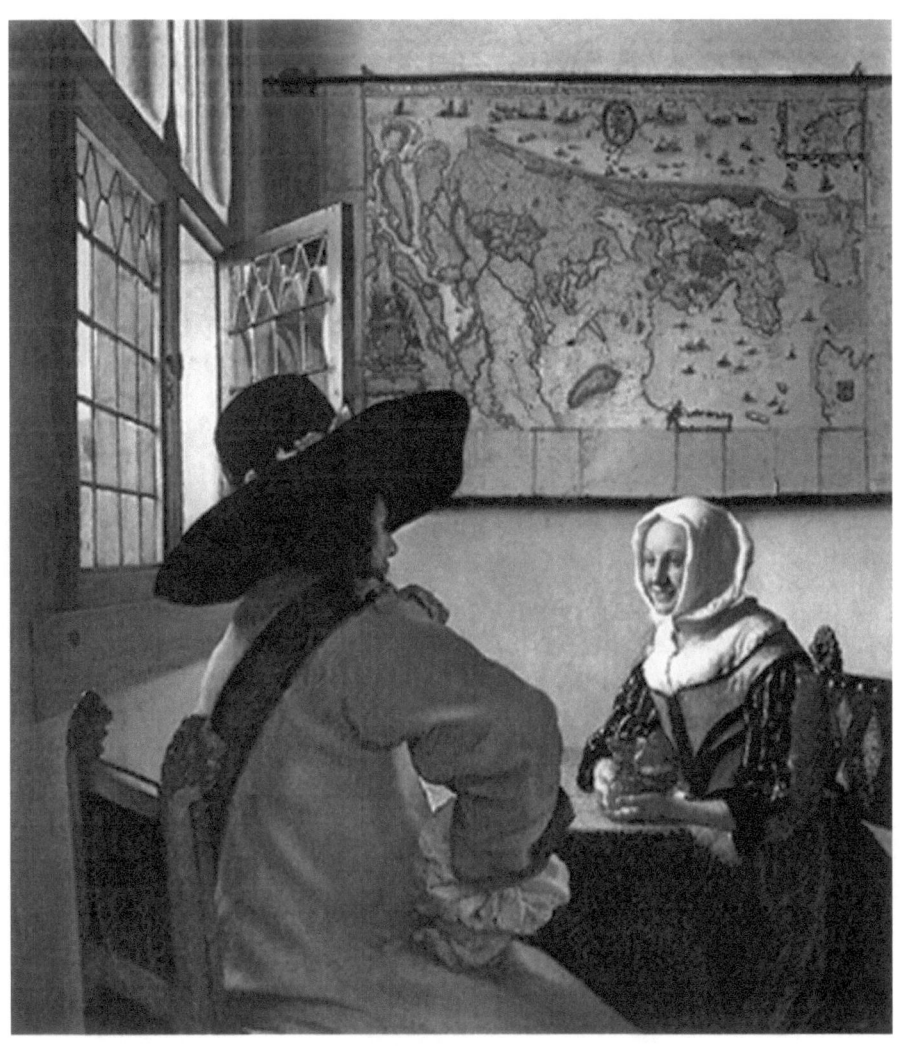

Across the street from the Mechelen house

THE LITTLE STREET
oil on canvas
21 1/16 x 17 1/8 in. (53.5 c 43.5 cm.)

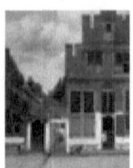

This picture, as well as a large outdoor painting of the city of Delft, were painted at the request of my friend, Pieter van Ruijven. He was interested in buying fashionable, contemporary paintings, suitable for interior decoration, rather than those painted for intellectual effect. Paintings of saints and characters of mythology were not appealing to him and did not support to his youthful passion for all things contemporary. Young people, especially wealthy ones, like Pieter, reject the past in an effort to emblazon an everlasting impression of their own unique identity in the moment. As this passion languishes with age it is rekindled by every new generation who would repaint the face of the past in their own image.

The details of this painting are noted on the most excellent Vermeer internet resource, Essentialvermeer.com:

"The (view of this building) is in fact a little painting of a small section of street. There is nothing to indicate how wide the street is, though we get the impression that the painter's view (which is our view) is from a house opposite, from an upstairs room, at no great distance. Topographical experts and local historians in Delft have spent much time trying to pin down where this was.

The Oude Langendijk, the Nieuwe Langendijk, the Trompetstraat, the Spieringstraat, Achterom, the Vlamingstraat, and the Voldersgracht are among the numerous streets put forward for the honor. The Voldersgracht has been a consistent candidate, for the back of Mechelen overlooked the little canal of the Voldersgracht and its narrow carriageway, on to which faced the Old Men's Home and - a few doors further east - the Flying Fox Inn.

In a few years the Old Men's Home was going to be partly rebuilt, with its chapel converted in 1661 into the hall of the St. Luke's Guild; drawings of the hall show a small house and archway similar to the part of the left-hand house and archway depicted in The Little Street. *But the house on the right in that picture has its gable-end facing the street, while the building which housed the chapel of the Old Men's Home stood side-on to the street.*

The two arched outside doorways in the painting, one with a closed door, the other with door open revealing a brick-paved passage in which a servant-woman is leaning over a barrel used as a washtub or cistern, and waste water runs towards us along a gulley form the heart of the picture.

What is behind the dark closed door? Its shut state, the openness and light of its companion, bring to mind those weather-predicting devices styled as miniature cottages out of which figures swing to declare that it is going to be fine or rainy.

There must have been many hundred such passageways in Delft then. However, an adjacent pair, with twin gates like those in the picture, is now not to be found in any of the favored streets. But given the artist's close relationship with Van Ruijven, it seems a possibility that the house on the right belonged to that gentleman. The Little Street *was painted around the time Vermeer and his wife borrowed 200 guilders from Van Ruijven.* [XII] (FOOTNOTE)

The house on the right has signs of a good deal of hasty repainting and patching of cracks, as if it was shaken severely by the Thunderclap, [XIII] (FOOTNOTE) *and we know that van Ruijven owned a house on the east side of the Voorstraat that was damaged in the explosion. The picture was in his collection."*

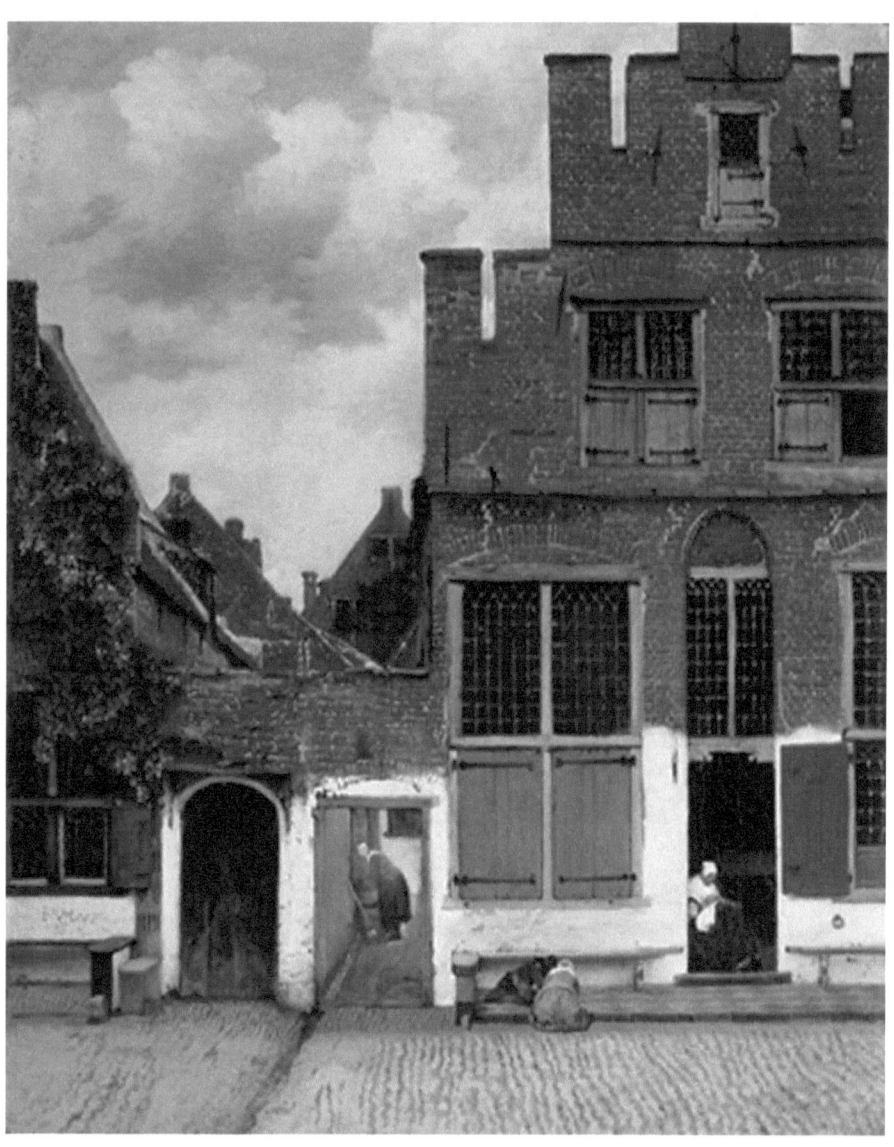

A Music Session

THE MUSIC LESSON
oil on canvas
28 7/8 x 25 3/8 in. (73.3 x 64.5 cm.)

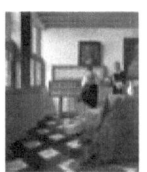

Catharina and my life-long friend and neighbor, Anthony Van Leeuwenhoek, [XIV] (FOOTNOTE) shortly after we moved into the house of Maria Thins. He visited us frequently over the years: sometimes to see me, for my professional and intellectual relationship, and more often to visit the girls with whom he shared an enthusiasm for music. He was, in every way, a gentleman. It seemed that he was successful at everything he attempted, both as an investigator, designer of scientific instruments and glass lenses, and as a practical, no-nonsense businessman.

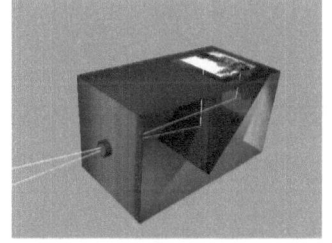

Anthony was exactly my age, (baptized at the Nieuwe Kerk in the same month and the same year), born only a few hundred yards away, near the fish market, on the western end of the Marketplace in Delft. We had other similarities in our lives: our fathers were both in the fabric trade,

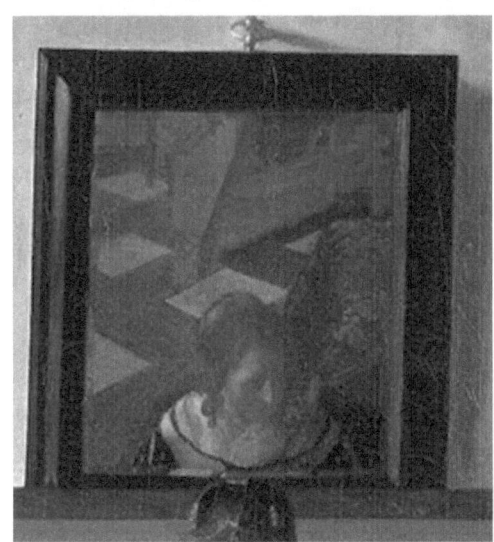

and member of the Guild of St. Luke. His only surviving daughter was also named Maria. She did not marry, but took care of him until his death.

Anthony was curious about everything. He was as keen an observer of nature and innovator of technology as I, myself, have been given credit for in the advancement of painting. He certainly influenced me own work in a significant way. It was he who introduced the camera obscura, and taught me the fundamentals of it's uses. He built one for me, and several times modified it for my purposes.

Reflected in the mirror shown in the painting of "The Music Lesson" is the easel, part of the artist's stool, the wall behind him, and a small wooden box, which is the portable camera obscura.

Neither of us thought it especially remarkable at the time, as my use of the camera was an interesting extension of his own experiments with light and lenses. He could never have applied it's use to my ends, as he had no skills of painting, any more than I could have ground a lens to fit a microscope. Nonetheless, the cumulative results were important to future generations.

My daughters spent many occasions with Anthony, learning and practicing music. He was as patient and meticulous with music, as with his scientific interests. I can't recall that he ever played an instrument, but he helped the girls learn how to play for him.

I have a very good feeling about him, and am honored to have known him, where ever he may be today.

The unique virginal instrument being played in this painting is one owned by friends and neighbors in Delft, Constantijn Huygens and his wife Suzanne, whose portraits are shown here. Constantijn was very instrumental in making scientific and artistic introductions to me on intermittent occasions.

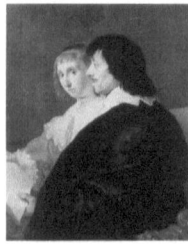

Huygens was not only a musical composer, and poet, but the owner of a *camera obscura*. He was also an enthusiastic champion of Antony's work with microscopes, as well as the wonders of the camera obscura, of which he was already very well informed before either Anthony and I was born, as he wrote in a letter to his parents from London in 1622:

Constantijn Huygens and wife Suzanne

"It is impossible to describe to you the beauty of it in words: all painting is dead by comparison, for here is life itself, or something more noble, if only there were words for it".

Fortunately, painting was not yet dead, and remains marginally alive today, in spite of digital photography and high definition video!

XV (FOOTNOTE)

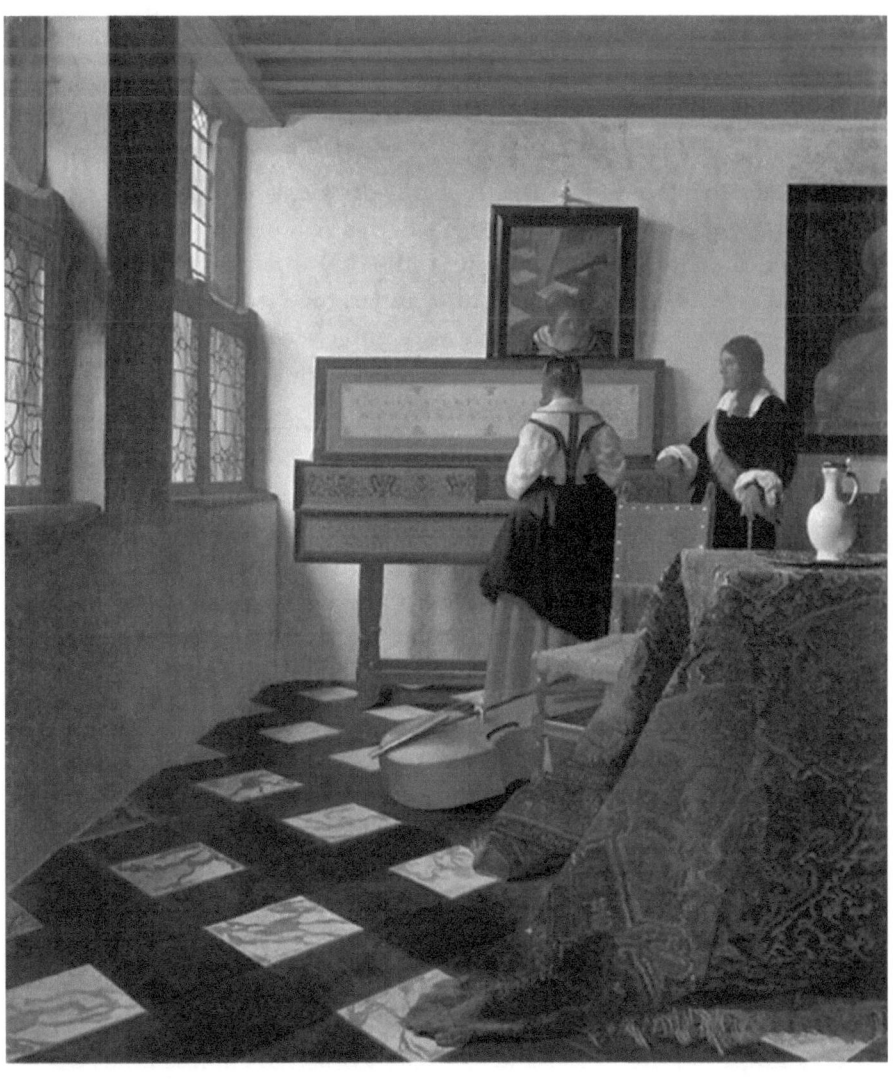

Delft in Pleasant Weather

VIEW OF DELFT
oil on canvas
38 1/4 x 46 1/4 in. (98.5 x 117.5 cm.

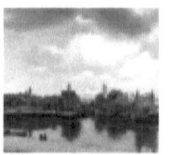

Delft, on a typical spring day the temperature is, is mildly temperate, mostly humid, a filled with coastal clouds. [XVI] (FOOTNOTE)

In winter this balmy scene turns to dismal drizzle, and then to a dreadfully icy, dead winter. Nothing is ever warm in Delft from December till May, if then. For me, with all it's special splendor and quaint quiescence during spring and summer, the North Sea region, on the average, was a brutally cold, and very unpleasant place to live in winter. [XVII] (FOOTNOTE)

I painted only in during mild weather. In winter and raining weather, very little was possible. The only source of light was the sun, which when blocked by precipitation, incessant clouds, or fog, made painting impossible. Likewise, cold weather froze my paints, as well as my fingers, which, if I could not feel or move, I laid down my brush. Shivering in front of a frosted easel is not my idea of fun! (How many artists, since Gauguin left Europe for the Pacific, who, while freezing in a wintry garret, have envied his time in Tahiti!)

Many art "critics" (men who can not paint, but only diminish the genius of others) have commented, or so I've read, that Vermeer didn't paint many paintings, (in their opinion) and wondered why. Obviously, if they could paint, and tried, in Delft, they would not ask this stupid question. Especially, in an age when everything stops at night, for lack of light, to await the breaking of the light! Candles were scarce and hardly a fitting tool for any artist. Heating fuel was even more rare, so indoor fires were not wasted. It is a lovely place, in spring and summer....

Many months were spent on this painting, cold air or none. Relentless observation, a hundred thousand strokes of brush in endless tones of blue-grey-white and umber. Working and reworking, piling paints on top of one another to create the illusion of depth, dimension and permanent peace. It is as real as I can make it!

The camera image made it possible for me to paint the objects with points of light, rather than the flat, monochromatic colors where were taught to use in school. I could never be satisfied with mere competence. I was bound by my maxim for myself, that it is the duty and responsibility of the artist to continually sharpen the cutting edge of art. Aesthetics are a subjective experience. If a picture were just "pretty" or only technically well done, it was not "artistic" in my own estimation. Where is the thrilling adventure of exploration if one remains behind the city gate, defended by tradition against a strange and marvelous world? For me, who rarely traveled outside of Delft on foot, adventure was my aesthetic experiments. My sword and lance were brush and paint, an easel was my steed, and the dragon I sought to slay was light!

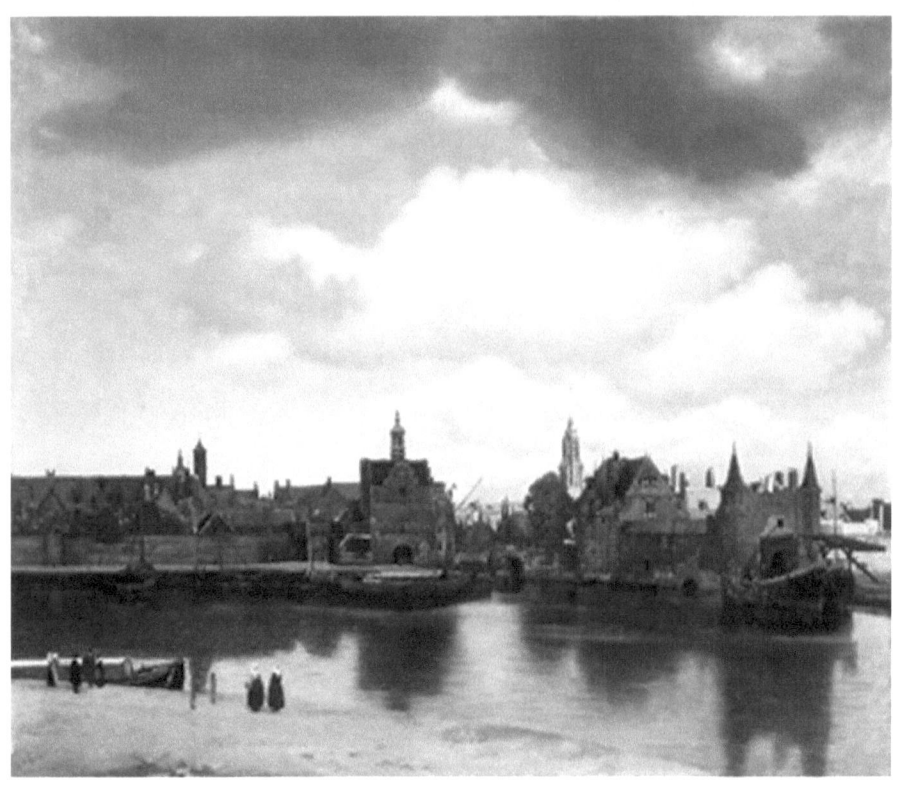

Maria Thins: A Matron with Her Cupid

A LADY STANDING AT A VIRGINAL
oil on canvas
20 3/8 x 17 1/4 in. (51.7 x 45.2 cm.)

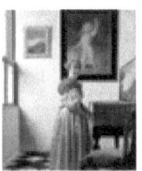

This is one of the few painting that features Maria Thins. The likeness of her is very accurate, and the composition and colors are most pleasant. It is the duty of an artist to flatter one's patroness, especially women, for whom Earthly beauty is so dearly held and highly prized. This likeness makes her appear as she did in her younger years. She was about 70 years old when we moved to live with her.

I loved the blue and white and golden elements of the floor, the chair, the paintings and the delicately laced shawl, her pearl necklace and gown. I think these colors suited her well. The light in the room is exceptionally pure. This is one of my finest paintings, which I worked on to improve intermittently over several years.

Maria Thins was quite stubborn and tenacious as woman and a grandmother. This painting was made to honor her love of music. It also features her beloved painting of Cupid. [XVIII] (FOOTNOTE) She always fancied herself an independent person. And, it is true, that she was a far more competent than the average women who resigned themselves to be wholly dependent on men.

Maria Thins fought for and won her freedom from a very abusive husband. Her generous fiscal support of myself, my wife and my children, made it possible for us to enjoy a life style I never provided through my own industry, neither as a painter, or as a dealer in the paintings of others. [XIX] (FOOTNOTE)

My greatest strength, and terminal ruin, were both that I was a dreamer. My common ground with Maria Thins was aesthetics and family. She indulged my avocation, and supported my children, so that they too could pursue music and the arts.

Maria Thins was a great enthusiast of music and the arts. She provided the virginal, seen here, stringed instruments, and musical lessons for her grand-daughters. [XX] (FOOTNOTE)

Maria Thins died on 27 December in 1680. She was buried near Vermeer in the Old Church graveyard in Delft.

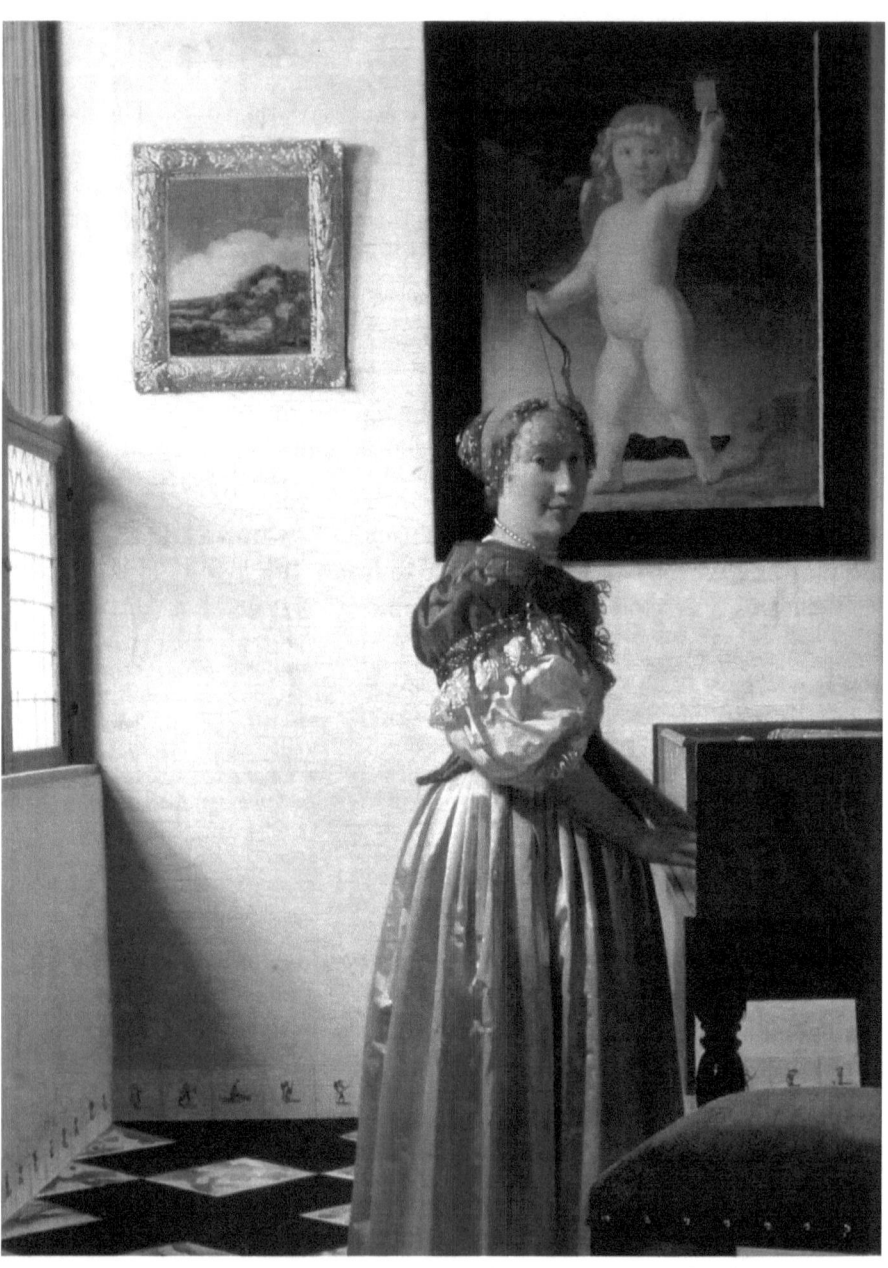

Catharina Vermeer, A New Hair Style

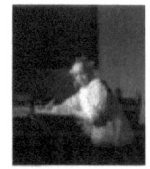

A LADY WRITING
oil on canvas
17 3/4 x 15 3/4 in. (45 x 39.9 cm.)

My wife, Catharina, poised over a sheet of paper, as if writing a letter. She is showing off her new hair style, which was very fashionable during the 1660s, with accessories of ribbons, pearls, silk and fur.

As with most women throughout the history of the human females, making oneself an aesthetic object, and sexually desirable, is a survival practice. The Puritans, Calvinists, Mennonites, and other conservative protestants at that time preached against ostentatious displays of vanity. This was not so among Catholics. Pretentious displays of wealth, possession and vanity, for them, were the order to the day!

Of course, pretension, ostentation and vanity for the priests, cardinals and Pope at the Vatican had long since been elevated to a high art form, and enforced vigorously with treachery, superstition and force! According to the Hebrews, god forbade the worship of golden idols: a prohibition that was never applied by the Pope, who idolized as much gold as he could lay his hands on!

This was especially true of gold that came from "heathen" sources, like the millions of Aztecs and Mayans who the Pope authorized to be murdered if they resisted coversion. Soldiers and priests stole all the gold the natives had mined for 2,000 years and carried it away by the boat load. The masterful metallurgy, and astonishing artistry of the native smiths was ignored so that their artistic treasures could be melted into gold bricks and chains for easy transport to the Vatican. There, it was transformed into "holy" idols and gold leaf to adorn the chapel halls to enrich the spiritual lives of "enlightened" Catholics.

Albrecht Dürer, the finest German draftsman that ever lived, whose father had been a successful goldsmith, visited the Emperor Maximilian in Brussels, in 1520, he saw an intact sample of Aztec gold art that Hernán Cortés had sent home to Holy Roman Emperor. Dürer wrote that this treasure "was much more beautiful to me than miracles." [XXI] (FOOTNOTE)

Albrecht was influenced by Martin Luther, a fellow German Catholic. As one of the most pious and diligent priests in Germany, Martin made a pilgrimage to the Vatican in Rome, where he witnessed the amazingly hypocritical corruption of the Pope in person. [XXII] (FOOTNOTE)

When he returned home, he started a revolt against the church that inflamed all of Europe, and is the foundation upon which the Dutch Republic has built an empire!

Of course we didn't care about any of this. The Papal propaganda line was safe and secure in our household. Our only interest was to enjoy as many of the pleasures and luxuries of life that we could afford, and as many as we could not afford also.

In this, all of the girls in the family were very close and worked together as a team. This flashy conspiracy was led by my mother-in-law, Maria Thins, with whom we lived for most of my married years. It was her money, inherited from her family and litigated from her former husband, that provided a few small luxuries for her daughter and grandchildren.

The universe of women is uniquely feminine, that is for sure. They are aesthetic creatures, and enjoy fine fabrics, jewelry, clothes and hair. In all, a string of pearls, some silk and fur trim were all they had to work with, and they certainly made the most of these modest treasures to make themselves as presentable as possible.

The girls enjoyed making themselves look lovely, more for each other, than to gain the admiration of men -- although this was essential, especially in an era when survival of the family often depended on getting the girls out of the house and supported by a husband! Unfortunately, all husbands are not as supportive of their wives, financially, romantically, and least of all spiritually, as the young maiden dreams they will be when married. Only two of my nine daughters were betrothed.

Personally, I enjoy the companionship of women, sexually, spiritually, and conversationally. However, some women and many men do not confide with other people except in a guarded, covert fashion. I find this very unsatisfying. Communication is the essence of existence for humanity. If we are fundamentally afraid to trust each other, life is spoiled. So, why bother living it. One might as well be a cow chewing cud in a pasture!

On the other hand, families are very good for propagating a protoplasmic population. However, the resulting necessity to care for and feed those physical entities is very bad business for a free spirit. I like privacy when I want privacy! I want to have the freedom in time and a quiet space, to enjoy the raptures of contemplation and imagination. Wives and young children have little tolerance of such inactivity, as they demand that one give your effort and attention to them first, and yourself last!

Nonetheless, I enjoy a existence balanced between chaotic action and contemplative recreation. There is no perfection in a universe made of matter, time and force. Perfection exists, theoretically, only in a universe made for and by oneself, if one is able to continue creating it before it fades, like a family that once was mine, 300 years ago.

As though a Tibetan sand painting, a tiny gust of time turns all matter into dust. In my world, they are always with me, and I with them.

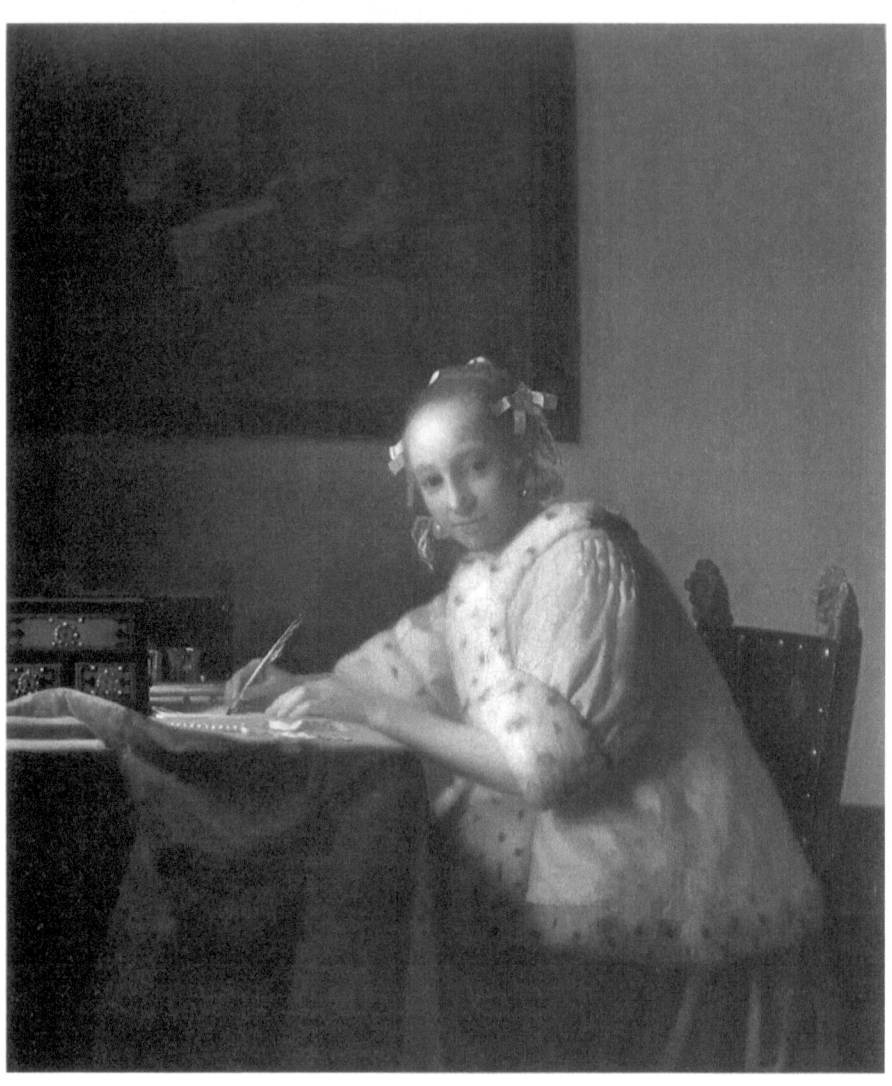

Self Portrait, With Elizabeth Vermeer

THE ART OF PAINTING
oil on canvas
47 1/4 x 39 3/8 in. (120 X   100 cm.)

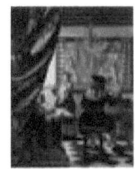

Painting embodies the most fundamental understanding of any existence, in any universe: the only Universe worth inhabiting is that of your Own Creation. And, when not continually created, it disappears, until you alter it, or create another.

In this universe, one can not be the Father, without merging with the Mother. Creation is a two-sided coin, positive and negative, joined. Only in one's own universe can there exist idyllic perfection.

Philosophically, this is a portrait of myself at work, with my daughter, Elizabeth, posed idyllically. For me, she represents the Spirit of Artistic Creation, and I portray the Father. Together, we bring into being a universe of our own, isolated from the rest. Only our own imagination represents any threat of intrusion into it. Whether the art is painting, music, poetry, literature, or any other joyful activity that brings something into being, conjured from imagination only, it is represented here.

In the physical universe, of course, it is also a painting of me, dressed in my "Sunday Best" shirt under a black, slashed doublet, with beret, baggy pantaloons and droopy over-stockings. This suit was out of style at this time, so I did not where it in public. However, it makes a flamboyant combination and the black and white colors compliment the other elements of the painting perfectly, particularly the floor tiles.

As always, my hand in balanced on a maalstick: a necessity for detailed brush work. Obviously, my easel is actually positioned at the vantage point of the viewer, rather than at the position shown in the painting. Two mirrors, one in front and one behind me, are used to reflect my own posterior, so that I might paint myself accurately without moving.

Meanwhile, outside the door of the room parades the incessant household clamor of the younger children playing, being groomed, scolded and schooled by their mother, mother-in-law and my older daughters. Elizabeth was excused from assisting them long enough to stand for me, posing with serenity. It was a reprieve which she enjoyed.

Elizabeth, in her teen years at this time, is an idealization of The Muse of music, art and literature. Some of the props were borrowed for the painting from other members of the Guild of St. Luke. These are carefully placed to create a layered gradient of perspective.

These objects were chosen, not only as symbols of the arts, but to reflect texture, light and color. The perspective and textures of light revealed, observed and captured with the brush was an extreme excitement to me as a painter! The camera obscura was an effective secret weapon in the conquest of light, the painters only adversary.

I am fundamentally a revolutionary. Therefore, I rebut the ordinary. At the time, in the 1660s I was artistically invigorated, and fortunate to be surrounding in Delft by many other artists and innovators who seem to be attracted to each other in various times and places when circumstances are favorable to freedom in thinking and doing. Those times are, unfortunately, too few and far between.

In fact, during those fleeting decades of my life in Delft, there were more brilliant artists living in close proximity to each other than nearly any other time in history. The confluence of intellectual freedom, religious tolerance, economic prosperity, transportation, and civil order, relative to earlier periods, attracted artistic beings like migrating geese to a wetland meadow. Holland afforded us the rare luxuries of time, place and abundance required to pursue art as a livelihood.

However, no matter how hospitable the economic and philosophical climate for painters in that age, there remained a fundamental antipathy, to the degree that the Dutch people were very pragmatic, materialistic and bound to reality. As such, dreamers and mystics were not acknowledge or compensated. Artists, by nature, are the creators of illusion. Dreams and fantasies, departures from reality, had no place.

In such an environment, a painter could earn enough money to eat only by placating the vanity of those whose guilders they had to seek. To this degree, we were forced, as artists, to become tedious copyists of the faces, places and accoutrements of those who could afford to pay the fee.

Contrarily, artistic beings require unencumbered time to practice their craft. If one must plow the field, or serve a master in order to subsist, there is no time for art. Wealth enables the artist to create, even if the content of that art is dictated and perverted by the patron. Unfortunately for all, the premise of the artist is that any art is better than none at all.

I was too unwilling to have the subject matter of my art determined by another. This is why Maria Thins, with whom we lived for the most part, and who supplemented us financially, was a most convenient champion.

Without her, I would have been forced to compete more aggressively with other artists in Delft, and Holland, who painted portraits of merchants for a living. Who would not prefer painting one's own beautiful daughters at home, to sitting for hours in front of fat, smelly old Burghers, whose only care is for their own self importance?

This painting was done at the height of my artistic fervor. Although we produced many more paintings together through the years, I think I was more mythically enthralled by the aesthetic and intellectual life at this moment than any other. Every detail of this painting evokes the essence of my effort to express my painterly technique and a romantic notion of myself as an artist.

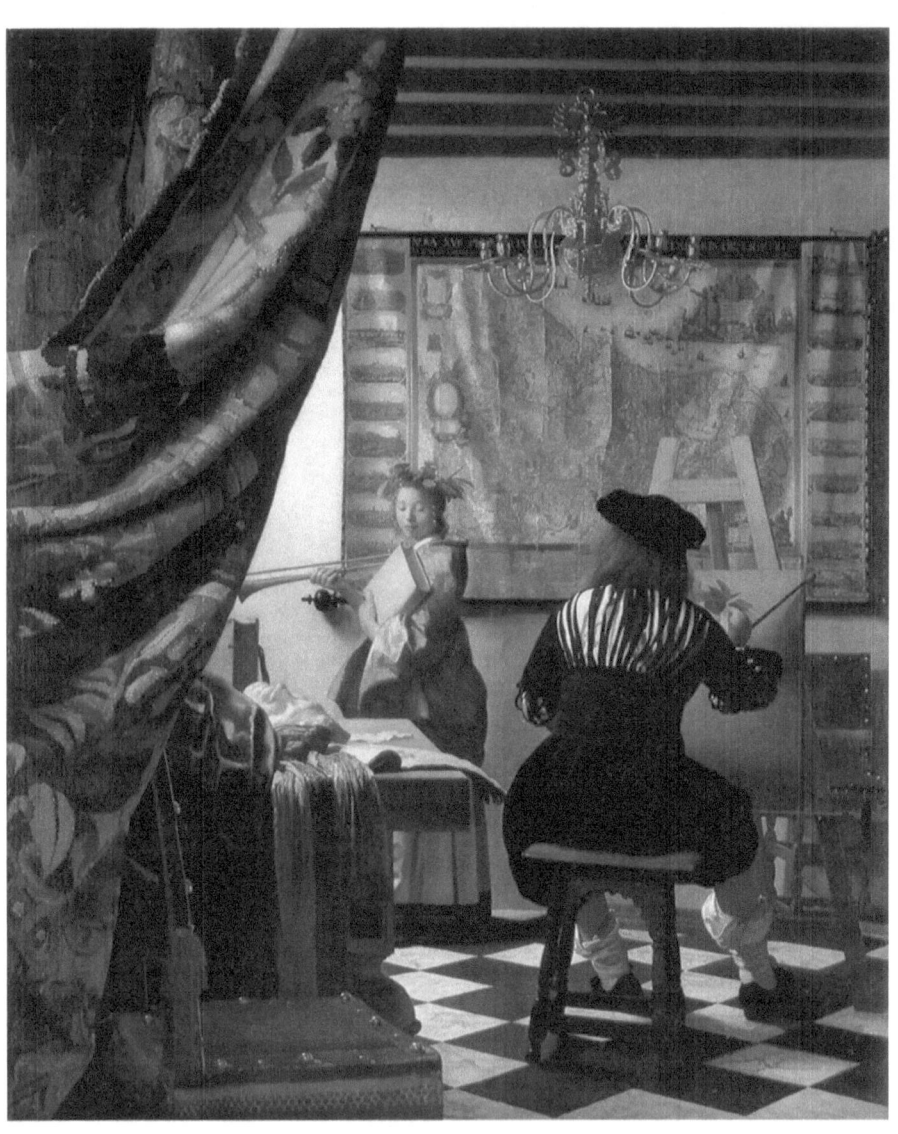

Elizabeth Vermeer Playing Tunes

A LADY SEATED AT A VIRGINAL
oil on canvas
20 3/4 x 17 7/8 in. (51.5 x 45.5 cm.)

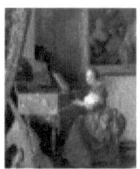

A portrait of my daughter, Elizabeth, when she was very young, about ten years old. She was very eager to dress up in her mother's grown-up clothes and be painted like her mother and sisters had been. The painting was done rather quickly, to please her, rather than choosing a construction and elements to paint as a technical experiment which I chose to give myself.

However, I decided to pose the problem of painting a scene as though it were in a room darkened by closed shutters to keep out the cold. Or a night time scene where there was no sun light used for illumination, not even a fire or candelabra. This is evident by the closed window, the shadowy corner behind the virginal, and the painting on the wall in the rear which is only partially distinct do to the lack of a direct source of light to illuminate the details. All of the light in the picture is from a source from the front, left side of the cello.

This was challenging, in a way, however, since color is a reflection of that portion of the visible spectrum we call light. Each gradient of that spectrum is divisible and reflected by the qualities of the surface it contracts and is reflected by. By necessity the intensity or luminosity of any color, even "black" or "white" requires bright light to reveal the detailed attributes which animate the subject being painted. There is no absolute color attainable, as each is a gradient scale relative to another gradient.

She was very pleased with the painting, as it made her feel more grown up and noticed by her father. I was pleased to make her feel loved and cherished, although the painting is not especially satisfactory for obvious technical reasons. It lacks sufficient detail to be worthy of painterly consideration.

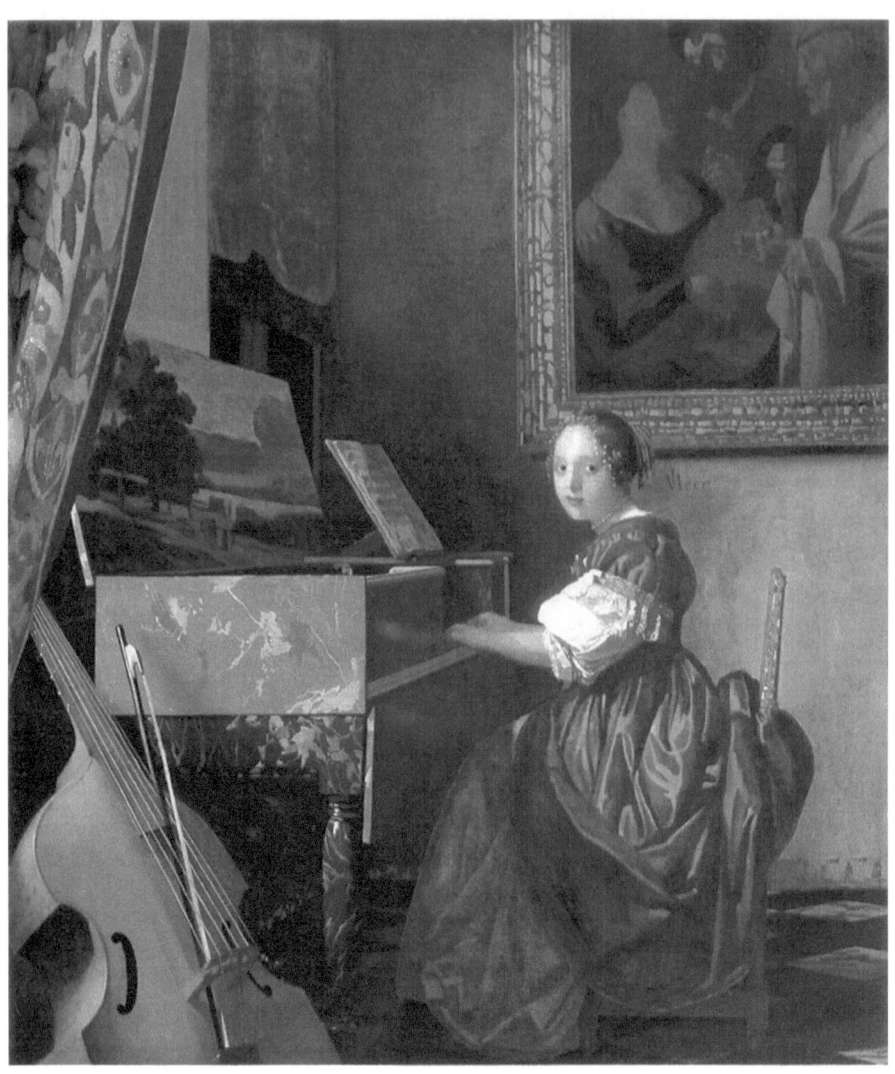

Anthony as an Astronomer

THE ASTRONOMER (Dated 1668)
oil on canvas
19 3/8 x 17 3/4 in. (50 x 45 cm.

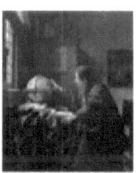

Our very good friend, neighbor, mentor, the lens maker and scientist, Anthony van Leeuwenhoek is the model in this of himself as an Astronomer. In exchange for providing me with the use of a portable *camera obscura*, as well as instruction in the use of it, which he constructed and loaned to me to use in many paintings, I painted two portraits of him. In this, we being the same age, he is 36 years old.

He is also included as a character in several others. Of course Carl Fabritius, my dearly beloved friend and mentor, shared my intrigue for the advantage of discerning perspective and light more effectively through the use of the camera obscura. But, Anthony was the only person I knew who actually made lenses and could construct these clever mechanisms.

Anthony was born in the same year as myself. Conveniently, his house was only a very short walk from the house of Maria Thins where we lived on the Oude Langendijk in "Papist Corner," the Catholic quarter of the city. At birth he was named Thonis Philipszoon. However, he became known as Van Leeuwenhoek from a young age because he was born in a house at the corner of Lion's Gate in Delft. Van Leeuwenhoek means, literally, "from Lion's Corner". Like us, he also had a daughter named Maria.

During the years of our friendship, we spent many, many hours together discussing the mysteries of the microcosm and macrocosm, both of which were boundless fascinating to both of us. His knowledge of the Earth, and the heavens were wonderful. The wonders he witnessed through is hand-crafted lenses allowed him to peer into a the unseen universe of tiny living forms so small that no one suspected they existed!

Anthony was continually exhilarated by the "new worlds" revealed under a microscope and through a telescope. He yearned intensely to experience the universes beyond the confines of his mortal form, like Alice, through looking-glasses [XXIII] (FOOTNOTE) of his own design, and ground by his own hand, to see through nearly infinite space, and extend himself in all directions, massively large, and incomprehensibly small.

I am consoled to know that Anthony was willing and able to lend assistance to Catharina to settle our disastrous financial situation after my death. I would have suspected no less from such a worthy friend and honorable gentleman. He lived his own life in the world of men, between the extremes of planetary bodies and microbial beasts, with grace, integrity and intelligence.

I regret that I departed that world in a less honorable relationship with it than he, being at a complete loss to cope with the overburdening obligations of my own creation. On reflection it seems that my disinclination to restrain myself from sexual activity with my wife, whose fertility was endless, led us to ruin. No person of ordinary financial means could support 15 children, much less as a small town artist in Delft!

I married Catharina, in part, for the allure of her mother's income, and her family indulgence of the arts, which made our match all the more inviting. I married, primarily, to placate my lusty loins. That her Catholic faith forbade her to refuse me in bed I thought all the more attractive, especially when combined with the former.

When I was young, I had no thought beyond satisfaction in the moment. Sensation, aesthetics and placation of desires were my quest! I was sure I would live forever! Or, so I felt at the age of 21 years. Alas, immortality is mitigated by the flesh. The sweet cream of youth curdles with age. Like bacteria, we swim in the microbial milk of life. We eat, excrete, spoil our environment and our own lives within it.

Through the brief interlude of earthly activity we measure ourselves with possessions, power, relationships and pleasant experiences. More pleasure than pain is a gauge of success. To cause pleasure, without responsibility for consequences, creates pain. Ultimately, one knows, that survival is a game that cannot be won. Everyone loses in the end.

What little is gleaned from playing is eventually negated. Painful experience accumulates in ruin. The final score is remorse, regret and death. Then, one forgets: identity, memory and possessions are erased, simply by departing from a location in space, a body, a time, a place.

Amnesia is our elixir. Painful memory is erased. Then, once more, we return to play: knowing, without knowing, fully prepared to lose again, and yet return to play. If only we learned to avoid this futility! We could gaze through the Lens of Eternity, span the extremities of this universe, as the spiritual beings we are, and inquire: Mortality, what place have you here?

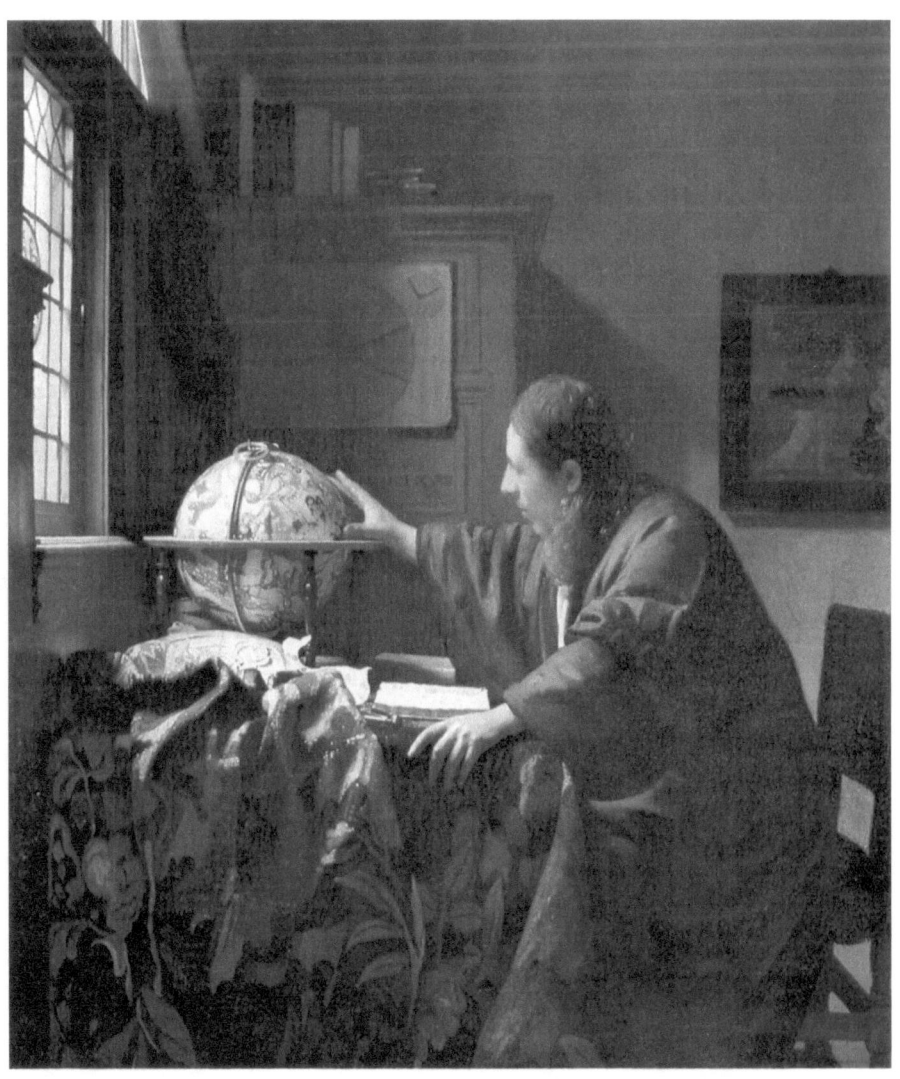

Anthony, The Surveyor

THE GEOGRAPHER (Dated 1669)
oil on canvas
20 7/8 x 18 1/4 in. (53 x 46.6 cm.)

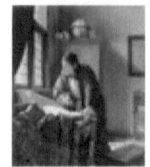

Antonie van Leeuwenhoek seemed interested in the entire spectrum of existence! Specifically, he qualified to practice the trade of a *landmeter* or surveyor in Delft in the same year as this paining of him was done. The staging of this painting was done at the opposite end of the same room as "The Astronomer", to create variety between the two portraits I made of him, using different windows and vantage points.

In this painting he plays at being an astronomer. In life he also played at being an astronomer in a most intensely professional manner! Here, he studies the sphere of the heavens, just as he studied, as a geographer, the globe of Earth: the macrocosm and the microcosm.

Since we lived on the North Sea during a period when the Netherlands operated the most extensive fleet of ocean going vessels in Europe, we had continual news brought to us by sailors who visited myriad exotic countries around the globe. [XXIV] (FOOTNOTE)

Unfortunately, the slave trade between Africa, the Americas and Europe provided revenue to the Netherlands that was the source of prosperity I benefited from as an artist. [XXV] (FOOTNOTE) Money from slave production bought more slaves, and the diabolical slave trade triangle [XXVI] (FOOTNOTE) between Europe, Africa and the Americas was repeated.

Financial prosperity from slaves enabled the arts to flourish in Europe. Factually, no matter how cruel a reality, without wealth, art cannot exist.

Although Anthony earned a fine living as a draper or clothe merchant, he always seemed to have the time and the means with which to purchase the instruments and tools of science and the cornucopia of curiosa he always needed for his experiments and science explorations.

All of the props in this picture were provided by him. I don't know much about the meaning of his paraphernalia. However, the arrangement of them within the scene makes a pleasing portrait of a man obsessed with observing the universe, and his relentless quest for knowledge.

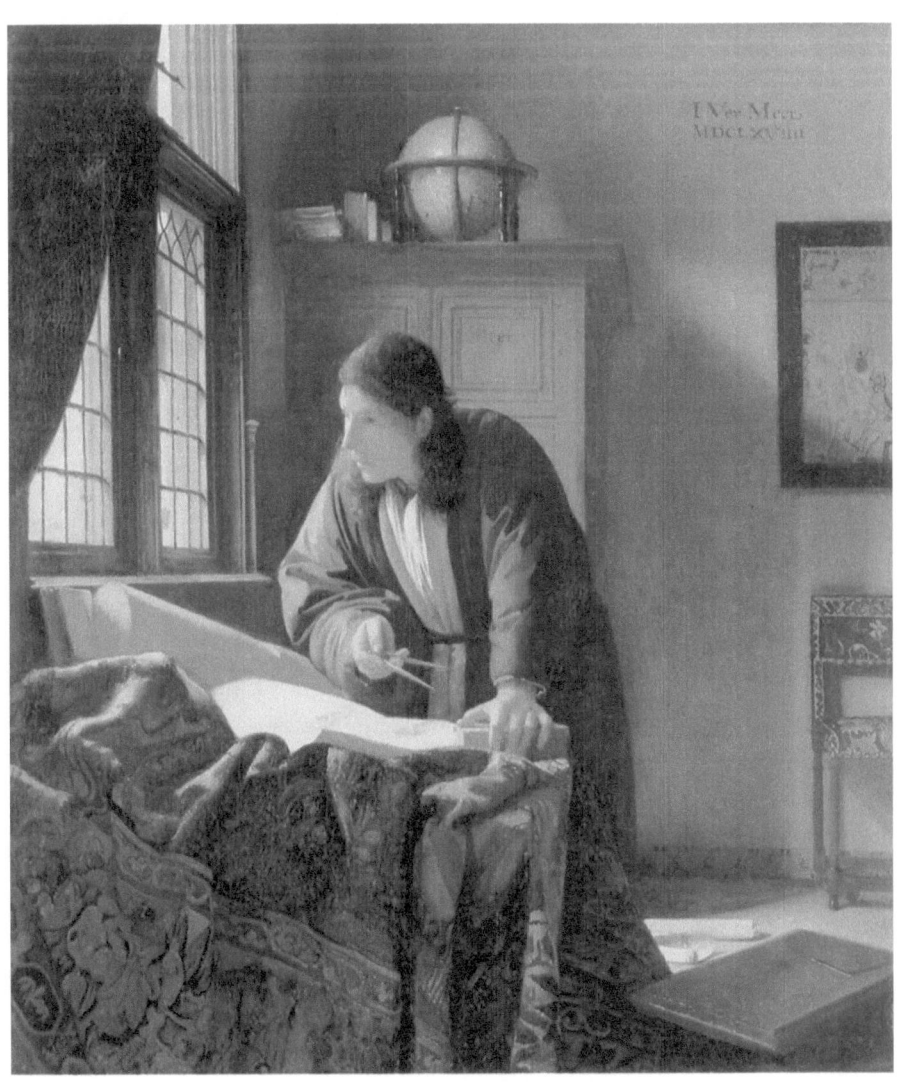

Maria Vermeer Reading Mail

A GIRL READING A LETTER BY AN OPEN
WINDOW
oil on canvas
32 1/4 x 25 3/8 in. (83 x 64.5 cm.)

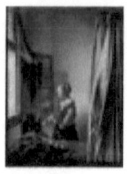

Even in her teen years, my eldest daughter, Maria as portrayed here, was quite literate, having been educated by her mother and at school in Delft. She could read better than I, and was generally astute with music, and other academic skills, as time allowed. I, on the other hand, was singularly focused on painting and matters related to the trade of paintings and the business of artisan members at the Guild of St. Luke.

Books were very expensive and not in ready supply. So, reading material was principally confined to correspondence, legal documents, business records, ledgers, accounts and miscellaneous pamphlets, unless aggressively sought after.

Our daughters were educated, like Catharina, in the Girl's School in Delft. The fundamental skills they learned there, reading, writing, a numbers, for the most part, were supplemented by training in musical instruments, singing, lace making a similar arts at home. This was the definition of home entertainment in the 17th Century!

My concern was not with the letter in this picture. I was more interested in mastering in the technical aspects of painting fabrics, the gradient shadows in the room, the reflection of Maria in the window glass and the air itself. Her pose, reading a letter, offered a subject standing still, which is most conducive to success when one is obsesses with replicating reality in every aspect.

The acceptable standard for a competent painter in that day, before expressionism, and other subjective art forms that later came into vogue, was strict obedience to reality. I was well pleased with this, as, in order to do so, one must emulate The Creator Himself! A perfectly rendered patch of light, place precisely with paint and brush is quite empowering.

At least it seemed so at the time, and until recent years of my most recent life. I have begun to admire more fully the artist who creates from nothing, from imagination only. What greater skill it takes to imagine a universe, before one paints, rather than painting one already made? The skill and ability required for the former is immeasurable more!

Although I respect and admire the "old masters", who faithfully copy the world, I envy an original creator even more for making up their own. This is true for all the arts: literature included. Fiction is much more difficult than documenting facts, or recording opinions, and is far more rewarding for the originator.

The imagination of a child, untethered by "now I'm supposed to..." is a lesson I learned as an aspiring artist. Not rhetoric taught in school. Beauty, truth and goodness are opinions of the viewer, I can not teach or learn. Techniques? Yes. Aesthetics? No. Morals? Yes. Integrity? No.

It has been said that the most I will know of god is myself. Personal integrity is the observance and application of those god-like qualities for which I hold myself accountable. I must live eternally with myself. As an artist, I am my only patron. I am my own most critical judge and enthusiastic audience!

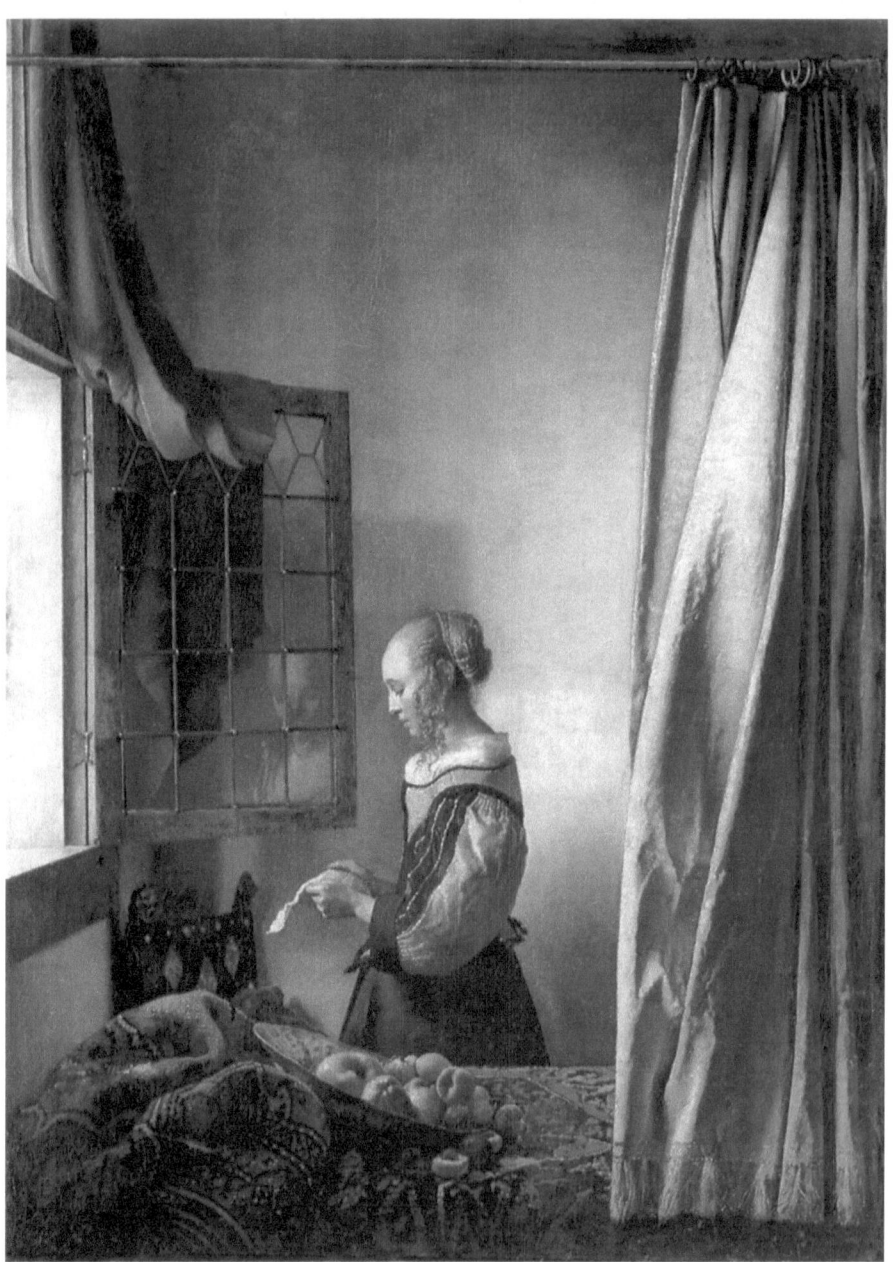

Catharina Bolnes: Holding Life In The Balance

WOMAN HOLDING A BALANCE
oil on canvas
stretcher size: 16 3/4 x 15 in. (42.5 x 38 cm.)

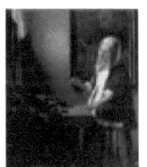

Catharina Bolnes, my wife. Pregnant, again. I'm not sure with which child. Of the 15 children to whom she gave life during our 22 years of marriage, 11 survived to adulthood. In 17th century Europe, only about half of children survived, on the average. Her prolific rate of birth is testament to her fertility and strength. But the fact that she was able to counter-balance the weight of death against life in that age, proves her determination to survive.

Diseases, propagated by scientific ignorance, and the centuries old prohibition against bathing, (an evil of the hated Romans) enforced by Catholic priests, made easy victims of human beings for vermin and bacteria. Indeed, the so-called "discovery" and conquest of the new world was accomplished by the deaths of one hundred million native "American" citizens who were instantly overwhelmed by bacteria carried on the filthy bodies of Spanish and Portuguese soldiers, sailors and priests!

This portrait of Catharina, although allegorical, is appropriate for her. Indeed, Catharina held my own life in balance for most of our years together. She was the stable, domestic shore for which I always found refuge from whatever storms blew outside the home. Fortunately, for the greater number of our years together, these were relatively few.

No matter how philosophical one may be, given the odds against surviving to adulthood in the 17th century, one can never bear the loss of one's own child without overwhelming grief and mourning. As a mother, Catharina balanced the scale between life and death with her care, attentiveness, industry and compassion. In spite of this, we lost four children to diseases bred in warm weather or exposure to frozen air of the North Sea during the winters of the Low Country.

In fact, our mortality was measured by Death in December: myself, Maria Thins, Catharina and several of our children died during the Winter Solstice month, when shivery days were short, and Cimmerian nights were made of ice.

Through all, Catharina created an illusion of confidence through competent, industry, and diligence. Regardless of turmoil, upset or obstacles she persisted and put chaos into order. The apparent order, tidiness, and pleasant interiors of my paintings, including this one, were orchestrated by her with a careful planning and a lot of toil!

In addition to the roles she played as a mother, educator, wife, housekeeper, lover and friend, which would consume all of the energy of any normal person, I must rightly give her credit for enabling and facilitating much of my work as an artist. It was her patience and hard work to keep order in the household that made it possible for me to focus on my painterly chores. And, as captured for posterity in this, and several other paintings of her, she was an exquisite model!

More than these, she lived the role Juliet to my Romeo while managing the stage, the lights and the score! All without a fee. Just for the joy of it. What husband, painter or person could ask for more?

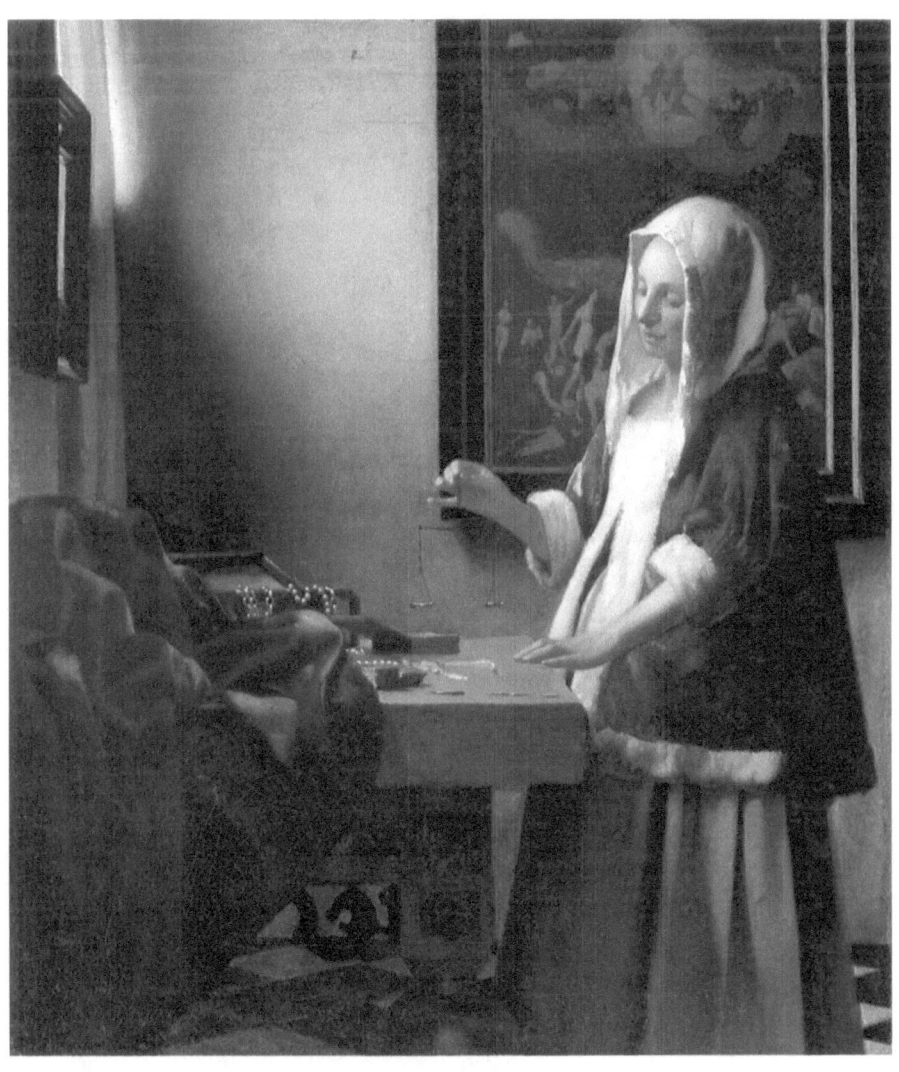

Mistress of The Light, Maria Vermeer

YOUNG WOMAN WITH A WATER PITCHER
oil on canvas
18 x 16 in. (45.7 x 40.6 cm)

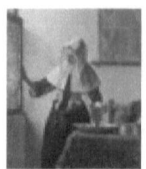

Shakespeare said it best, when he wrote:

"But, soft! what light through yonder window breaks?

It is the East, and Juliet is the sun.
Arise, fair sun, and kill the envious moon,
Who is already sick and pale with grief,
That thou, her maid, art far more fair than she.
Be not her maid, since she is envious;
Her vestal livery is but sick and green
And none but fools do wear it; cast it off.
It is my lady, O, it is my love!"

 -- Romeo and Juliet: Act 2, Scene 2

These lines could have been written, fittingly, for a scene for the tragic love-drama, "*Johannes and Catharina*". The story line is similar. Only the dates, places, and names have been changed to protect the participants.

In this case, Maria, acting a the model for this painting, holds the window carefully, as though inspecting it for flaws. Her mother, by the time of this painting, when Maria was a teenager, was far too busy with household duties and caring for the younger children to spend very many of her daylight minutes modeling for my idyllic, ethereal pictures.

Much of Catharina's time was spent dealing with the <u>consequences</u> of romance: nursing babies at her breast, cleaning dirty bottoms, washing, rinsing, scrubbing, mending and a thousand other menial messes enforced on Motherhood. The pain and blood of childbirth are a crass contrast to the fleeting joy of orgasms!

Romantic sentiments, nonetheless, the soft light of the sun streaming through "yonder window", are the principle subject of this painting. The polished brass pitcher, and tray, create an interactive reflection of the sunlight. The relatively course, ruddy carpet, by contrast, intensifies the reflected light of the other objects in the scene, just as the beauty of Juliet is enhanced by the adoration of her suitor. Just as bearing a child is the consequence of sexual bliss: lovely and messy intermeshed.

Maria's translucence mantel is exquisite white! So much so that it is highlighted by the blue from her dress. The effect is diffused, yet precise. It is an act of magic! Just as soft light streaming through a window in Delft is a miracle of photons interacting with atmosphere and canals.

What more perfect colors can there be, on Earth, than blue, gold and white? The earth, sun, the moon, the stars, water, and sky are gradients of red, blue, gold or white, made visible to the human eye by a spectrum of reflected light.

As always, the attention to minute details of light and objects in the painting is my attempt to embody a three-dimensional world on a two-dimensional plane. Art emulates the spirit, but cannot be it. Beauty is the opinion of the spirit, not the object admired. Painting an idea leaves much to be desired. One cannot know an apple by seeing the skin. One must taste the sweet texture and savor the juice within!

To experience life, one must be the essence of it. Yet, to observe is not to permeate! To Be the essence of life, without becoming the adverse effect of it, one must occupy the space, without becoming the objects in it. Can one love without demanding love in return? Can one be free, yet be enslaved? This is the agony of a painter: it is the scent that cannot be smelled.

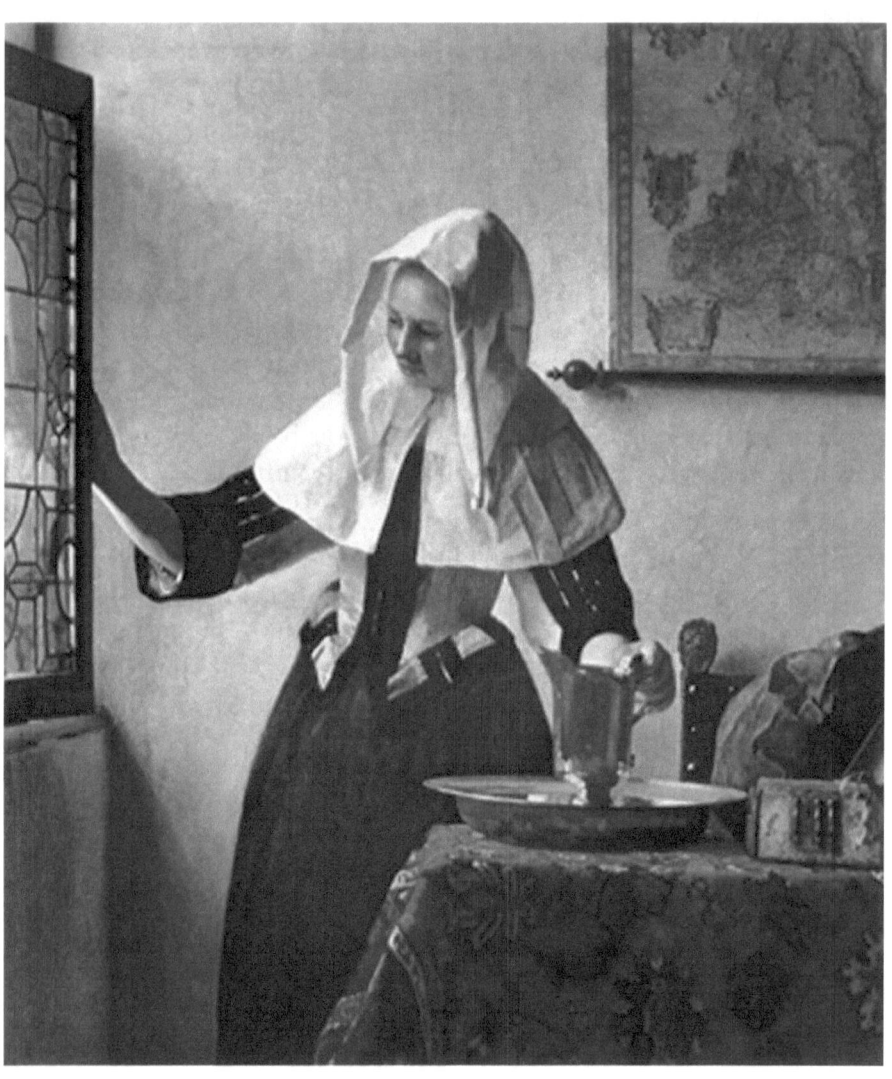

The Faith of Maria Thins

ALLEGORY OF FAITH
oil on canvas
54 x 35 in. (114.3 x 88.9 cm.)

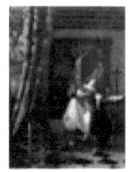

To please Maria Thins, and as an unofficial payment to her, in exchange for her many years of generous financial support of our family, I painted this tribute to her.   Without her support I could not have existed as a painter. It does not intend to portray anyone in the family in particular. The girls took turns posing. The focus of the painting is intended to be intellectual, rather than personal or biographical. Rather, the subject matter is the religious symbolism embodied in the work.

Maria was a Catholic, who eagerly embraced the manufactured mythos of the Papal superstition machine. [XXVII] (FOOTNOTE) Faith is an apt description of her personal resolve that all would be well in the long run. She was sure that we were each seeking a predetermined destination. God was guiding each of our insignificant lives. His Omnipotence had a plan which we mortals only need to trust, regardless of the tragedy, (embodied in the painting by the snake), that constantly tests one's faith.

Faith, by definition, demands a state of mindless obedience to self-anointed authorities, who, in the name of a god or monarch, suppress the intelligence of others for their own, personal gain. If one does not look or investigate or think or ask questions, one can have faith or become a "believer". Christianity, and every other "-ism" or "-anity" that ever crushed to spirit and intellect of man, depends wholly on others to have faith in the institution and the self-serving persons who dictate dogma and instill ignorance and superstition in them.

The painting is full of the Christian symbols. The theme of the work is an expression of Maria Thins trust that God, through His Son, ruled benevolently on Earth, and would continue, posthumously, in Heaven.

Personally, I would not have considered or conceded to paint this kind of painting, except to please her. I did study and embrace Biblical philosophy. But, in spite of my baptism at marriage, for the sake of winning Catharina' s hand, I didn't trust the institutions of organized religious practice, especially the Catholic Church, who, followed closely by Protestants, have spilled the blood of billions and ground it into the dust to ensure that their beliefs are the only beliefs! The armies of a

---

panoply of "the only true religion" have butchered and pillaged more civilians than any other assembled force in history, with the notable exception of Ghenis Khan, and his progeny.

The Khan, at least, had the unabashed self-esteem and willingness to take responsibility to enforce his personal decree that he, solely and personally, was <u>the</u> living god on Earth. He didn't cower behind the legend of a dead man or superstitious priests or philosophical ideology to justify his power or authority. He was, literally, a "god" among men. And, if you didn't agree with him on this point, you promptly became a disembodied spirit! Faith or no faith.

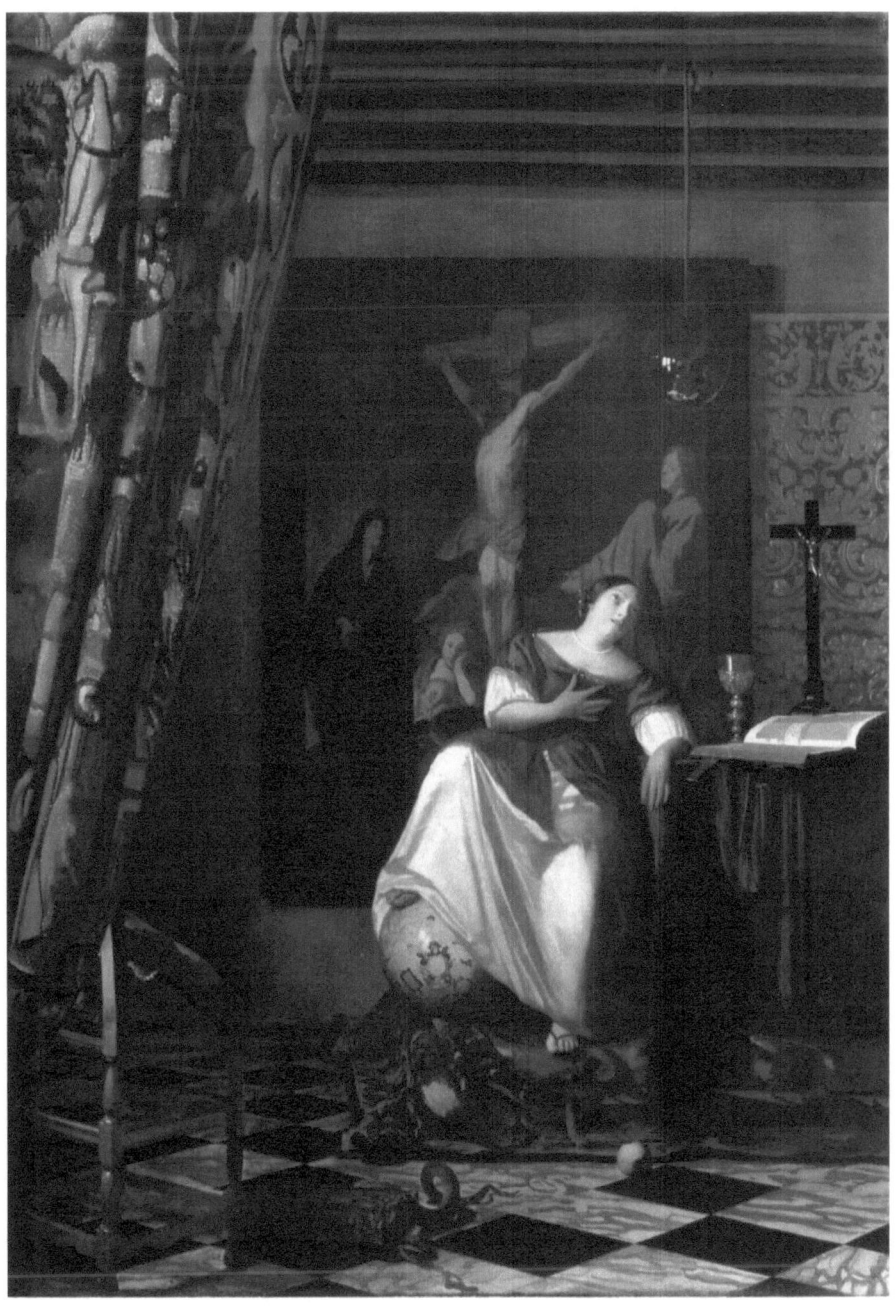

My Maria Mona Lisa

THE MILKMAID
oil on canvas
17 7/8 x 16 inches (45.45 x 40.6 cm.)

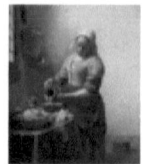

Much like Leonardo da Vinci, I worked intermittently on this single painting over a period of many years, never satisfied that it was finished, and continually improving upon the original. This painting is my personal Mona Lisa, my daughter, Maria.

We had a live-in servant for many years, named Tanneke Everpoel, hired and paid by Maria Thins. She did all of the "heavy labor", as it were: cooking, cleaning, washing clothes, carrying water, tending fires, and a myriad other chores, including helping with the children. However, the expense of paying her wage and room did not include standing for endless hours, day after day, while I painted this portrait! My daughter, Maria, was lovelier and much more readily accessible for the task of standing for this portrait.

> *By yon fair mirror, deft,*
> *My window is bereft*
> *Of light and air - a theft*
> *From golden Sol, himself! It's*
> *All my mirror's pelf - it's*
> *Jan Vermeer of Delft's.*
>
> -- by Dean Blehert

It is argued, convincingly, that the immortal painting by Leonard was his own self-portrait as his own, feminine reflection. What man, or woman, regardless of sexual preference in a given lifetime, has not inhabited the flesh of ten thousand bodies, some human, many not, through a nearly infinite cascade of galaxies, stars and planets come and gone. Is not survival a nearly infinite game, in which we interchange ourselves as the players of many parts?

Leonard kept his portrait with him all his life. He never considered that it was complete or perfect. Nor did he ever intend to sell it. How could one sell a most cherished reflection of himself? It is more meaningful than one's own body, which only disguises the inner self, the essence of spirit that animates the fragile flesh.

In fact, a body hides the reflection of the soul! How can any substance, especially that as rude and fragile as meat, reveal the inherent qualities an immortal nothingness? Indeed, it is the fundamental challenge and the most formidable task of an artist to reveal it!

The name given to this painting by others, "The Milkmaid", is a sacrilege! It rivals the incomprehension others have for Leonardo's personal masterpiece. Yet, how can anyone truly understand that a painting is meant to reflect the essence of an immortal being, seen through the eyes of another?

She is painted with angelic colors: blue, gold and white, in contrast to the menial nature of her station in life. From her issues, for me, the Milk and Bread of Life. Life is embodied in her and through her. Women, are the source of children, the source of energy, the source of care. There is no more vital responsibility for any being who plays the game of life, than to confront dreary daily tasks. To humbly make the daily loaf. To soak that bread, mix and soften it with milk, make it warm and feed it to a teething child. Survival is made of such things.

When done with love, survival is not made of daily chores, but is a blessing and a joy of creation! These duties are usually done by women, and rarely appreciated by men. The stench of body sweat, vomit, urine and stinking bowels demand constant cleansing. Aching muscles full of cold, menstrual cramps, and exhausted patience are rewards for being equal to the tasks of sweeping, mopping, scrubbing floors on hands and knees, boiling water, and tending fires to repel incessant waves of filth and cold into a home.

Pealing produce, gutting ducks and mending clothes, soothing tears, scolding and teaching are all done while nursing a small children on a hip. All the while, making oneself look beautiful. Should one reveal this hellish life in a portrait of a woman? Or, is it more humane to honor her with a picture of innocence and wholesome grace? Can one honor their toil more perfectly?

In those days, the measure of a competent artisan was an ability to duplicate minute details of a domestic scene. In this, I went overboard: rough brush strokes used for smooth surfaces, make the coarser objects compatible with polished brass and glass, in a rustic scene. The nail holes, and textures of the wall, water stains below the window, a broken pane of glass, roughly sewn garments, a foot heating box, litter on the floor, are all acceptable decor in a kitchen corner. In the original painting, there was once a laundry basket on the floor, which I brushed out for the sake of composition. It should have been left alone, to more accurately portray the actions of a woman.

Our bread was baked with whole grain flour, coarsely ground. Milk came from real cows, with fat enough to grow a calf, in half a year, from birth to 600 pounds. Food was eaten fresh from the market square, or from the ground. Sugar -- an evil of the aristocracy -- was used only for pastries. All food was what we now call "organic". Without chemicals or preservatives, there was none but fresh food, no rotten or tainted food. Shopping for was a daily chore. Few things could be stored. *semelbrood,* "black," rye-kernel bread, is shown in this scene, as it lends itself to the rustic theme of the scene.

Generally, food was plentiful, and much enjoyed, during several meals each day. [XXVIII] (FOOTNOTE) Nonetheless, few people were fat in those days. This portrait of Elizabeth makes her look more plump than she was in reality. She is dressed in heavy clothes against the cold. Robust women were not feared, but cherished as healthy, hearty stock, capable of heavy work! Plump thighs are a sign of health (and soft to sit or lay on). She was always soft, and warm, in body and in soul.

In those days I viewed life as idyllic. My dreams were more real than reality. All things were a possibility. Tragedy could not find me. Until it did, of course. Even when we lost a child, which we did with several, my wife, Catharina, remained resolute in her Faith. God guided us. He did what was best. We knew not why and need not question His purpose for us.

I have no such faith in predetermination. A loaf of grain, clean water and a bed was my fare. Time and a place to paint, uninterrupted, were necessities. My love, shared with wife and family, was the staple diet of my life. I assumed, as a Fool who knows not his own mortality, that they would endure, even when I was gone.

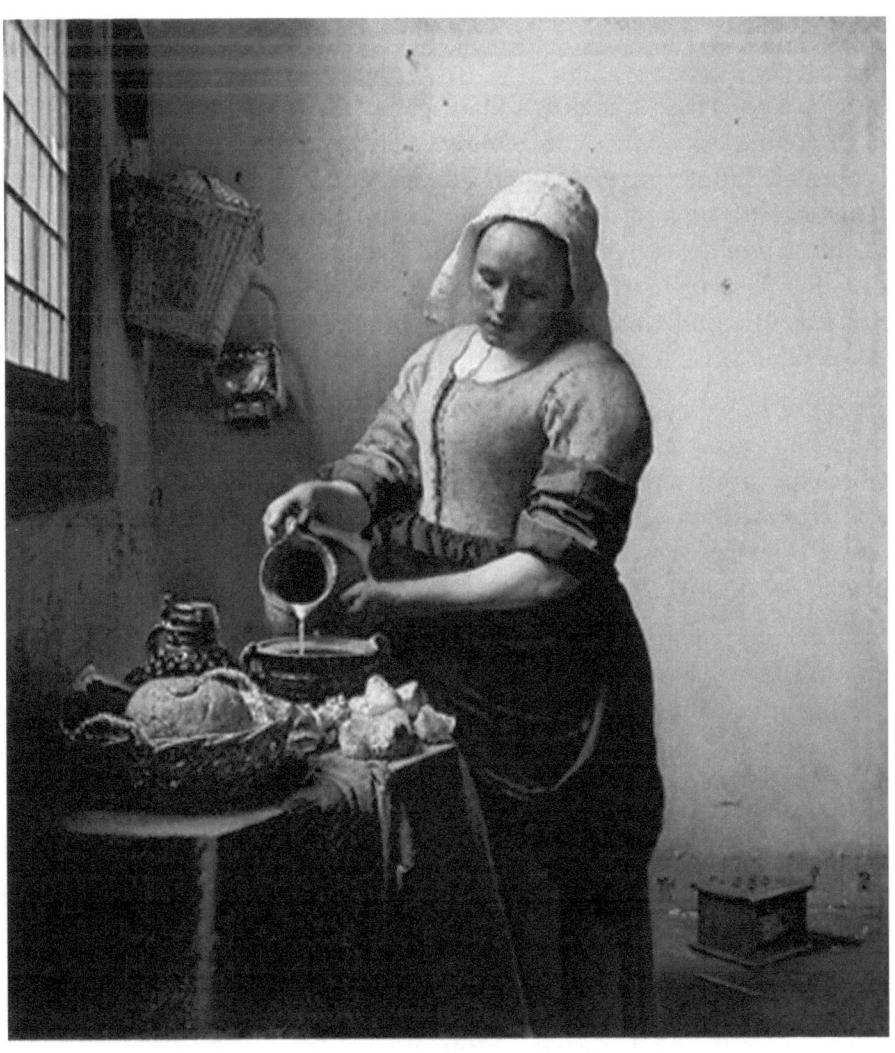

Elizabeth Vermeer: Turban and Kimono

THE GIRL WITH A PEARL EARRING
oil on canvas
18 1/4 x 15 1/4 in. (46.5 x 40 cm.)

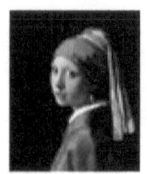

N umerous false scenarios and imaginary identities have been
conjured, by critics and admirers alike, to identify the face in this
exquisitely simple portrait. Much like the Mona Lisa, which may be a
feminine reflection of the face of Leonardo, the face in this painting is a
manifestation my own genetic material. This young woman is my second
daughter, Elizabeth, who was perhaps 15 years old when this was
painted. Of course, she is also the girl with the flute, and with the red hat
in the other small tronie portraits mentioned previously.

The "pearl", so much discussed by those enamored by this painting, is
not really a pearl at all. It is cosmetic jewelry imported from France,
where they form a thin sphere of glass filled with a concoction of *l'essence
d'orient*, a mixture of white wax and the silvery scales of a fish called an
ablette. This false jewel is then varnished to emulate the luminosity of a
pearl. [XXIX] (FOOTNOTE)

Further, I have enhanced the size of it with brush and paint, to make it
appear larger than its actual size, for the sake of composition. It creates a
striking effect, and at a small fraction of the cost of a genuine pearl of
such size, which would cost more than any but bankers and kings could
afford to adorn their brides.

A source of intensified light was used in this portrait to augment
Elizabeth 's innocent beauty. The effect was achieved by using a mirror
to reflect sunlight from a nearby window, directly on her face, thus
intensifying the luminosity of the image. Combined with the
"photographic" effect provided by the camera obscura, the portrait
seems more lifelike than other portraits. I used a the same staging
procedure in the small portrait of Beatrix.

I was able, with brush technique, to further enhance this effect, using
broad, unrefined strokes to render the garments, while finely polishing
the features of her face using brushes made with very soft hair.

For this reason, also, a very dark background was used, devoid of any
other objects. This applies an ancient painting technique which contrasts
dark and light, called *chiaroscuro*. This further intensifies, by contrast, the
light, and therefore makes the features of Maria's face much more

distinct and striking than in the other portraits of her. Compare this portrait of Elizabeth with the two other "tronies" wherein her eyes and face are shaded by large hats, and the relatively low level of lighting in the room.

This technical effect was suggested to me by my friend Van Leeuwenhoek, who used a mirror to reflect and intensify light for his microscope, so as to gain greater clarity in the tiny subjects he studied. For example, he was able to see the fluids coursing through the veins in a leaf when reflected light was directed to the underside while viewing the leaf through his lens from above.

A cloth turban, and the simple kimono, against a black background, create a genesis of light on her face which appears to magically radiate from within her skin! It is no wonder that people are enraptured by the glow of her innocent, exquisite gaze. The luminescence of Elizabeth's vestal visage and pubescent complexion diminishes the earring, by comparison, to an incidental highlight not worthy of mention!

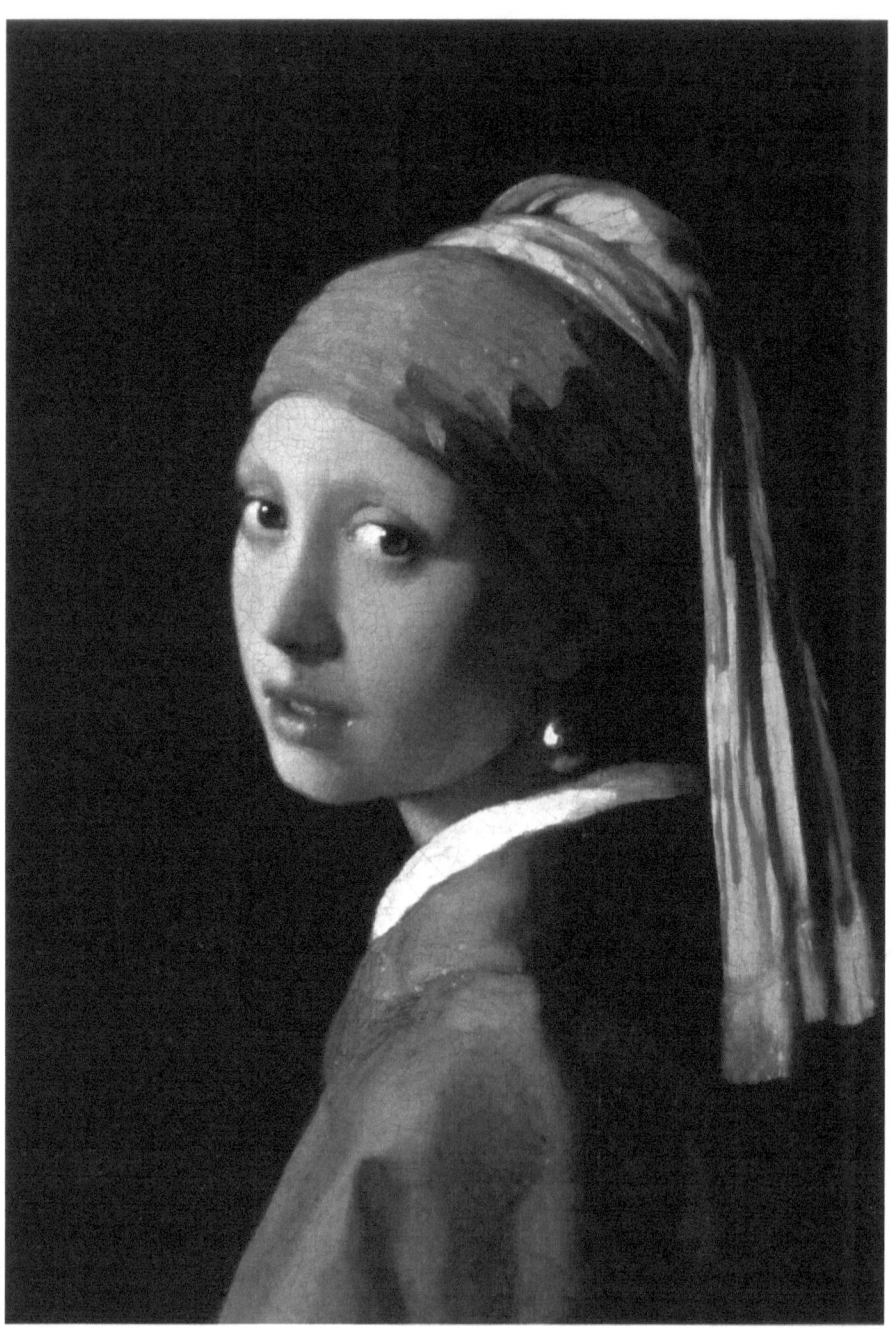

A Portrait of Beatrix Vermeer

STUDY OF A YOUNG WOMAN
oil on canvas
17 1/2 x 15 3/4 in. (44.5 x 40 cm)

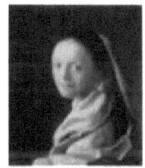

More than a priceless pearl, to a man pure in heart and unpretentious, there is nothing more precious to a father than his daughters.

One of my younger daughters, Beatrix, when she was about 10 years of age, is the subject of this small portrait, or *tronie*. She has many more of my features that the other girls, especially my mouth, with a more narrow chin, and thinner lips than her mother and sisters. I will never forget how intensely attentive she was to having her picture painted.

The silvery silk draped around her shoulders is contrasted against a black background or *chiaroscuro* effect. Her turban provides a perfectly nondescript background to augment the features her soft eyes and gentle face. She, like her sister Elizabeth, wears the large, false pearl which compliments the color of her cape, but as the light of the shawl is reflected its form is lost to casual observation.

I think she relished, more than anything, having my complete, undivided attention for the many hours we spent together during our painting sessions. I must say that the likeness of her in this painting is extraordinarily accurate. I think it is one on my best works of portraiture, in defiance of the diminutive size of the canvas.

Beatrix was always a favorite delight to me! She was eternally effervescent and energetic. She loved me dearly, and was devoted to having my admiration whenever possible. She is an innocent, impish soul whom I will always love with all my heart!

Although I have always loved and cherished each of my children, in any lifetime, for the unique beings they are, I always smile to myself with a special, quiet joy, when see this portrait or whenever I think of Beatrix.

The kingdom of heaven is like unto a merchant man, seeking goodly pearls; who, when he had found one pearl of great price, went and sold all that he had, and bought it.

-- Matthew 13:45

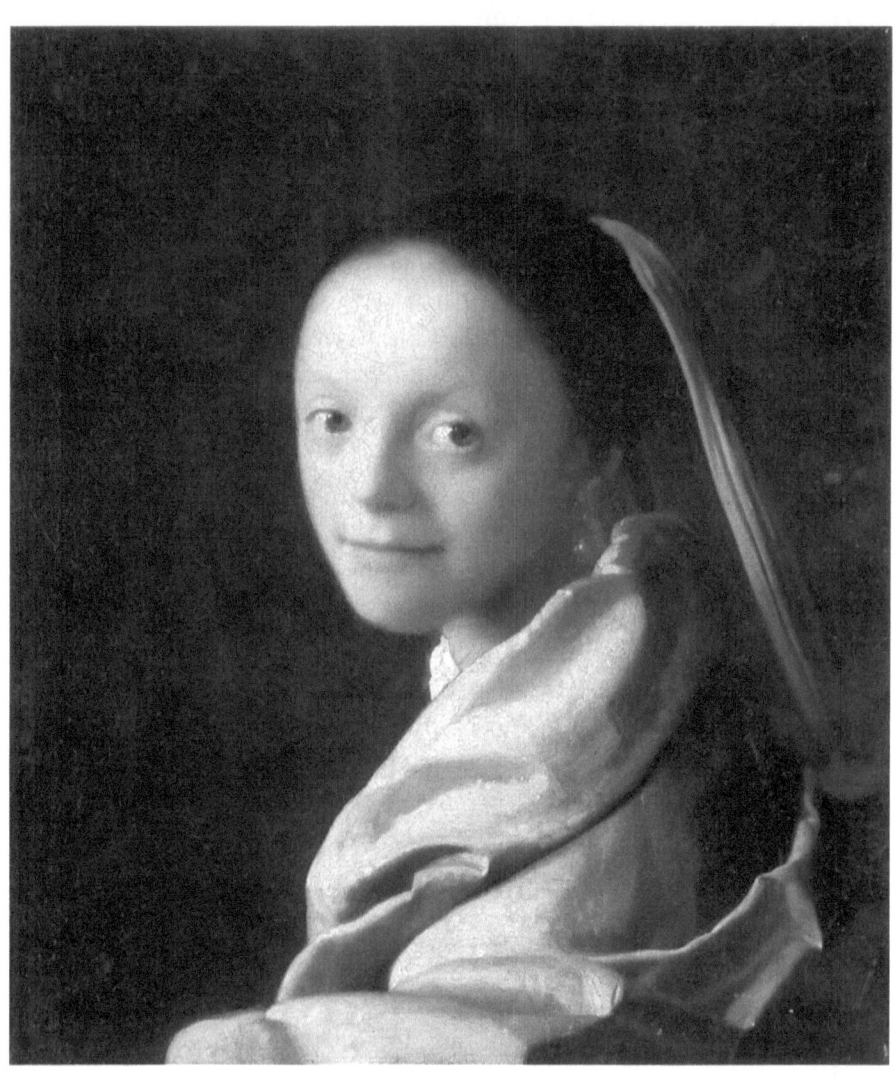

Cornelia Vermeer, Musician

A YOUNG WOMAN SEATED AT THE VIRGINALS
9 7/8 x 7 7/8 in. (25.2 x 20 cm.)

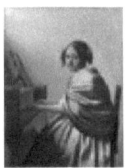

Cornelia, whom we named after Catharina's sister, wore a characteristic curl of her auburn hair, which was similar in color to my own hair. Cornelia was naturally artistic and a diligent student of music. She is pictured in several paintings having to do with music - at least those painted when she was grown up enough to sit still for a portrait.

The younger children were too full of impatient energy to pose for a portrait! I did not paint my son, Johannes, for this reason as he was far more interested in scampering about with his friends than remaining seated and motionless indoors for extended periods!

Music, fabric arts and literature were acceptable pursuits for women in that age, rather than those crafts or trades that might compete with men for a livelihood. Women were not accepted as members of the Guild of St. Luke, at least in Delft, as only men were allowed to participate in artistic vocations that could earn money.

Women, although immensely talented, intelligent, tough, tenacious, wise and industrious -- and often more determined to survive than men, such as myself -- were kept suppressed into domestic servitude. As only women are brave and strong enough to bear children, they are fundamentally feared by men.

Men are comparatively weak and cowardly, when compared to women on the whole. Warfare is proof of this. Is not the fact that men kill each other with guns and swords an overt admission that they are incapable of creating reasonable accord between themselves with words?

The primary failure of womankind has been to allow their sons to grow up to become brutal, morally bereft, barbarians. As in the ancient Greek play, *Lysistrata*, (loosely translated to "she who disbands armies"), the story's female characters barricade the public funds building and withhold sex from their husbands to end the Peloponnesian War and secure peace. After several days, the men begin to experience physical pain from lack of sex. They quickly settle peace negotiations between the countries. Lysistrata declares the sex feud over and allows the women to return home with their husbands. [xxx] (FOOTNOTE)

Men and women are so thoroughly overwhelmed by the emotional and psychological effects caused by the glandular secretion of bodily fluids, testosterone and estrogen, that they are literally -- in the most thorough sense -- drug addicts. They are addicted the bodily chemicals over which they have no ability to regulate, other than the sentient ability to reason.

This faculty, in theory, is the principle difference between men and animals. One could propose a scientific hypothesis, easily demonstrated and proven, that men and women are, in fact, only animals to the degree that they are unable to control the effects of their bodily hormones through the exertions of their own intellect.

I know that this was certainly true for me, personally. The 15 children born by Catharina and I are proof enough that we were intellectually incapable of controlling the stimulus-response mechanism of our loins.

Giving children a very thorough understanding of the consequences of the sexual act and the responsibilities of reproduction could tame sexual aggression significantly. It has been the quest of many a monastic order to overcome this grossest of human impulses, in an attempt to enable to body and soul to separate.

It has been said that all the angles of paradise can not hold down an aroused penis. When paradise and angels fail, we must perfect, through intellectual disciple, the control our own sexual appetites. If this was the highest priority of cultivating adolescent homo sapiens into behaving as humane and sentient citizens, we would be the angels, with Paradise as our home!

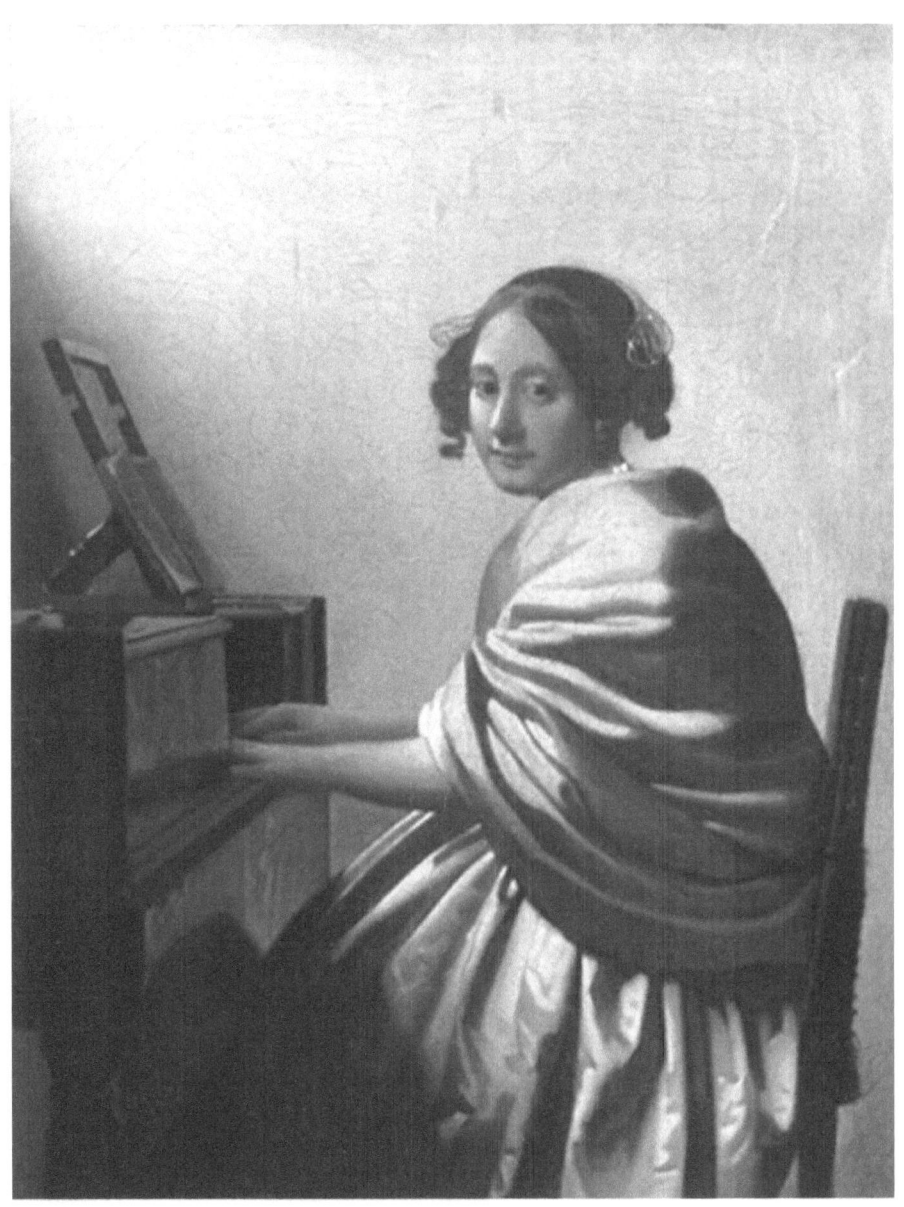

Cornelia Vermeer Making Lace

THE LACEMAKER
oil on canvas
9 5/8 x 8 1/4 in. (24.5 x 21 cm.)

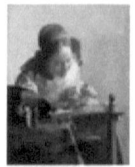

Cornelia in one of two miniature portraits of her. In addition, she is posed for one of the small virginal pieces, and with the guitar and a table.

In fact, Cornelia was a skilled Lacemaker, XXXI (FOOTNOTE) as were many of the ladies of Delft, partially out of necessity to have pretty, decorative garments to wear. Lace was very expensive to buy as it was an art form that required many hours of patient attention to meticulous details. This art form requires considerable tutoring and practice to gain the skill required to produce delicate, lovely masterpieces of thread.

Pieces of lace worn by ladies, as part of head a covering for attending Mass, were an ancient tradition of the Catholic church.

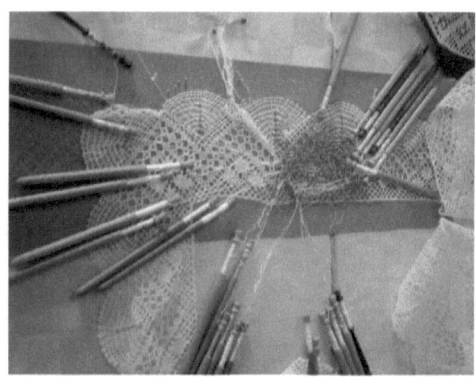

I have done some needlepoint work and found it to be quite relaxing and satisfying as a pass time, although is not challenging enough technically. Needle and thread do not provide the virtually limitless gradients of color and texture that are facilitated by blending oil and pigments.

The pigments used in my paintings I sometimes ground by hand in the attic of my home. These, I mixed with linseed or walnut oil to create the correct opaque or transparent viscosity. When available, I sometimes purchased pigments and other items ready made from the apothecary in Delft, XXXII (FOOTNOTE) who usually kept a good supply of necessities for members of the Guild of St. Luke.

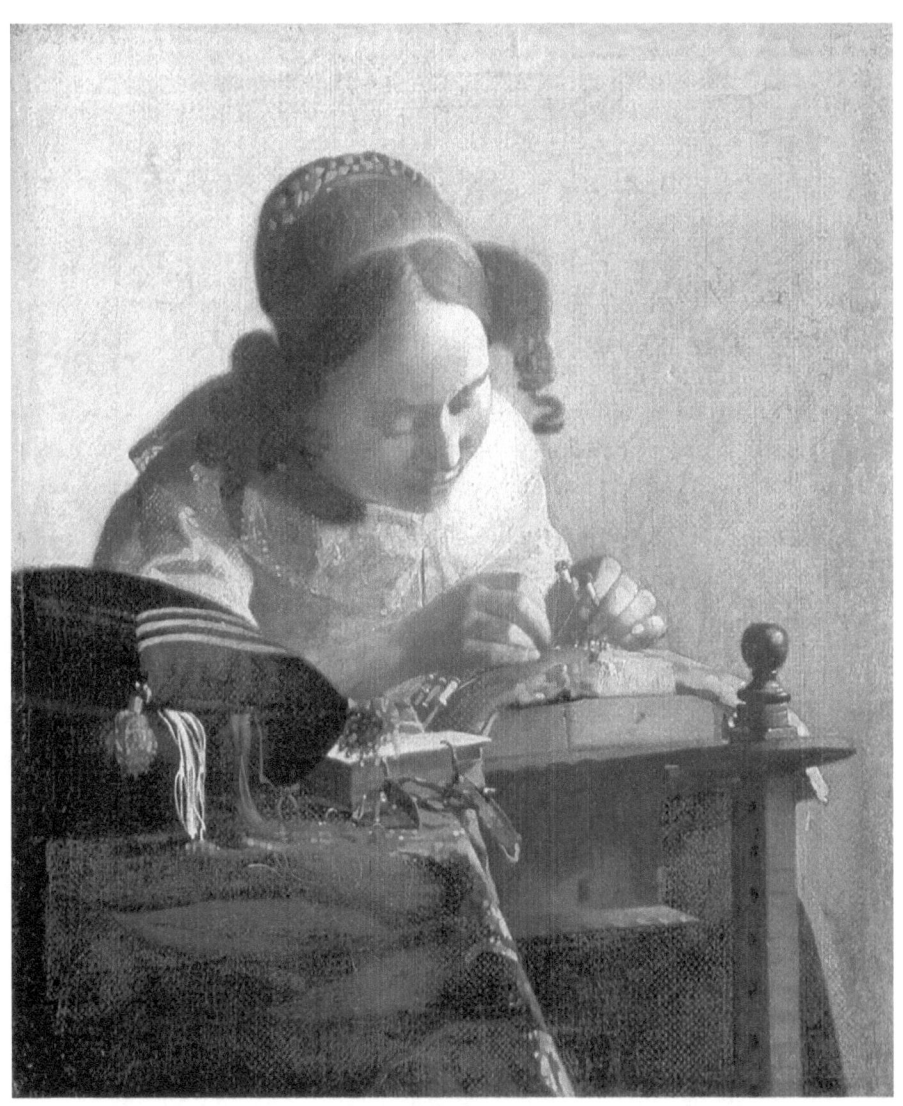

Aleydis Vermeer, Dressing Like Mother

WOMAN WITH A PEARL NECKLACE
oil on canvas
21 1/8 x 17 1/4 in. (55 x 45 cm.)

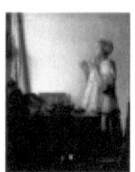

My lovely daughter, Aleydis, at about the age of 12, dressed up like her mother, before the window light. This window is in the upstairs room I often used for painting while we lived in Maria Thins house. I never felt this house was my own home, as we moved out of the house my father owned when we outgrew it. Nevertheless, ownership is an idea, not only an act.

As I recall, dimly, my impression is that she was very domestic and aspired to be so. I think she was very practical, actually. Although, she was more a dreamer, than her mother. That is, she still suffered the "delusions" of youth, before the painful ardors of reality beset her. Any dreams are far better than none. Art, music, love and laughter were her escape from reality. I am very pleased to say that she had some of these.

As for this painting, I think it is a good study of light, as is the case with any painting, if fact. One paints light. That is all one paints. Light in it's gradient, nearly infinite, subtlety. The greatest challenge to me was to render the soft, moist light of Delft as it actually appeared. Humidity intensifies, and magnifies the reflected photons from the sun. In ten minutes, the sun has moved, that <u>exact</u> light is changed or lost. To that very large extent, one paints a <u>memory</u> of light, as it appeared in one, most desirable, instant before it is faded or intensified.

The gradual affect on our perception of the light spectrum we call "color" is the entire subject of painting. There are, truly, no lines, or shapes in things. There is only our subjective interpretation of light, fallen on a form, reflected and filtered through the retina of the eye. We assign the significance to it, we endow it with the quality of beauty or ugliness, or somewhere in between.

No two beings perceive the universe exactly alike - in spite of the "authorities" in art, who deem themselves more worthy to see existence than we, the unwashed, unholy, heathen. Only the sophomoric idiot, who can not <u>do</u>, pretends to know more than the rest of us. Art is a quality, not taught in schools, but rendered by the soul.

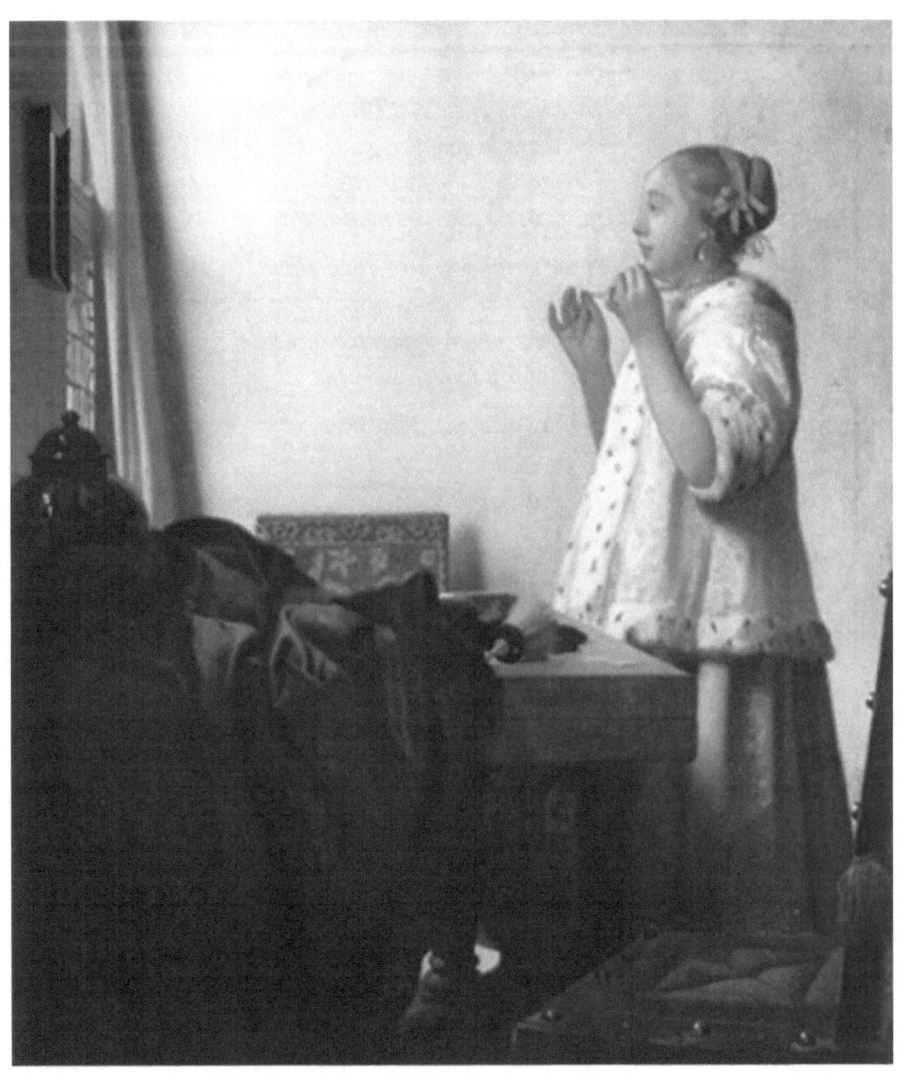

Woman, Thou Art Beauty

WOMAN IN BLUE READING A LETTER
oil on canvas
18 1/4 x 15 7/8 in. (46.5 x 38 cm.)

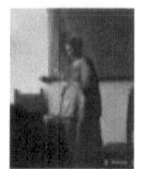

Woman, Thou Art Beauty!
born beyond being...
rare and simple purity
fragile power -- timeless immortality.

Complex simplicity, perfectly sublime:
undying, yet reborn.
Serenity in action, uncompromised by time:
wrinkled, though unworn.

No dance can sway Thee
No psalm can say Thee
No sight can see Thee
No sense can be Thee

You Are that You Are
as ever You will be.
Thou Art Beauty.

A more mature Elizabeth, posing as her mother would have, had she taken the time away from caring for our very large family during the later years of our marriage. Many, many people have mistaken this painting as a portrait of Catharina Bolnes. It is not. This is an allegorical painting, exemplifying the true source of the human race. Men cannot exist without women to bear babies.

(Yet, it is now possible for women to impregnate themselves with the sperm of a dead man to sustain the species. Therefore, it is theoretically possible for men to be eliminated from the reproductive process and subjugated by women. A convincing argument can be made that the potential survival of the human race would be enhanced by eliminating testosterone driven males who thrive on the urge to murder and destroy for fun and profit, a pass time in which women rarely indulge.

This notion occurs to me as one to be greatly desired, particularly after having my livelihood wiped out by the megalomaniacal monarch, King Louis XIV in his quest for personal wealth and physical immortality!

May he, and all the Macho Maniacs of Mankind agonize in the Infernal Netherworld for All Eternity!   I deem that this fate is the sole inheritance of such degraded behavior here on Earth, of which we are all their witless victims.)

Elisabeth is portrayed here, as though pregnant, just as her mother was most frequently. Due to the overwhelming demands of caring for 10 children, at the time of this painting, Elizabeth, posed for me, as though she were her mother. The object of the painting was not intended to be a portrait. Rather, it is a tribute to women and motherhood, personified beautifully by Elizabeth who had much more time available to pose for me than her mother.

Elizabeth never married, thus escaping the burden of child bearing. However, she was very familiar with child rearing, as she spent many years of her life helping her mother care for and raise her siblings.

The relatively monochromatic coloration of this picture was intended to accentuate and glorify an allegorical vision of Womanhood. It is Womankind, in all of Her magnificence, that inspired me! Women are the beauty of Mankind. Women are the Nurturing Force of Mankind, without which the Species of Humankind would not exist.

Elizabeth, as seen in several other portraits of her, has characteristically darker hair than her mother. The trait that predominates her portraits is her parted lips. As mentioned earlier, she was plagued by a chronic sinus condition that demanded that she breathe through her mouth.

I understand, from reading historical accounts, that Elizabeth never married, although she was certainly as beautiful as any woman can be. It seems she never gained exposure to the bachelors in the community. Her marriageable years were consumed, after my death, as she remained at home with her mother, helping to care for her sisters and brothers. She sacrificed her own future for the greater good of the family. Maria, who was married before my death, and Beatrix, where the only two girls to get married. Maria helped Catharina to raise Johannes, my son, and helped her mother greatly until her death 12 years later.

The beauty of my daughters was eclipsed only by their integrity.

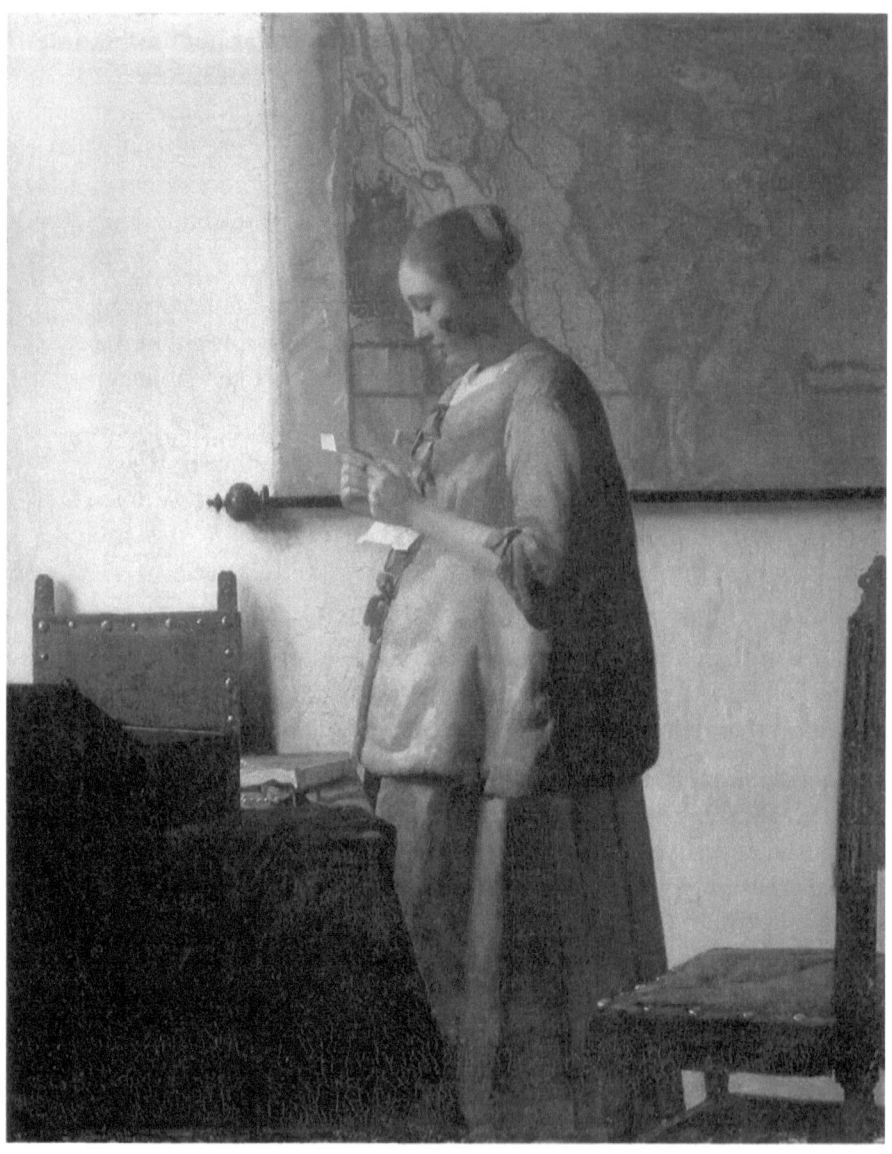

Elizabeth Vermeer: A China Hat

GIRL WITH A FLUTE
oil on panel
7 7/8 x 7 in. (20 x 17.8 cm.)

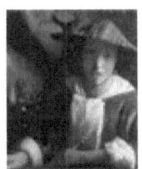

A tiny painting of my second oldest daughter, Elizabeth. It is smaller than a piece of letter-sized paper! The canvas is one of four miniature portraits I made of my daughters. Each is less than one-half the size of the largest of the three "tronie" paintings of Elizabeth, i.e. the "pearl earring". Painting in miniature is a great challenge, technically. It requires tiny brushes and a highly controlled use of the brush hand, balanced against a maalstick.

However, one of the primary goals of painting is to create illusions of light: to guide the eye in directions chosen by the artist, rather than by reality. Even at this diminutive size the painting was never finished with the detail, relative to it's size, of most other painting. When viewed from a distance, it creates the illusion of a thoroughly detailed image. Yet, in proportion, the brush strokes are coarse and gross. Such illusions were masterfully refined by later artists, the so-called "impressionists".

You will note that Elizabeth has her mouth open slightly, and she appears to be somewhat listless. During the process of re-examining these pictures, I recall that Elizabeth had a predilection to suffer from head colds, or sinus problems. As many people who live in cold, damp climates, such as Delft, will readily attest, chronic sinus drainage, especially during cold weather, is a common malady. For this reason, Elizabeth, usually carried a handkerchief. Her sinuses were constantly stuffed up for which she often compensated by breathing through her mouth.

Her tiredness, if not attributable to her sinus discomfort, was suffered, like her mother, to sleepless nights spent attending to the infants and younger children in the house, and having to awaken a daybreak to tend to the multitude of chores during daylight hours -- sleep or no sleep!

The responsibilities which befell Elizabeth, being an older daughter, included helping her mother, sisters and grandmother take care of all the younger children. With a houseful of children and adults to feed, clean and care for, this was never a small task.

To compound the magnitude of work already necessary, just to maintain fundamental survival, the women in my household were almost obsessed with cleanliness! In addition to food preparation, fetching fuel for the fire, preparing food, cooking, mending, sewing, tending the fires for warmth, chasing the smaller children about, and a thousand other tedious tasks of domestic living in the 17th century, they managed to keep themselves looking beautiful and presentable in public!

I have never, personally, displayed such tireless industry. Any man who deems himself superior to women solely due to his greater height, and musculature, is an outright, blithering fool! Female stamina, endurance and tolerance of pain inevitably, and universally, transcends that of men.

Combined with perennial, belligerent stupidity, induced by testosterone, it is a marvel that human civilization has endured at all. We would be extinct as a species already, if not for the nurturing strength of women.

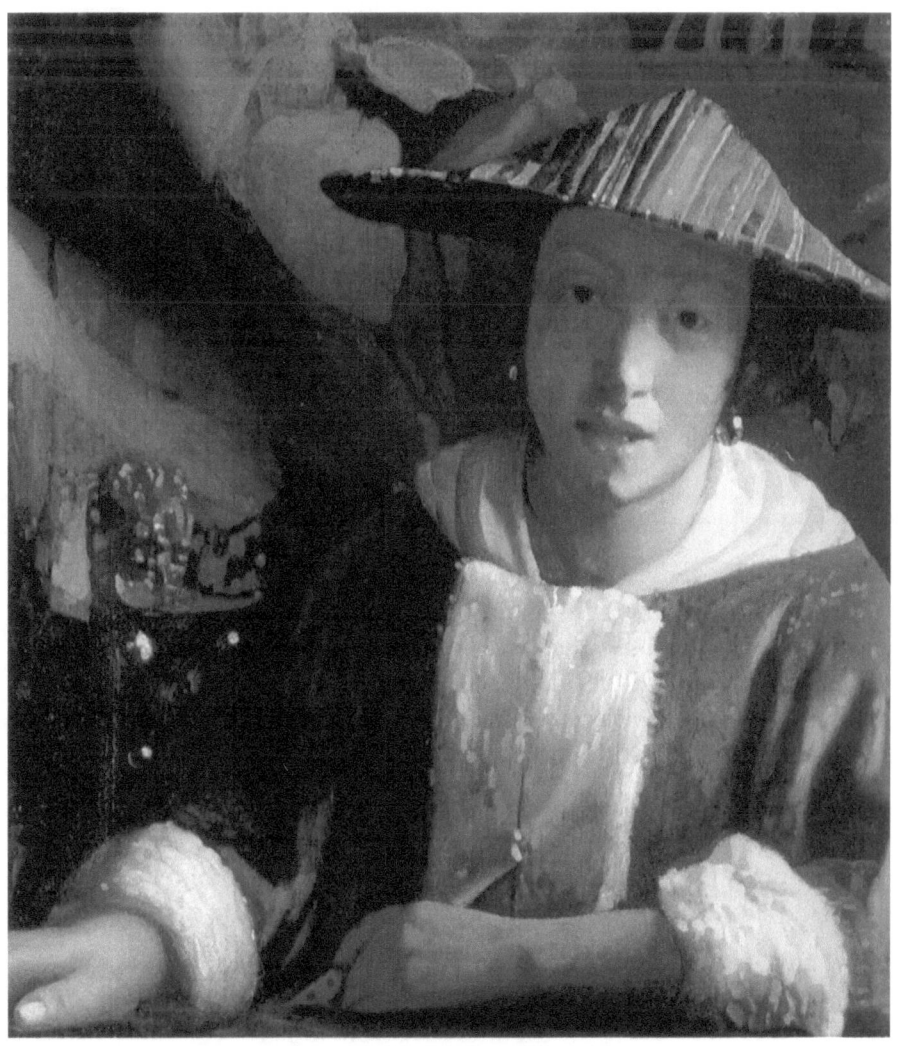

Elizabeth Vermeer: A Fuzzy Red Hat

GIRL WITH A RED HAT
oil on panel
support: 9 1/2 x 7 1/8 in.   (23.2 x 18.1 cm.)
painted surface: 9 x 7 1/16 in. (22.8 x 18 cm.)

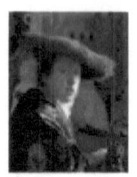

A very small, almost miniature, painting of my second oldest daughter, Elizabeth, dressed in an imported hat and gown. It is one of the 2 miniature portraits of Elizabeth.

Dutch trading ships frequently docked in Delft to deliver merchandise brought back from unnamable destinations around the world. I was technically invigorated by the challenge of painting light effected by feathers, fir, fabrics, textures and patterns.

Elizabeth enjoyed getting dressed up in any fine costume. It was a game of "let's pretend" in which we   transported ourselves to other lands and times, without leaving the house. This painting, and the painting of her in an oriental hat, use a similar theme, but different gown and hat.

These small portraits of a head or facial feature were called a *tronie* painting. This hat and costume, made of fine, exotic materials, were especially wonderful subject for light as seen through the lens of the camera obscura. The lens created an effect on the light which seems to condensate or coalesce in into small, intense pools. It is like gathering sun beam flowers into a bouquet.

These paintings, as all the others, were given names by others people. In this case, the name is not appropriate, as with most. The "flute" or "red hat" or "pearl" are quite unimportant to the theme and content of these pictures. They should be named "Foreign Fantasies".

Titles are assigned for the convenience of those who, over the decades since they were painted, bought, sold, re-sold, profited, speculated, and evaluated them. During my lifetime they were mostly neglected. Later, they were detected, inspected and injected with mystery and mystique born of misunderstanding and false assumptions. Finally, they have become objects in which a few wealthy people are heavily invested.

This effect always excited me aesthetically, but I felt as though I was "cheating" the traditional discipline of painting by using such a tool. To that degree, I never considered these paintings, although very appealing, to be "real" portraits. One does not observe nature with the unaided eye in this way. So, to that degree the painting, artificially aided by this tool, could not be considered to be a "serious" work of art.

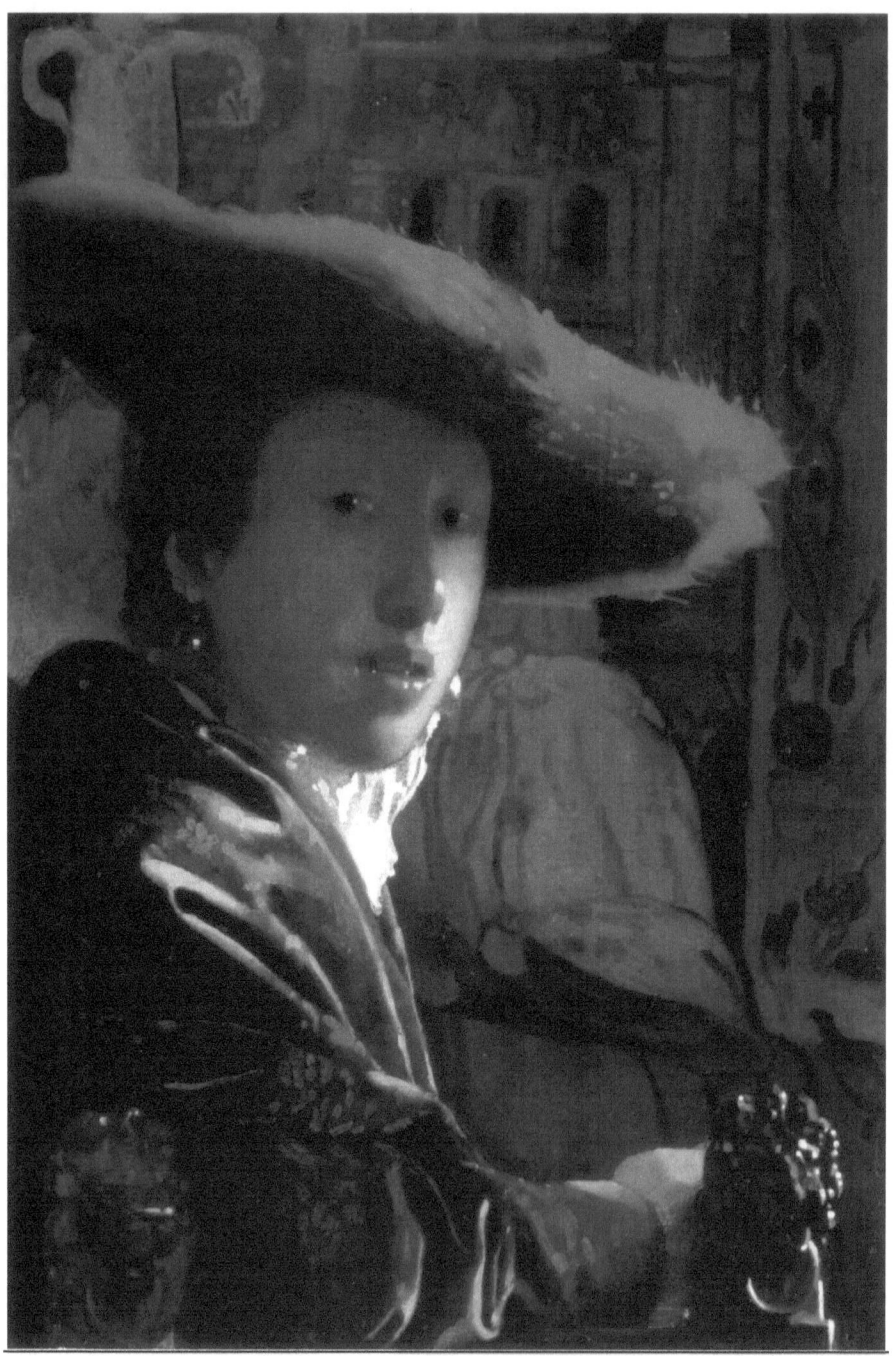

Aleydis Vermeer, A Hidden Secret

THE LOVE LETTER
oil on canvas
17 3/8 x 15 1/8 in. (44 x 38.5.cm)

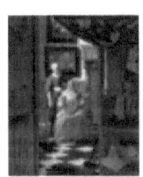

This painting conveys multiple dimensions of space, as well as a mysterious intrigue. It features the ubiquitous trappings and props used in so many of my paintings: the yellow cape with fir trim, (her "manteltge", with spotted squirrel fur trim, was owned by Maria Thins, but worn by Aleydis in this painting. It was more expensive that those worn by my wife and daughters, which were trimmed with cat fur.) pearl necklace and earring, and satin gown. These were all possessions of Maria Thins, lent to Catharina and my daughters on many occasions so they would appear presentably well dressed.

The servant is Tanneke Everpoel, the live-in maid hired by Maria Thins to help with the heavier duties of the household. She was a part of the family, and privy to the various intrigues which the women of the house may have gossiped about between themselves.

The theme of the painting was suggested by the work of my friend, and fellow at the Guild of St. Luke, Pieter de Hoogh. [XXXIII] (FOOTNOTE) I admired the intimate, impromptu nature of his paintings which I felt were much more suggestive of the natural events of life than many of my own works, which are more classically posed.

Although we were certainly not ostentatious, it was an agreed upon convention that we create the illusion of prosperity by wearing our best clothes when making a painting that might be seen by the others -- even though the "Sunday Best" was shared between of the ladies of the family.

This picture is intended to convey a secret vantage point from within a closet, looking out into the kitchen, so as to eavesdrop of an intrigue over a letter. A guest in the home would never be allowed to see a cluttered room full of laundry, rags, brooms and general untidiness. As it was often her purse that paid for daily necessities, Maria Thins often sat in the kitchen, even if not working, which she usually did with great industry, so she could supervise household affairs. More often she stayed warm there during cold, damp weather, which was nearly constant.

Only once was their an actual intrigue worthy of notice by the neighbors. Her indigent, drunken son, Willem, came to the house and threatened her over withholding his rightful share of the money she received in the divorce judgment against his father, her former husband. Of course, this money was not his inheritance and he had done nothing whatever to earn it. After a vocal row with Mara Thins, he withdrew.

However, he was foolish enough to return at a later date, and accused his mother of spending "his" money on Catharina and her children, while ignoring him! He also threatened my pregnant wife with a walking stick! When I returned home from the Guild to hear this report, I made quite sure that Willem received a just reward.

I am not a violent man, by any means. I have always avoided combat whenever possible, except when attacked, because I have learned that I am unable to control my temper once set off! However, his parries toward my wife and unborn child inflamed a homicidal rage in me that was restrained only by my wife and my good companions with whom I served as a member of the Delft militia. They, mercifully, attended to the dirty work of bashing Willem themselves, thus preventing me from dispatching him, at the risk of my own imprisonment for murder!

Revenge is sweet. However, a very thorough "accident" of well-placed blows delivered by practiced professionals is a more practical and legal remedy in such matters. Maria Thins happily paid a considerable sum of 74 guilders to the two surgeons who were required to stitch his wounds, and set his bones.

I persuaded my mother, who was still the proprietor of the family inn at Mechelen to provide Willem enough wine to drown the pain of his broken bones after my battle-ready friends from the militia visited him at his house in the country! Needless to say, we had no trouble with him after that occasion.

Life in Delft was serene and devoid of violence, with two overwhelming exceptions: The first was the cataclysmic explosion of the weapons arsenal, which took the life of my very dear scruffy friend, Carl Fabritius and many other neighbors. I was at the height of my youthful vigor at that time, which absorbed the ruinous reality of this general carnage and sequestered the pain of it in the dark depths of my psyche.

The other was the infernal war with France and England. Although the battle never quite reached the threshold of Delft, the constant threat of it growled at our door with daily, deadly menace. That year consumed my energy to assist the Delft militia with whom I fully expected to fight if the French troops were to advance far enough to meet us. Had that been the case our lives and those of our wives and children would have been most gravely at risk.

After the armistice, our economy, and the art trade, were in a stat of collapse by the greed and treachery of the usual suspects: the idiot aristocracy, malicious military madmen, and brutal bankers who funded the destruction for personal gain.

Personally, I did not recover from that overwhelming wound. I exhausted my own credit with lenders, and the demands of daily living consumed the funds of Maria Thins. My depression was fatal to the body, as my poor dear wife described to her creditors afterward.

After I died Catharina sold as many of my paintings as remained, including those she would rather have kept, in her attempt to survive long enough to raise our children, to whom she remained tirelessly dedicated until her final end.

Apart from these, our lives were free of violent incidents. On an average day, we bet our lives that the shiny gleam of Joy would win the toss over Tragedy. Yet, predictably, the death of our infants, friends and family member that we loved, and inevitably, ourselves, exposed the obverse side of the Mortal Coin.

In spite of death, we remain the Eternal Hypocrites:

We kiss the sensuous Face of Life, yet curse the Foulness of it's Breath!

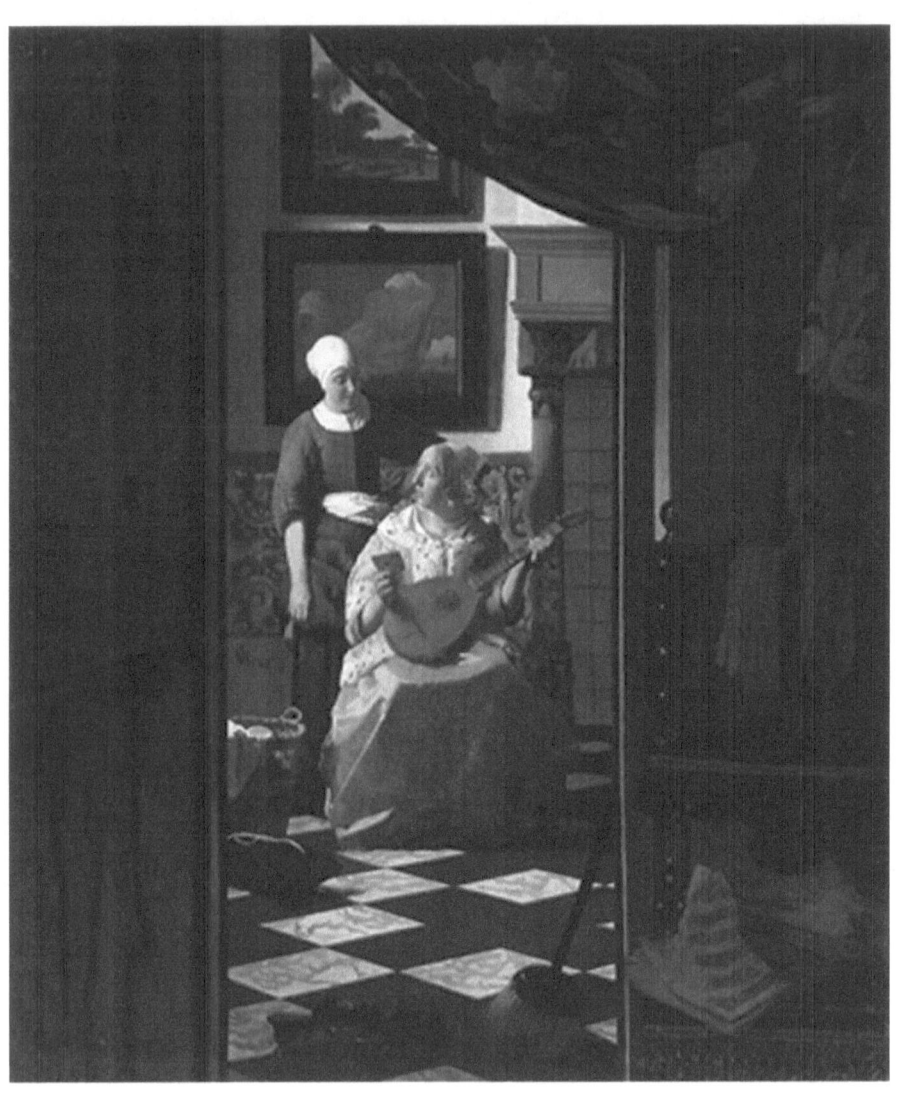

Maria Vermeer, Keeping Up Appearances

MISTRESS AND MAID
oil on canvas
35 1/2 x 31 in. (90.2 x 78.7 cm.)

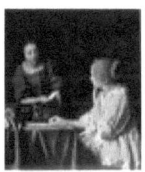

A family matron, discussing the household affairs with a servant is played by my oldest daughter Maria, with Elizabeth as the maid, once again.

Maria was engaged to be married when this was painted. In June 1674, when she was about 20 years old, she was married to the son of a prosperous Delft silk merchant named Gilliszoon Cramer.

In our household Catharina, and her mother, Maria Thins managed the household affairs, shopping, budget and all matters domestic. It was uppermost in their minds that an appearance of prosperity must be maintained at all times. For this reason, careful money management was an important activity.

This painting contrasts the routine setting of the household and with the most opulent apparel and jewelry that a woman of means could afford. Her "manteltge", with spotted squirrel fur trim was more expensive that those worn by Catharina and the girls. This was intended to purvey the appearance of a wealthy citizen who could afford to indulge their vanity and ambition or "keep up with the Jones".

The contrast in apparel between the maid and the "mistress" in this picture is designed intentionally to create an artificial distinction in social standing, financial well-being that did not actually exist in reality. Although we were relatively secure, due to the underlying support of Maria Thins, and having a house to live in that was paid for, the apparent wealth of the lady seated is largely a myth, in that the ostentatious use of jewelry is overdone.

On the average, we brought in only about twice the meager salary of a brick layer, or similar artisan, which was considered an vocation of the lower-middle class: honorable, but menial. When divided by the number of meals required to feed 3 adults and 11 children in all, our financial situation bordered on desperation continually. This painting illustrates the careful and meticulous concern that matron of a household was expected to gave to planning the household budget.

The purpose for which the paper, ink pots and pen are being applied by her and the nature of the paper being handed to or received from the maid are intentionally ambiguous. Many similar paintings of this nature, painted by other artists, were based on a theme of romantic intrigue, wherein the paper would be the composition of a love letter. Though fanciful as a subject for art, our household had none of that kind of romance.

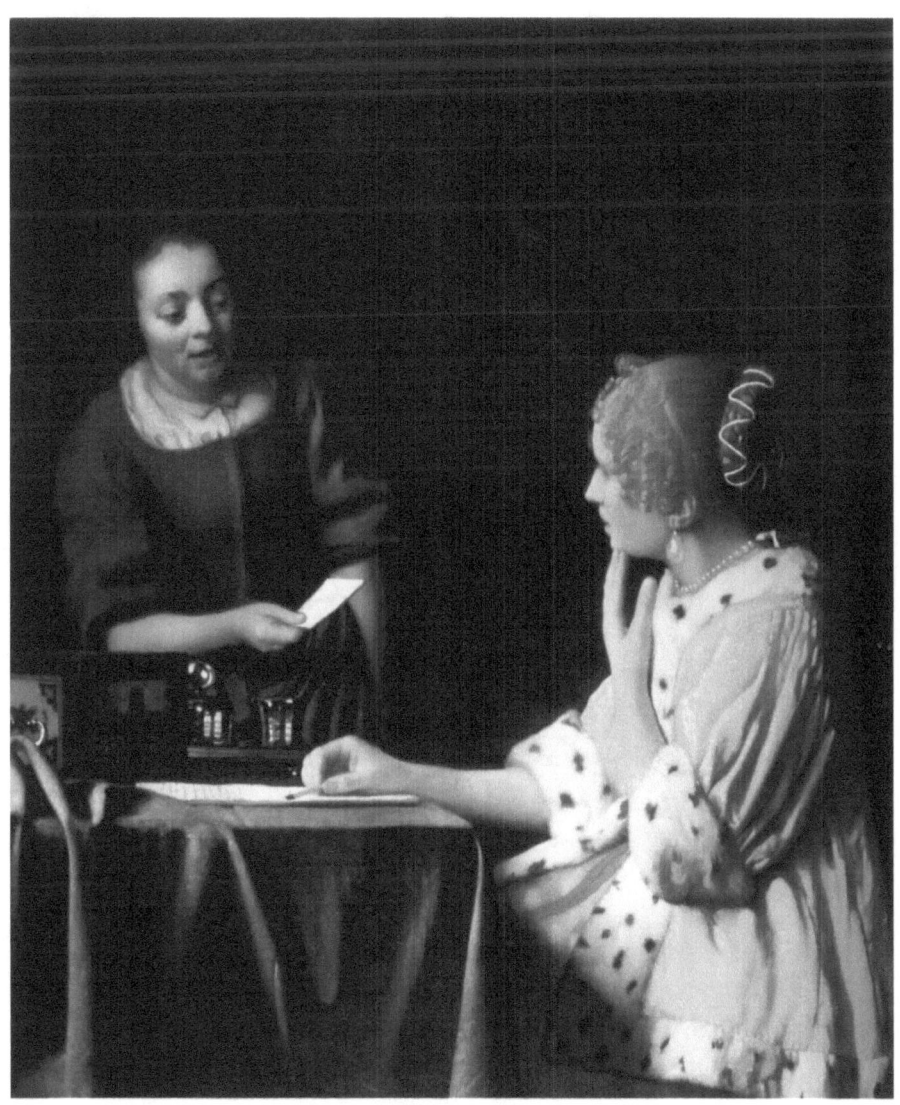

Maria Vermeer Writing a Letter

LADY WRITING A LETTER WITH HER MAID
oil on canvas
28 x 23 in. (71.1 x 58.4 cm.)

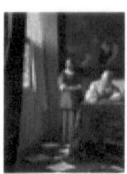

My first born daughter, Maria, with her younger sister, Elizabeth, posing as a household servant, dressed in a plain, practical garment. She muses absently, while awaiting instructions from the lady of the house when she has finished writing a list of daily duties to be done. The air is casual, the mood is sober, a scrap of paper has fallen to the floor. Unpretentious drudgery, manual chores, another day, another loaf, honest labor: life as a servant girl.

Most of the time, we could not afford more than one servant, other than Tanneke, the lady who lived with us, to help with cooking, washing clothes and cleaning in the kitchen. She and my wife, Catharina, assisted by Maria Thins, and later, our older daughters, managed the menial necessities of survival. Scrubbed floors, bed linens washed, garbage and piss pots disposed, clothing mended, wiping a child's nose.

Every single inch of the house on *Oude Langendijk*, was relentlessly defended against a never-ending attack of dirt, mud, mold and soot. Every minute of interminable drudgery was taken for granted. No thanks, no glory, no recognition: the rewards of womanhood.

Catharina was burdened with constant child care most of the time. Nevertheless, many of the heavy and dirty chores were done by her.

This picture is posed and pristine, with only a small hint of disorder: a scrap of paper on the floor. Neither of these ladies are sullied with the soot of menial labor. This artificial unreality defined my paintings. I refused to acknowledge or glorify grit and grime in my art! The conquest of chaos, the imposition of order by human sweat and will are the qualities that make human beings the dominant species on Earth!

Above this bland domesticity, the women in our house were literate. They could read and write as well, or better, than any man. They were trained in music, lace making and sewing. Womankind, for lack of muscle strength to defend themselves against brutal men, who in recent history had been owned like chattel, attained beauty and lived with grace in our house, in Delft, in Holland, in the 17th Century. What better depiction of courage and integrity than these ladies?

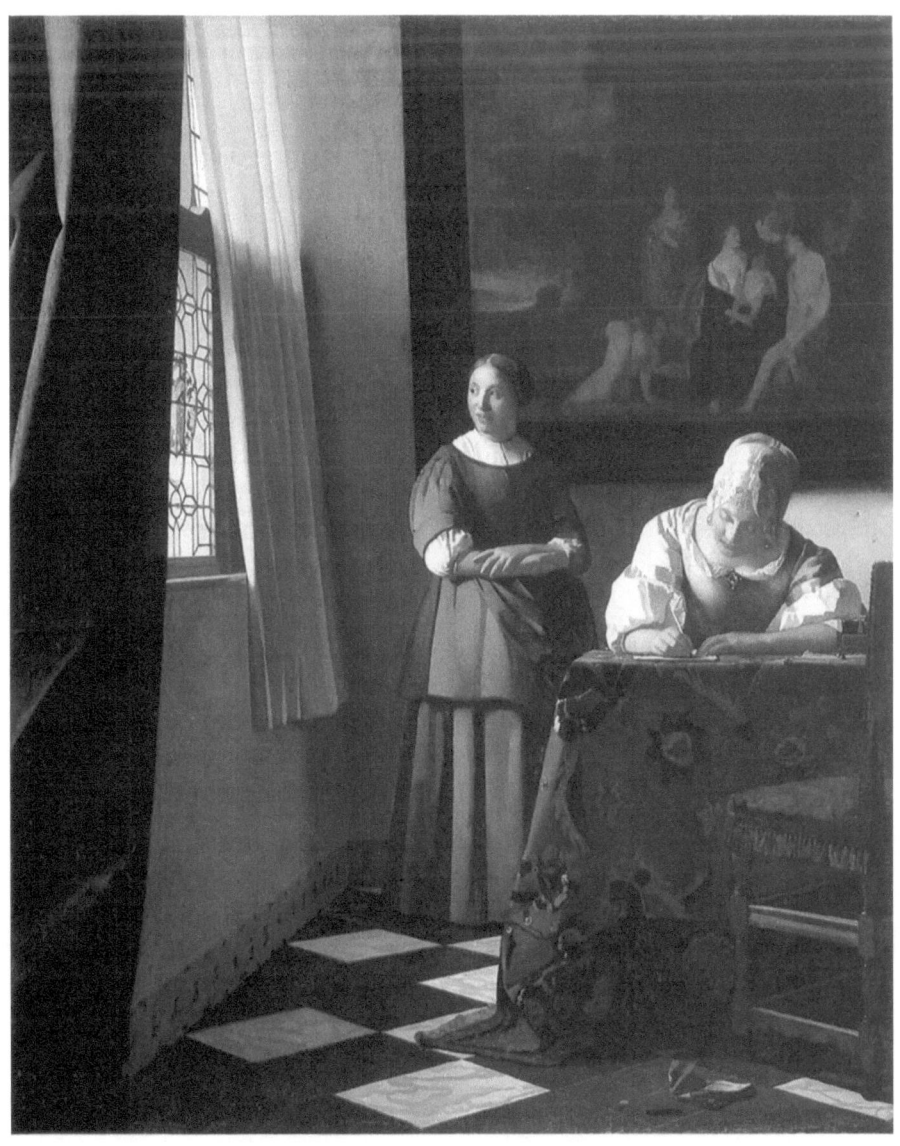

Beatrix Vermeer Musing

WOMAN WITH A LUTE
oil on canvas
20 1/4 x 18 in. (51.4 x 45.7 cm)

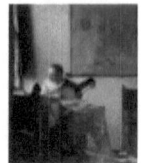

My daughter, Beatrix with a lute. As with many other portraits of my family, she wears the finery -- provided by her grandmother -- to put forward the most presentable appearance. The clothes and jewelry nearly became a trademark of the women in my family. It seemed they all wore the fur fringed cape, pear jewelry, and skirt, even if painted a different color, for the sake of composition.

She didn't know how to play well yet, she studied music and used the prop convincingly, as a consummate model always does. I think Beatrix would be an excellent actress in the modern age. She has natural theatricality. She invites the viewer to sit contentedly and muse with her. She is absorbed in her own world with no thought to the painting voyeur in the room. Her relaxed, improvisational manner was never contrived, even when posing for this carefully staged portrait.

Although she was still quite young when I passed from life, a recall that Beatrix was steady and serene, as far as I remember her, yet impish, playful and gay. It seemed that nothing bothered her, though her love and empathy were always evident. She lived outside herself, rather than within. She mused, and dreamed but was never introspected. Unlike me.

Selfless extroversion was her strength. Great performers and great leaders keep the show on the road, no matter what the odds against them. If we are Actors on The Stage of Life, Beatrix was one for The Ages. She played every line to the *nth* of her gentle core as though it were carefully studied and rehearsed, then performed with effortless certainty.

"All the world's a stage,

And all the men and women merely players:

They have their exits and their entrances;

And one man in his time plays many parts."

William Shakespeare - (*from* "As You Like It")

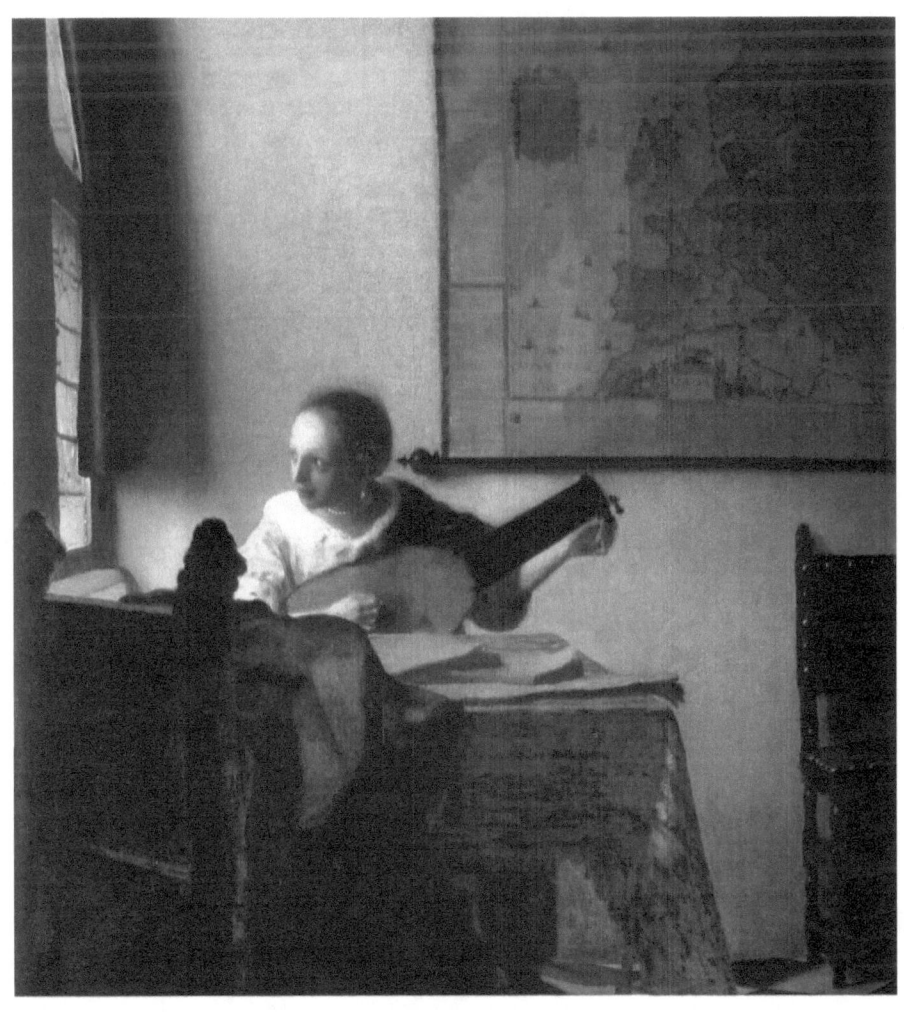

Aleydis & Cornelia Enjoying Music with A Friend

THE CONCERT
oil on canvas
28 1/2 x x25 2 in. (72.5 x 64.7 cm.)

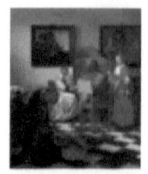

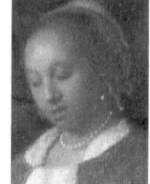

The women in my family were musically accomplished and very much enjoyed singing. In this case, Aleydis (inset top) and Cornelia (inset bottom), sing and play. This art form, along with embroidery, lace making, sewing, writing letters, reading and few others were afforded to women as an endowment of literacy and culture in a continent barely emerged from the Dark Ages of cultural suppression. The arts, and the working-class affluence that bought the leisure time to study them, were finally being rekindled in Europe for the first time since the cultural flame of the Roman Empire flickered and died 1200 years earlier.

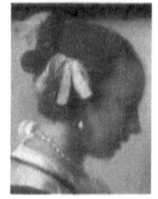

The man who is seated with a cane, and playing a lute, is our old friend, the music composer, poet and statesman, Constantijn Huygens who lived nearby, and visited frequently to teach and enjoy music with our daughters. Although he was somewhat advanced in age at the time of this painting, he lived a vigorous life. He is the owner of the virginal being played in this painting. As I have mentioned, he also owned a *camera obscura*, and was very conversant in the uses of it.

He and his wife, Suzanne, owned an expensive, custom virginal made by the firm of Ruckers, in Antwerp, purchased with the help of a gentlemen banker named Duarte at the healthy price of 300 guilders. Later, Huygens arranged for one of my paintings of the girls playing a virginal to be sold to Duarte.

I may have used my own reflection in a mirror to model for this picture, as I did before and after this picture was painted. A painting of "the procuress", owned by Maria Thins, in on the right background, which decorated her house, as in several other pictures. Maria Thins came from a wealthy family who could afford to indulge the arts, and she owned a collection of paintings before Catharina and I were married, and moved to live with her in on the Oude Langendijk in 1660.

This scene, like most of those I painted, were my personalized versions of pictures painted by other members of the Guild of St. Luke, or other

Dutch artists who paintings I was exposed to, as I earned part of my livelihood, as my father did before he, as a dealer in paintings. As a member of the Guild, and sometimes as an official officer of the Guild, I have the opportunity to work with the members daily. Many of these artisans were my personal friends, of course. We shared and discussed our ideas about painting, and competed with each other commercially as well.

I served several times as an officer of the Guild of St. Luke. My duties included handling administrative and business affairs of the Guild. This also included, occasionally, mediating disagreements between artisans, or interceded on behalf of the membership to prevent the intrusion of artisans who attempted to sell their work in Delft, who were not paid members of the Guild, or residents of the community.

I served in this capacity, in part, so as to save on paying membership dues, so to speak. The position also gave me some altitude with the other members. However, like most unpaid positions, the work was, for the most part, a thankless labor of love which had no financial, social or political advantage to me personally, other than business and artistic networking opportunities.

One of the benefits of membership gave me the advantage of borrowing props, such as pictures, carpets, garments, musical instruments, and the like, from other members, or patrons of painters, who were members of the Guild or who were patrons of the members. My wife and daughters did enjoy playing music and singing, which they did as frequently as the demands of maintaining a large household would allow.

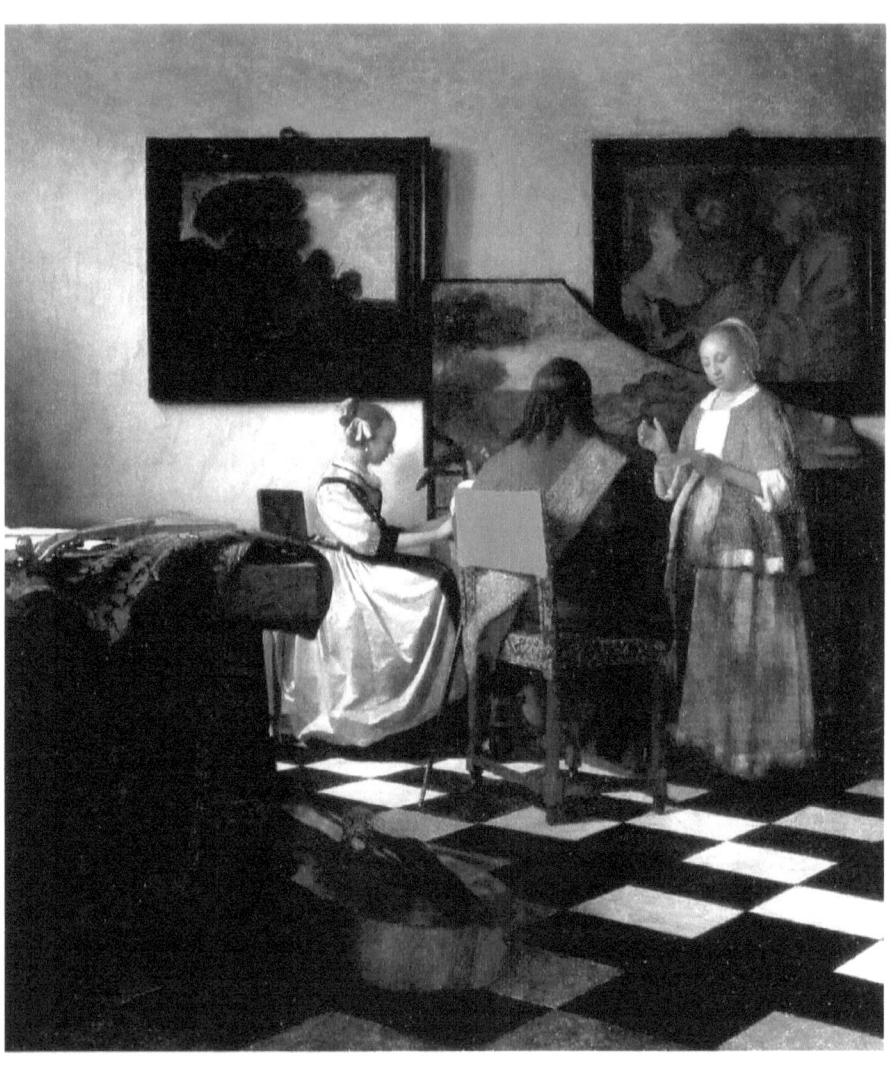

Cornelia Vermeer Playing Guitar

THE GUITAR PLAYER
oil on canvas
20 1/4 x 18 1/4 in. (53 x 46.3 cm.)

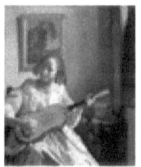

This painting is not entirely finished, as can be seen clearly in the face of my daughter, Cornelia, which is not painted in the usual fashion. Her overly red cheeks make her face almost a caricature, rather than an accurate portrait.

We never owned a guitar, especially not an expensive one, as this appears to be. It is borrowed from our friend, and music composure, Constantijn Huygens, who owned diverse musical instruments. As I have mentioned, I often borrowed objects from members of the Guild of St. Luke to use as props also. This was an unspoken advantage of membership in the Guild, one which all members were able to share in.

The arrangement of the room is in reverse, the windows being on the right, rather than the left of her. My feeling is that this painting served as an experiment with the camera obscura or mirrors in an attempt to produce a varied effect.

The painting on the back wall was as not one we owned, but one that I might have been dealing with, or one loaned to me by our friend,

It seems to have been painted while looking in a mirror, in order to reverse the position of the girl with respect to the window, then, with other elements added separately. This would also account for a certain lack of detail and quality that is disturbing to my sense of order.

In any case, recovering many fine details from a life lived 300 years ago is difficult at best. I prefer to rely on my own knowingness and observation about it, rather than make assumptions or circumstantial guesses.

This painting is only partially complete, a during this period in our lives all of us were greatly disrupted in our daily routines by the calamitous war against the invading army of the maniacal French king, Louis XIV, advancing from the south by land, as well as the neighboring English at sea to the north and west. [XXXIV] (FOOTNOTE)

As a member of the Delft Militia, I was fully expected and prepared to fight to protect our land and home against a certain fate of death at the hands of mercenary soldiers sent to rob our homes, rape our women, pillage our lands and place all survivors under the subjugation of foreign monarchs, as had been the case historically.

The time of opulent self-indulgence for the majority of middle-classes Dutch was near an end. The French had inundated and spoiled us with aristocratic fineries, and a lust for luxury. Our sailing fleet ruled the world of trade, literally sailing around the globe, nearly unimpeded. The fleets came home loaded to their creaking decks with the bounty of a planet: exotic foods, commodities, luxuries and curious items beyond imagining.

But in 1672 King Luis, in an alliance with England, decided that what we had earned by industry and ingenuity, should become his by military conquest and theft. Every tyrant in history knows the first rule of "leadership": *if you can't tax it, steal it.*

Such terror, instilled in our citizens by horrendous atrocities committed against our people by French troops in southern towns, caused many other cities, including Utrecht, to surrender without a fight! Had it not been for inundating the land with water by opening of the dikes, we would have surely been overwhelmed by land. This strategy, combined with Dutch victories against English ships at sea, at last secured our homeland. But not without great turmoil and economy chaos.

Our own people, who revolted violently against our own, incumbent government, so much that there were riots in Delft! Johan de Witt, our good and able leader for so many years, was overthrown by supporters of William III of Orange, who were convinced that his rule would be better for the rest of us. On August 20th, 1672, shortly after his resignation, a craven mob of Orange supporters ambushed Johan and his brother in the Hague with guns, knives, bludgeons and savagely slaughtered them!

I was sickened to my chore by this meaningless massacre. These good men were torn, by the mob, into a thousand tiny bits of flesh, which each of these self-imagined "patriots" grabbed up from the ground and took home with them as trophies, to store in jars of oil or alcohol! Their body parts were later bought at sold in the marketplace at high rates, so each deranged citizen could personally own a piece of the "traitors".

Since that date, I have lost all faith in the essential goodness of my fellow men, whether Dutch, Catholic, Protestant, beggar, king, neighbor or painter. The human race has proved to me that it is beyond redemption! I trace my own, personal "decadence and decay", as my own wife observed in my subsequent behavior, to that day.

The war and economic collapse that followed across the land, led to my end. Maria Thin's income was greatly affected, adversely, by the flooding of the land against the French, as I could not collect the rents from the farmer who leased the land she owned there.

The market for art objects disappeared, as necessities were scarce, which we ourselves could ill-afford even the barest essentials of bread and clothe. Only our good will with the baker, an admirer of my art, with whom we had bartered earlier, kept ourselves and our children alive. To further compound our suffering, we lost a child in the next year to disease. My life long friend, and mentor, Leonaert Bramer, died in February, 1674. How much more loss and grief can one endure?

My small income from painting, and trade in the works of other masters, was gone forever. I had not the will to paint, nor a patron to support my efforts at this easel, as my only patron had died the year before. My own father, mother and sister were dead, and our small property was more in debt that it was worth.

This was the beginning of my dismal, declining days. I collapsed a week after St. Nicholas's Day, having drunk myself into a state of physical and mental depression from which I had no will to recover.

My regret at this dismal end was beyond reconciliation or amends. All of the beauty in the universe could not rekindle faith in the goodness of the souls of men, nor the goal to survive, once lost.

Mortal existence is temporal. Eternal existence is inevitable.

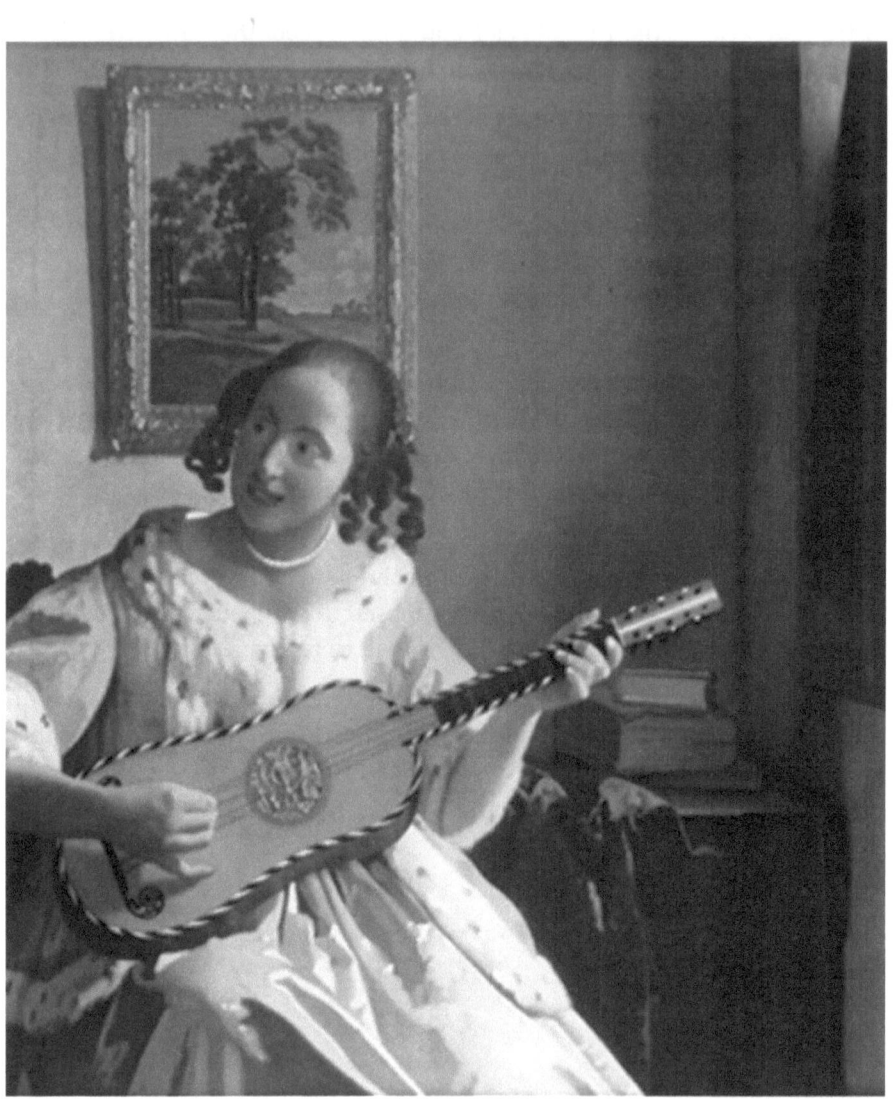

SELF-PORTRAITS OF JOHANNES VERMEER

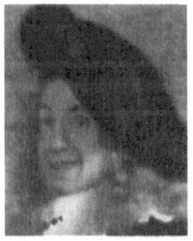

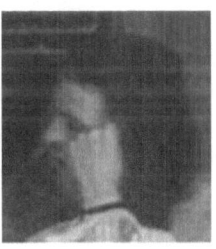

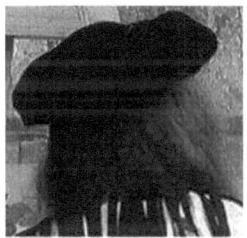

| from
The Procuress | from
A girl with a
glass of wine | from
The Art of Painting |

These are the only visibly recognizable self-portraits of Johannes Vermeer. Although none of these images are documented self-portraits, an educated assumption can be made that these are images of the artist that he included in three of his own paintings.

The striking similarities in coloration, hair color and style and facial features (of the two left-hand images) are self-evident. The insouciant theme of *The Procuress* and *A Girl With A Glass of Wine* lend themselves to a playful inclusion of the artist as an incidental character in scenes of his own creation.

It is known that after his death that his wife, Catharina Bolnes, and his mother-in-law, Maria Thins, went to great lengths in a failed attempt to keep *The Art of Painting* and to protect it against being sold to pay debts as part of the bankruptcy settlement administered by the family friend, Anthony van Leeuwenhoek.

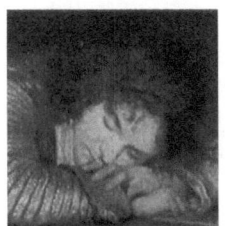

Compare and contrast the image of Vermeer painted by the master, Gerard ter Borch, (left) with those, above, painted by Vermeer of himself.

(from: *"Woman Drinking with a Sleeping Soldier"* by Gerard ter Borch painted c. 1660-1669)

Considering the documented relationship between the two men -- many argue that ter Borch was Vermeer's mentor, being 15 years older -- I assert that this is the same person: Vermeer, posing as the "soldier". In fact, ter Borch traveled to attend Vermeer's wedding! They painted much of the same subject matter, lived a short distance from each other, and share preferences in painting technique which have many commonalities.

MANY FACES OF CATHARINA BOLNES VERMEER

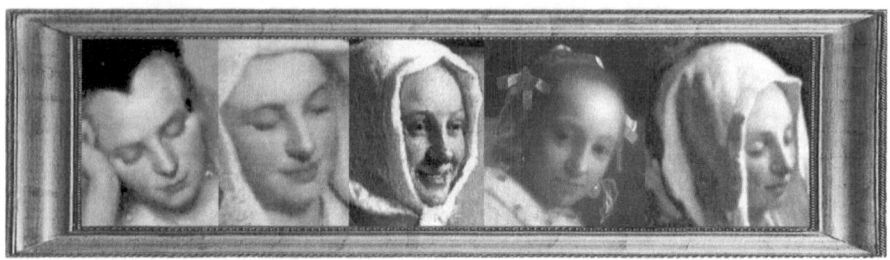

A tremendous number of speculations have been made as to the identity of the ladies represented in the paintings of Vermeer. It is easy to understand why so many contradictory opinions have been made on this subject. Those show above in the "group portrait" are a few of many renditions of my wife, Catharina. Shown here are various poses, costumes, lighting, coloration, hair styles, and demeanors, made of a single face to suite to purpose of the scene depicted.

One need only understand that Catharina was a collaborator and accomplice and constant companion during their lifetime together. Who else, other than his older daughters, during the later years of his life, would be so readily and cooperatively available to stand or sit for the long hours required to pose for a painting? The answer is simple when one confronts the obvious: these are all the faces of his family.

As I mentioned earlier, as the family grew, the hours of free time Catharina could devote to serving as a model grew proportionately fewer. The demands of caring for a large family, even with the help of Maria Thins, and our older daughters, were constant, to say the least!

Catharina, because of her Catholic convictions, never allowed herself to go out in public without covering her head. Likewise, she would not submit to being painted without head covering, if the painting was a knowing portrait of her. Since he aspired to paint a greater variety of portraits, more amenable to the general Protestant population in Delft, he began to use his daughters as subjects when they were old enough.

In addition, as his daughters grew up, he used them more frequently as his models because the demands on their time were less than that of their mother. Vermeer's older daughters -- Maria, Elizabeth, Cornelia, Aleydis, and Beatrix -- were all included from time to time. Even Maria Thins sat for him on at least one occasion.

Obviously, the differences between the portraits notwithstanding, these pictures were painted over a period of at least 22 years. During that time they produced 15 children, 4 of whom did not survive. During these 22 years Catharina underwent many changes in appearances due to emotional stress, weight gain, and loss, illness and discomfort during her pregnancies, as is evident in several of the paintings.

Throughout her lifetime, even though his technical ability as a painter improved, some of these paintings of Catharina are, frankly, not very good likenesses of her. These should be obvious, even on casual inspection. Part of his difficulty was that he do not paint very well from memory. As a painter, Vermeer was a realist, or copyist. Most of the subject matter or ideas for his painting were borrowed from his colleagues, or from pictures to which he was exposed as an art dealer.

Vermeer, like many of his contemporaries was a painter of objects and people and places. When he was able to observe and scrutinize an object or face carefully and continually, I can make a fairly accurate copy of it.

However, as was usually the case, he did not have the luxury of having a live model sitting in front of me during the entire painting process. So, once the original drawing or sketch was completed, he no longer had a model sitting in front of him. Thereafter, he had to rely on his drawing, or memory to render the likeness of the model. As you can see for yourself, in the many paintings wherein Catharina is the model, her appearance, although very similar, varies to a greater or lesser degree from one to the next.

In the case of the portraits of his daughter Elizabeth, e.g. "the pearl earring" portrait, she was probably able to sit in a still pose for many long hours while he continually referred to her features, the lighting and other facets of her face and eyes. The result is that her portraits are probably a very close likeness of her actual appearance, and more consistent from one to the next.

This is definitely not the case with some of the women shown in his paintings. Genre paintings, commonly produced by many Dutch painters in the period, were not necessarily intended to be a precise portrayal of anyone: the face of the woman in many of the paintings could by "any woman". However, it is obvious that Vermeer preferred the company of women, on the average, over the company of men as subjects for his paintings.

The 3 tronie pictures of Elizabeth, the so-called "girl with a pear earring, red hat, and flute", however, are very much more precise portraits of his beautiful daughter. Likewise, the portrait of Beatrix titled, "Study Of A Young Woman" is an exact likeness of her, as she had the time and the willingness to sit for me as I painted. She is obviously the same girl, although a little older, in the painting called "Woman With A Lute".

It should be noted, that for the most part Vermeer was not considered, and never aspired to become a portrait artist. There are many, many very talented painters in the world who make marvelous, meticulous portraits, usually of wealthy patrons, whose vanity they have the time, money and inclination to indulge. Vermeer is not one of these painters.

He always painted what interested him, primarily for his own, inexplicably selfish, aesthetic or technical reasons. I trust that his attention to the details of a face were a secondary consideration, compared to the entire composition and the universal serenity they purvey.

To the degree that this phenomenon may cause difficulty in identifying, or cataloguing his pictures, by those who are unable to paint themselves, but can only criticize the efforts of others, I do not think that Vermeer need offer any apology.

THE VERMEER DAUGHTERS

These are the eldest daughter of Johannes and Catharina Vermeer, in order from left to right in age. According to official documents discovered by the preeminent Vermeer scholar, J.M. Montias, the birth dates of all of the Vermeer children are not know, although most of the names are know. The eldest daughters who would have been old enough to sit for portraits during my lifetime, are noted in the descriptions of each of the surviving Vermeer paintings in the preceding pages of this book.

The composite that follows are the best examples of each daughter, cropped from their individual portraits, showing a frontal view of their faces. There are other portraits of each of them, described elsewhere. They all have the soft, innocent features of youth. Some appear nearly indistinguishably the same as the others, and all, very much like their mother. However, each is their own, uniquely beautiful individual.

As you can see, the excellent portrait of Beatrix uses the same intensely luminous lighting effect used in the "pearl" portrait of Elizabeth. It is, in every way, an equally excellent portrait, and the canvas and pigments have survived the tempests of time more completely, I believe, although I have not seen any of the paintings in person.

The portrait of Beatrix could just as easily have been titled the same, i.e. the "girl with a pearl earring". Actually, there is hardly a single painting of any of the girls, including Catharina, in which they are not wearing the same, exact pair of false pearl earrings which they all seem to share! This famous earring gleams more conspicuously in Elizabeth's portrait, but all the other girls wore it too. Appropriately, the pearl as a symbol: a lustrous, multi-layered jewel, of the women who wore them.

An Estimate of the Approximate Ages of the Vermeer Children at the Death of their Father in 1675:

Maria ....born c. 1654	(21) married
Elizabeth.......born c. 1657	(18)
Cornelia......... (?)	(17)
Aleydis.......... (?)	(16)
Beatrix.......... (?)	(15)
Johannes.......born c. 1663	(12)
Gertruyd........ (?)	(11)
Franciscus.....born c. 1664	(10 ?)
Catharina....... (?)	(5 ?)
Ignatius.........born c. 1672	(3)
unknown child...........born c. 1674 - 1678	(infant)

It is documented that the Vermeer's buried four other children who did not survive infancy. This means that Catharina gave birth to a total of 15 children during the 22 years of marriage.

Maria, Vermeer's eldest daughter, about 20, married the son of a prosperous Delft silk merchant Johannes Gilliszoon Cramer, who followed his father's profession. The wedding was held in Schipluy, as Maria's parents' wedding had been, and presumably with Catholic sacraments.

RIGHT PROFILES OF THE VERMEER WOMEN

NOTE: The portraits shown below of Catharina and each of her daughters who appeared in Vermeer paintings are arranged, youngest to oldest, (left to right) at the time each respective portrait was painted.

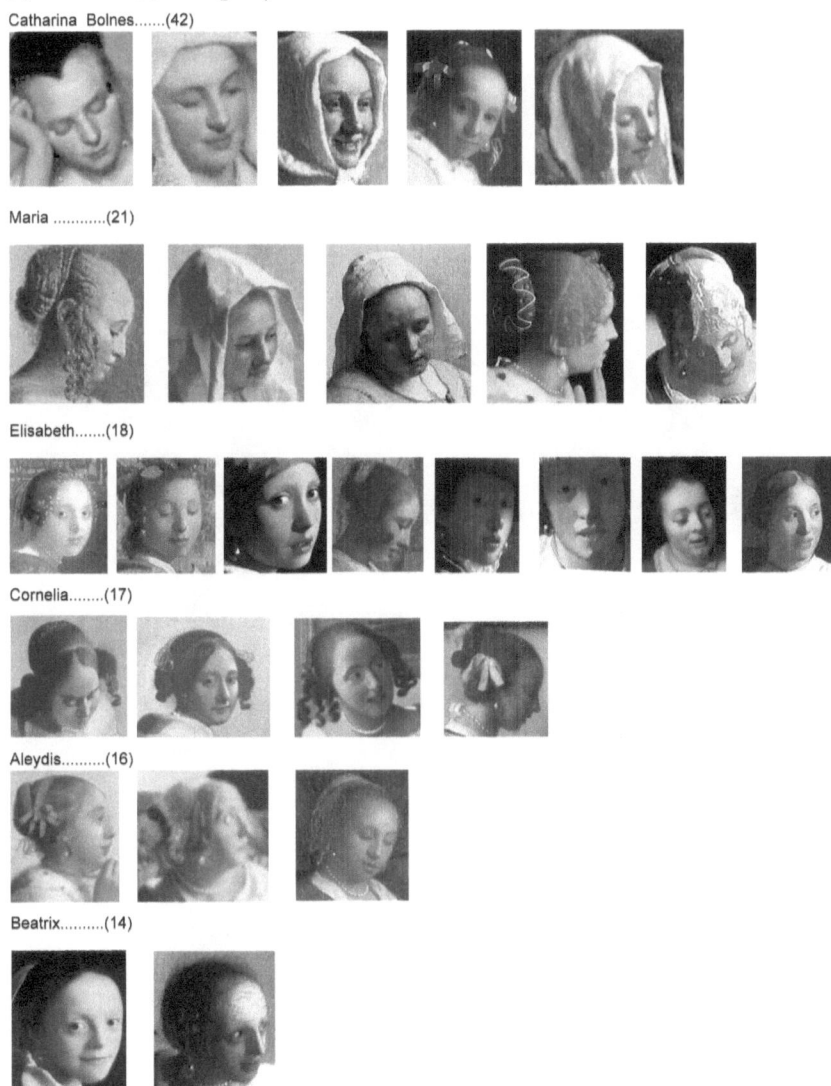

APPROXIMATE AGES OF THE VERMEER WOMEN AT HIS DEATH IN 1675:

Catharina Bolnes.......(42)

Maria ....(21)

Elisabeth.......(18)

Cornelia........(17)

Aleydis..........(16)

Beatrix..........(14)

LEFT PROFILES OF THE VERMEER WOMEN
The portraits shown below of Catharina and each daughter who appeared in a painting are arranged, youngest to oldest (left to right) at the time of the portrait

APPROXIMATE AGES OF THE VERMEER WOMEN AT HIS DEATH IN 1675:

Catharina Bolnes.......(42)

Maria ....(21)

Elisabeth.......(18)

Cornelia........(17)

Aleydis..........(16)

Beatrix..........(14)

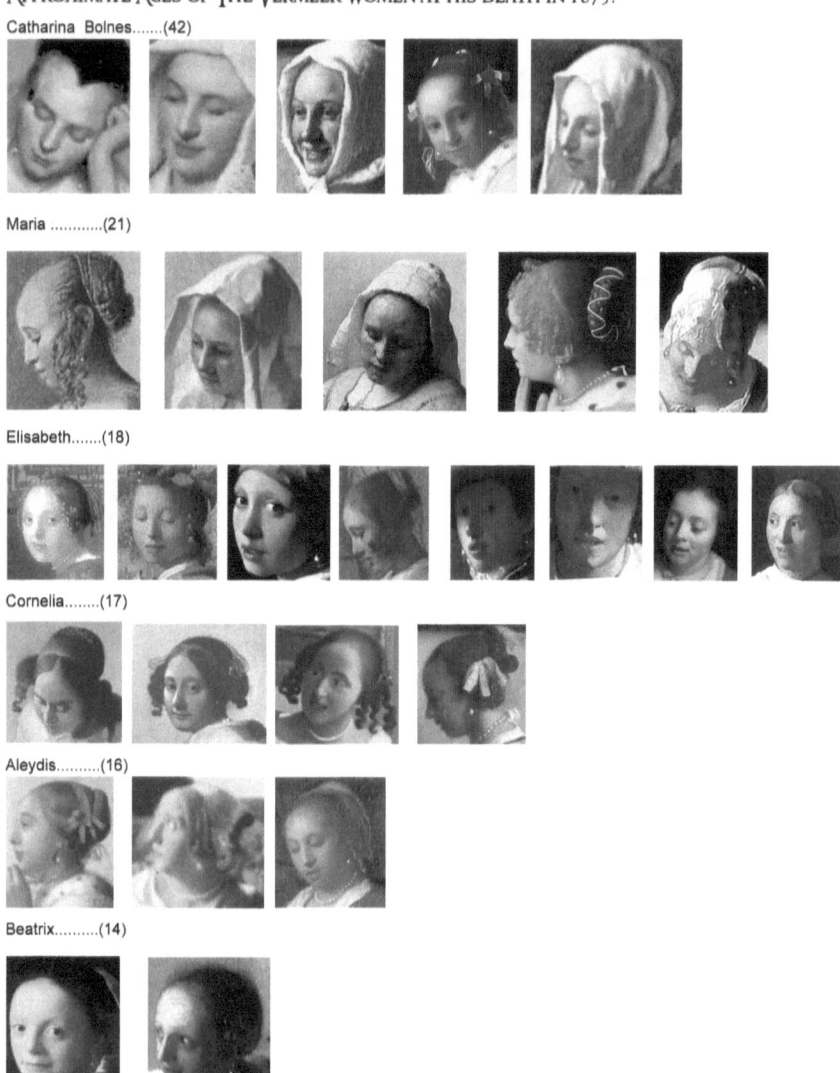

MARIA THINS: GRANDMOTHER and PATRONESS

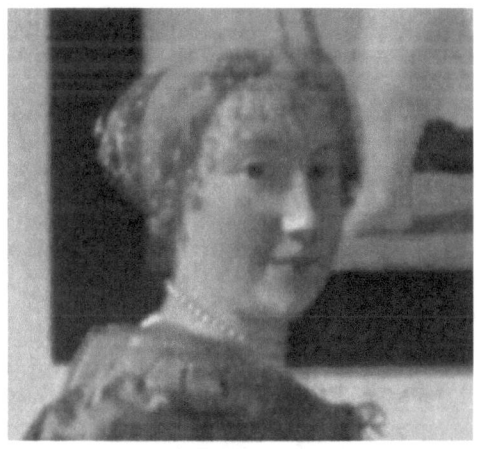

From Wikipedia.org:

*"**Maria Thins** - Born in Gouda, ca. 1593 - died in Delft, December 27, 1680. was a member of the Gouda Thins' family. In 1622 she married to Reynier Bolnes, a prominent and prosperous brick maker. In 1635 the marriage deteriorated; her sister found her crying in bed after her husband had beaten her. The couple moved to another house, where previously Wouter Crabeth had lived. There Bolnes had his dinner in the front room, together with his son, while he refused to talk to her and slept in a room upstairs. At one time her daughter Cornelia was locked up by her father. In 1641 Maria Thins decided to move to Delft, where her brother lived. Her husband refused to divorce her, but in 1649 she received a considerable sum of money from him.*

In 1653 her daughter Catharina married Johannes Vermeer in Schipluiden and at some time the couple moved in the rather spacious house on Oude Langendijk. Vermeer had his atelier on the front side of the second floor.

Vermeer and his wife buried a child in the Old Church in 1660. The same document states that at the same time, Vermeer and his wife were living in the house of Maria Thins on the Oude Langendijk in Delft. Although Maria Thins lived to be 87, surviving Vermeer, she was already about 67 years old in 1660 when the family moved into her house.

At the time, the household included Vermeer, his wife, his mother-in-law, and three children , not counting an infant who had died and at least one female servant. The house had a basement, a lower hall with a vestibule, a great hall, a small room adjoining the hall, an interior kitchen, a little back kitchen, a cooking kitchen, a washing kitchen, a corridor, and an upper floor with two rooms, one of which was taken up by Vermeer's studio.

Vermeer's family situation was unusual. Very few married men in the Netherlands lived with a parent or parent-in-law for an extended period of time. Vermeer's marriage too, must be considered exceptional in as much as he married outside his own family's religion and social class. He moved from the lower, artisan class of his Reformed parents who lived on the Delft Square to the higher social stratum of the Catholic in-law who instead lived in the somewhat segregated "Papist Corner," the Catholic quarter of the city.

Maria Thins was a devotee of the Jesuit order in the nearby Catholic Church. The third son of Johannes and Catharina was named Ignatius, after the founder of the Jesuit Order. It is not known if the children were baptized in the Catholic Church, because the baptize books from that period did not survive.

In 1663 her son Willem, a jobless bachelor, was locked up in an institution after an argument with his mother, and attacking his pregnant sister Catharina with a stick. In 1665 Maria Thins was entrusted with her son's property. She was not required by law to limit his share to legal minimum, but she said that he had been calling her names since his youth.

In 1672 Maria Thins got into financial difficulties: her land near Schoonhoven was flooded to prevent the (invading) French army (from) crossing the Dutch Water Line.

In 1675, when Vermeer went on several business trips for his mother-in-law, first to Gouda, when her husband died, and then to Amsterdam. In 1676 she lived in the Hague but moved back to Delft, where she was buried in the Old Church, next to Vermeer."

TANNEKE EVERPOEL, LIVE-IN SERVANT

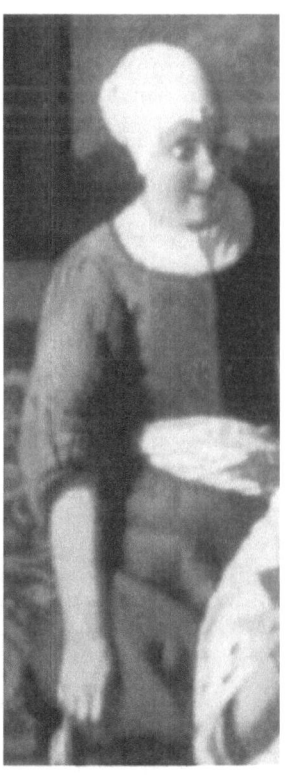

This face is immortalized in a Vermeer painting. Tanneke Everpoel was a servant hired and paid for by Maria Thins to help with the heavier household chores, especially cooking, cleaning and washing. According the Anthony Bailey, author of the authoritative book, "*A View of Delft, Vermeer Then and Now*", she stayed on as a servant, even after the death of Maria Thins. Her will, of May 1669, Maria left her a bequest of 20 guilders.

She is named in a legal deposition concerning the misbehavior of Catharina's brother, Willem, a perpetual trouble-maker for her mother and for a short time, in our home. Apparently he attempted to assault her sexually on several occasions. It was considered by some, that unmarried servants were "fair game" for sexual advances. This was apparently the case with Willem, whose obnoxious behavior toward his own mother, encouraged by his father, whom Maria divorced because of violence and abuse, was documented in the records of Delft.

Shortly after Willem came to our house to threaten his mother and my pregnant wife over money, while I was not at home, he met with a serious "accident". That was the end of his intrusions into our lives, once and for all!

In spite of this, Tanneke remained in the service of the Vermeer family, even after the death of her employer, Maria Thins. After as many years living in under the same roof, she would certainly have been considered to be a part of the family, if not legally, at least by verdure of her shared experiences.

A PERSONAL NOTE BY THE AUTHOR:

REMEMBERING THE ABILITY TO PAINT

How does a two year old child, like Mozart, and countless other examples, know how to compose complex musical scores before they can talk? The phenomenon of the "child prodigy" is almost common-place today.

However, the ability of self-proclaimed Western "experts", for which psychiatry has gained a well-earned reputation for incompetence and stupidity, to observe the obvious explanation that the spiritual being ALREADY KNOWS! They attribute the ability to some aberrated mutation of the brain, or genes, simply because they do not what to acknowledge that spiritual beings are the essence that animate all physical life forms. The ability inherent. It is too simple to be explained with complex, mechanical solutions.

That they now inhabit the body of a two-year old child is irrelevant. As soon as they develop the use of sufficient motor skills with the new body to write music, or play the piano, violin, etc. they training and understanding accumulated in previous life-times returns effortlessly. Many child musical prodigies have been asked "How to you know how to play the violin / piano, etc.?" They're usual response is, "I don't know how I do it. I just know how".

In India, whose culture and religions are based on awareness of oneself, and all life-forms, as immortal spiritual entities, who inhabit many, many bodies through time, do now struggle with or resist the obvious phenomena of remembering places, skills and knowledge learned during past lives.

However, the precedent for regaining one's lost abilities as an adult is far more common than ever before since the discovery and development of the mental/spiritual therapies described in the book, "Dianetics: The Modern Science of Mental Health", written in 1950 by L. Ron Hubbard.

One of the results of Dianetic counseling is the gradual recovery of the ability to remember details of many of the lives one has lived in the past millennia on Earth, and beyond. Remembering is best done as a gradient process, like peeling layers of an onion. The further back along the time track one goes, the more difficult it becomes to confront overwhelming forces at work in the past which were the original cause of memory loss.

In 1976, I saw one of Vermeer's paintings for the first time -- in the bargain books section of a Hollywood bookstore. I will never forget casually flipping through coffee table art book. There were replications of paintings by many of the "great masters", most of which I thought were mildly interesting, but not especially compelling.

When I flipped through to the section about the Dutch painters, there were several by Vermeer. I was transfixed by an almost electrical shock of inexplicable recognition about which I did not have any analytical understanding, but an emotional wave nearly knocked me down, and flooded through me.

In an instant I "knew", there was something very significant about this. Having experienced similar recollections from other lives I'd lived which were charged with trauma of one kind or another, I realized that the period during which Vermeer painted was one in which I had lived also. The intensity of emotion and perception rekindled were many times more powerful than a fleeting feeling of "deja vu" while sight seeing in Rome!

That moment reignited an excitement of sublime passion for painting I had known 300 years before! In subsequent months and years, I became gradually more aware that one my previous lives was spent as a painter. This was accompanied by confusion, and emotional turmoil that turned my whole life upside down! Until then, as far as I was aware, I didn't have an artistic bone in my body.

The exhilaration of regaining some ability to remember one's own identity is truly exhilarating, and validates the greater truth of one's own immortality as a spiritual being. Conversely, the pain of a lifetime lost: a body, possessions, beloved family, friends, and the accomplishments of that temporary identity, must be remembered and relived also.

The upsets and failures in life that precipitated an overwhelming apathy and ultimately the death of the body, are filled with emotional agonies that are very uncomfortable to resurrect, to say the least!

Pain is an abandonment and disappointment of unattained goals, betrayal of sacred vows, and promises unfulfilled. Ultimately, the most painful revelation to reconcile is the original decision, in that lifetime, to survive, and the failure to do so. This is the most fundamentally difficult to confront: betrayal of a promise to one's self.

Fortunately, life is an eternal, cyclical experience wherein second changes to learn from mistakes of the past can be had in an eternal now, through which each one of us makes our own future. We can improve.

PAINTING IN ONE'S OWN UNIVERSE

None of the paintings of Vermeer were given titles by him. However, through the years, for the sake of cataloguing, selling and identification, each painting has been given an agreed upon name by the art community.

The transcendent reverence assigned by audiences and astronomical prices paid for his paintings today, did not exist 300 years ago. Art collectors, promoters, auctioneers and speculators are a relatively recent phenomenon that have caused an artificial, super-inflated value to be placed on paintings that received only limited notice during his lifetime.

One is reminded that Holland, in the early 1600s, was afflicted by an epidemic of financial speculation built on tulip bulbs! Every citizen wanted to get rich quick. Men traded herds of cattle, and paid thousands of guilders for a single flower. This inferno of greed finally flamed out in 1637 and impacted the national economy! [XXXV] (FOOTNOTE)

During Vermeer's life, paintings, like other decorative craft objects, such as tapestry, pottery, engravings, etc. were traded as a commodity. The worth of decorative paintings was often evaluated by the number of figures in the painting, or the obvious technical skill required to render the subject matter, or the current popularity of the theme, and the number of readily available pictures of similar nature. Therefore, the prices paid were very modest indeed, and the marketplace was intensely guarded against competition.

Holland, until 1675, was relatively prosperous financially. Any civilization must have an abundance of necessities, in order to afford to indulge in the support of luxury items, like paintings. Typically, a very few aristocrats control all of the resources, and the lives of the peasantry. Bankers monitor and limit access to goods and services to make them sufficiently scarce so as to serve their own vested interests first and everyone else afterward.

Therefore, artists tended to work for the wealthy, employed to glorify their patron, as did DaVinci or Michelangelo. A large, prosperous middle-class is virtually unknown except during very brief periods.

Self-motivated artists, like prophets and visionaries, are often disdained as heretics or lunatics when they are alive. When they do not agree with the "normal" people in society, and are treated with contempt. It has been said that "reality is agreement".

Therefore, many artists did not achieve fame, fortune and critical claim until hundred years or more after their death. How many were starving, abandoned, scorned, ignored, diseased or bankrupt during their lifetime? The phrase, "starving artist" has become a cliché in Western civilization.

Vermeer considered himself to be a craftsman, and as an area of specialization, a painter. Within that context he was primarily a copyist. That is, he did not draw pictures from imagination, like any competent draftsman might. It appears that he emulated themes commonly circulated by contemporary like his friends Carl Fabritius, Pieter de Hooch, Gerard ter Borch, and other members of the Guild of St. Luke.

Likewise, he used the "camera obscura" as a tool for making a copy of living subjects or objects. Today, an overhead projector, copy machine or camera will accomplish this quickly and precisely.

However, the ability to create something purely from one's own imagination separates artists from copyists. To copy is human. To create is divine.

Aesthetics should be applied to the task of uplifting the spirit. Unfortunately, it is too easy to apply an aesthetic wave to subject matter that is debased, depraved, or demeaning to the spirit. Using art to glorify the physical universe is the stock and trade of the Hollywood film industry. Where is the immortal human spirit portrayed on film?

As a painter Vermeer tried to innovate the ability to communicate a subjective experience, or personal point of view. He wanted others to see a universe, a subjective reality, through his eyes. Necessarily, he wanted to perceive and purvey the essence of a thing, the spiritual source.

Painting, no matter how technically expert one becomes, is ultimately limited to the perceptions and conveyances of the physical universe: light, paint, brush and canvas. The camera obscura was an attempt to enhance the perception of light and the color reflected through it. Vermeer wanted to see beyond the ability of an unaided eye. This fascination and innovation he shared with his friends Huygens and Van Leeuwenhoek. Each in their own way, revealed the microcosm and the macrocosm.

The limitation of a draftsman, no matter how accomplished, impede the fundamental desire to create a universe from ones own imagination! Paper, pen and paint cannot reveal the full extent of imagination. There are many masters of drawing and painting who possess extraordinary ability to paint from imagination.

Yet, there are several who come close, including Michael Parkes (ww.michaelparkes.com). His works draftsmanship, painting, and sculpture are meticulously rendered with inhuman technical precision. However, it is his subject matter that are most compelling, recollected straight from the mists of a far ago backtrack in a universe where magic was the mainstay of reality.

Frank Frazetta, (www.frazettaartgallery.com) who was a child prodigy of art at the age of 8. He freely admits, as an adult, that he does not know how he knows how to draw or paint. We just "knows". Nonetheless, the ferocity rendered through his paint is wrenched from primordial depths of visceral barbarity. His ultra realistic sensuality purveys a monstrous playfulness that defies the maxim that muscles don't have soul.

The cartoonists Bill Watterson (Calvin & Hobbes) embodies a calculated, comic insouciance, drawn with ink and a magic wand! No real life 6 year old boy has ever been as fancifully cunning and delightfully creative.

Jerry Van Amerongen (www.ballardstreet.com) is another cartoonist with masterful technical skills and a comedic sense that converts the mundane into a magical menagerie of imagination.

However, everything that is aesthetic is not necessarily "artistic". Clever artisans, like actors or musicians, often make very good slaves who serve the destructive agendas of war lords and power mongers. Hollywood is overflowing with writers, designers, actors and cinematographers who spew out endless mounds of steaming, aesthetic manure every day to glorify the police state, the sex object, and the beauty of being "in agreement" with beings trapped in a body: oblivious to ones own immortality, potential freedom and power.

Control is the tool of the politician to tax the productive, enslave the worker, order soldiers to pillage, and priests to instill fear. Aesthetics, rendered by talented artists, writers, actors and musicians carry out the orders of these cruel beings, all in the name of "art".

The intention and demeanor of the artist should surpass the technical skill required to render an image or a song. Simply making a copy of a mundane, domestic scene, or painting a pretty face -- no matter how alluring -- is not a skill worthy of the word "aesthetic".

Emulation, duplication and glorification of the physical universe is a crime against the spirit. To use aesthetics to attract and trap the attention of a spiritual being into playing the trite and tired games of the material world is a betrayal of the immortal essence of every being who ever loved another or themselves.

As a painter Vermeer tried to elevate the spirit by painting love and light. Fundamentally, the only universe worthy of the essence of You is one of your own imaginative creation. This is difficult to attain and sustain as everyone in this universe agrees to the ultimate lie that it is the only universe.

By definition, an aesthetic must approach the no-wavelength of a spirit as closely as possible. By this, is not meant religious spirituality - which is designed intentionally to entrap and control every spirit who enters.

A spirit, even while inhabiting a body, is not a physical universe entity. A spirit -- an individual, immortal spiritual being -- imagines, endows and animates a universe. Such universes are as numerous and varied as the individuals who think them up!

Every being can imagine a universe of their own without any restrictions imposed by the brittle regulations of time, matter, form, space and energy -- the finite boundaries of the material universe. Such universes can include qualities that do not exist in this universe: love, beauty, compassion, action and unrestrained emotion!

Every quality worthy of the spirit is conceived and conveyed by a spirit. These qualities are, in fact, the genesis and the antithesis of the frigid foundations of this universe. Our quest to discover or create spiritual qualities in this universe is a source of perpetual pain.

The artist can abandon this brutal abyss of creation. We can recall and resurrect the fundamental source of creation: our simple, yet omnipotent, immortal, spiritual self. Remember? You are, as always, who you really are. And, we can create new universes of our own.

APPENDIX

A LESSON IN DUTCH POLITICAL / ECONOMIC HISTORY

The following brief historical background concerning the circumstances life in Holland at the end of Vermeer's life (1675) is extracted verbatim from Wikipedia.org:

"The largest cities in the Dutch Republic were in the province of Holland such as Amsterdam, Rotterdam, Leiden, Alkmaar, The Hague, Delft, Dordrecht and Haarlem. From the great ports of Holland, Hollandic merchants sailed to and from destinations all over Europe, and merchants from all over Europe gathered to trade in the warehouses of Amsterdam and other trading cities of Holland.

*The **rampjaar** ("disaster year") was the year 1672 in Dutch history. In that year, the Republic of the Seven United Provinces was attacked by England, France, and other allies. The invading armies very quickly defeated the Dutch army and conquered a large part of the Republic.*

As a result the cities of the remaining coastal provinces of Holland, Zealand and Frisia panicked and the city governments were taken over by Orangists, opposed to the republican regime of the Grand Pensionary Johan de Witt. This signified the end of the First Stadtholderless Period in Dutch history.

A famous Dutch saying describes the condition of the Dutch population at that moment as "redeloos" (without reason), its government "radeloos" (witless) and the country itself "reddeloos" (beyond rescue).

During the 1650s and 1660s the existing tensions between Dutch trade interests and English trade interests grew. The First Anglo-Dutch War was fought between the republics, resulting in a victory for the English.

Later, an English attempt to take over Dutch trade and colonies led to the Second Anglo-Dutch War. After the previous war Johan de Witt had supervised the expansion and improvement of the Dutch navy at the cost of neglecting the Dutch army. With the new fleet and the help of France, with whom they had allied again, the Dutch ultimately defeated the English at sea through the Raid on the Medway and put pressure on the English ally Münster.

The French had advanced from the IJssel to Utrecht. There negotiations started. (The megalomaniacal murders) Louis XIV and Charles II of England had intended that William became Sovereign Prince as head of a Hollandic rump state principality, a joint protectorate (with the British occupying key Hollandic cities and the isle of Walcheren) and Louis halted his army to allow the Orangists to take over Holland and come to an arrangement with him. He offered the Dutch peace in exchange for either the southern fortresses, religious freedom for Catholics and six million guilders or his keeping his present conquests and sixteen million guilders. These demands, especially the financial part of them, led to a public outrage and the Dutch mood abruptly changed from defeatism to a dogged determination to resist the French.

While the negotiations took place, the French had failed to prevent the Dutch from starting to inundate the Dutch Water Line and for Williams III's small army to withdraw behind it. Before they came to understand the nature and importance of this defense system their further advance was blocked by an impassable water and mud barrier. **(NOTE: Maria Thins owned land that was ruined by this military strategy that devastated her financially.)**

This small success for the Dutch was followed by others. The Dutch fleet under admiral Michiel de Ruyter had already defeated the Anglo-French fleet at the Battle of Solebay and on 28 August 1672.

On the diplomatic front, the Holy Roman Empire and Spain took the side of the Netherlands. In 1673 Bonn fell to a Dutch army. This made the French retreat from most of the Republic. England, Münster and Cologne made peace in 1674."

THE GUILD OF ST. LUKE:
A SUCCESSFUL EDUCATION SYSTEM

Had in not been for the Guild of St. Luke, to which my father arranged for me to study as an apprentice painter, I would have not become technically accomplished as an artist. Painting is highly technical. It is full of chemicals, techniques, rituals, time tested processes, and practical methodology, which at that time, and rarely since, have ever been committed to writing in a book.

The only way for a young man (women were not allowed) to learn an art or craft was through years of practical apprenticeship working daily with a man who had already paid his dues with years of successful application of these tools and techniques of the trade.

In only way to perpetuate the skills required of a trade was to train children to replace their parents. The most successful method for artisans and tradespersons to do this in that day was to organize themselves into a system of "guilds". Each trade eventually established and supported a guild. In addition, the guild was responsible for the administration of the business affairs and regulation of the master craftsmen who were members.

Eventually, the "guild system" was widely practices, with great success, as a fundamental system of education in Europe for many centuries. It was especially effective for practical trades, crafts and arts, that required the close tutelage of a master artisan to teach an aspiring apprentice by demonstration, repetition and application.

Drawing by Gerrit Lamberts of Saint Luke's Guild seen from the Old Men's Alley, the facade on the left represents the inn/house owned by Vermeer's father

This is some background information about Guilds from the on-line encyclopedia, Wikipedia.org:

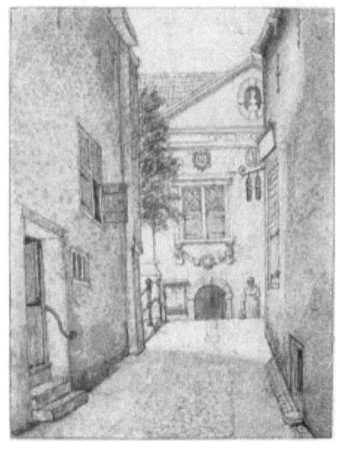

"In pre-industrial cities, craftsmen tended to form associations based on their trades, confraternities of textile workers, masons, carpenters, carvers, glassworkers, each of whom controlled secrets of traditionally imparted technology, the "arts" or "mysteries" of their crafts. Usually the founders were free independent master craftsmen.

During the Indian Gupta-period (AD 300 - 600) Indian craftsmen's associations, which may have

had archaic antecedents, were known as shreni.

Islamic civilization extended the notion of guilds to the artisan as well — most notably to the warraqeen, or "those who work with paper." Early Muslims were heavily engaged in translating and absorbing all ilm ("knowledge") from all other known civilizations as far east as China. Critically analyzing, accepting, rejecting, improving and codifying knowledge from other cultures became a key activity, and a knowledge industry as presently understood began to evolve. By the beginning of the 9th century, paper had become the standard medium of written communication, and most warraqeen were engaged in paper-making, book-selling, and taking the dictation of authors, to whom they were obliged to pay royalties on works, and who had final discretion on the contents. The standard means of presentation of a new work was its public dictation in a mosque or madrassah in front of many scholars and students, and a high degree of professional respect was required to ensure that other warraqeen did not simply make and sell copies, or that authors did not lose faith in the warraqeen or this system of publication. Thus the organization of the warraqeen was in effect an early guild.

Local guilds also served to safeguard artisans from the appropriation of their skills: The publication industry that spanned the Muslim empire, from the first works under the warraqeen system in 874 and up to the 15th century, produced tens of thousands of books per year. A culture of instructional capital flourished, with groups of respected artisans spreading their work to other artisans elsewhere, who could in turn copy it and perhaps "pass it off" as the original, thereby exploiting the social capital built up at great expense by the originators of techniques. Artisans began to take various measures to protect their proprietary interests, and restrict access to techniques, materials, and markets.

In the Early Middle Ages most of the Roman craft organizations, originally formed as religious confraternities, had disappeared, with the apparent exceptions of stonecutters and perhaps glassmakers

The guild was made up by experienced and confirmed experts in their field of handicraft. They were called master craftsmen. Before a new employee could rise to the level of mastery, he had to go through a schooling period during which he was first called an apprentice. After this period he could rise to the level of journeyman. Apprentices would typically not learn more than the most basic techniques until they were trusted by their peers to keep the guild's or company's secrets.

Like journey, the distance that could be traveled in a day, the title 'journeyman' derives from the French words for 'day' (jour and journée) from which came the middle English word journei. Journeymen were able to work for other masters, unlike apprentices, and generally paid by the day and were thus day laborers. After being employed by a master for several years, and after producing a qualifying piece of work, the apprentice was granted the rank of journeyman and was given documents (letters or certificates from his master and/or the guild itself) which certified him as a journeyman and entitled him to travel to other towns and countries to learn the art from other masters. These journeys could span large parts of Europe and were an unofficial way of communicating new methods and techniques, though by no means all journeymen made such travels - they were most common in Germany and Italy, and in other countries journeymen from small cities would often visit the capital.

After this journey and several years of experience, a journeyman could be received as master craftsman, though in some guilds this step could be made straight from apprentice. This would typically require the approval of all masters of a guild, a donation of money and other goods (often omitted for sons of existing members), and the production of a so-called masterpiece, which would illustrate the abilities of the aspiring master craftsman; this was often retained by the guild.

The medieval guild was established by charters or letters patent or similar authority by the city or the ruler and normally held a monopoly on trade in its craft within the city in which it operated: handicraft workers were forbidden by law to run any business if they were not members of a guild, and only masters were allowed to be members of a guild. Before these privileges were legislated, these groups of handicraft workers were simply called 'handicraft associations'.

The town authorities might be represented in the guild meetings and thus had a means of controlling the handicraft activities. This was important since towns very often depended on a good reputation for export of a narrow range of products, on which not only the guild's, but the town's, reputation depended. Controls on the association of physical locations to well-known exported products, e.g. wine from the Champagne and Bordeaux regions of France, tin-glazed earthenwares from certain cities in Holland, lace from Chantilly, etc., helped to establish a town's place in global commerce — this led to modern trademarks.

In many German and Italian cities, the more powerful guilds often had considerable political influence, and sometimes attempted to control the city authorities. In the 14th century, this led to numerous bloody uprisings, during which the guilds dissolved town councils and detained patricians in an attempt to increase their influence.

*Two of the most outspoken critics of the guild system were Jean-Jacques Rousseau and Adam Smith, and all over Europe a tendency to oppose government control over trades in favor of laissez-faire free market systems was growing rapidly and making its way into the political and legal system. Karl Marx in his **Communist Manifesto** also criticized the guild system for its rigid gradation of social rank and the relation of oppressor/oppressed entailed by this system. From this time comes the low regard in which some people hold the guilds to this day."*

Tragically, presaging the ultimate disappearance of a vast number of arts and technologies, the demise of the Guild System occurred with the advent of the aristocratic learning system, or the university. The use of books and verbal instruction in a school room, and ultimately in a university auditorium, removes the student from being able to personally <u>observe and apply</u> the object of study in <u>reality</u>. Books can not replace <u>doing</u>.

No modern university as ever produced a competent craftsman or artist, unless that student served (outside of school) as an apprentice to a master. Indeed, the modern Western world will ultimately be lost because there has been no effective replacement for this very effective method of education.

Contemporaries of Vermeer in Delft

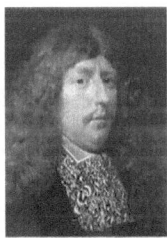

Master Painter
Gerard ter Borch (or Terburg)
(1617 – 1681)

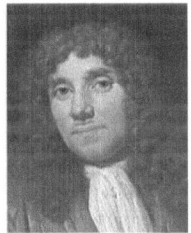

Scientist and Inventor of the Microscope
Antonie Philips van Leeuwenhoek
(1632 – 1723)

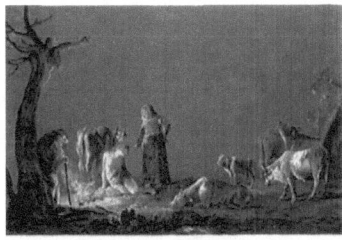

Leonard Bramer (alias Nestelghat)
(1596 - 1674)
Painting by Leonaert Bramer
Peasants by a Fire c. 1660

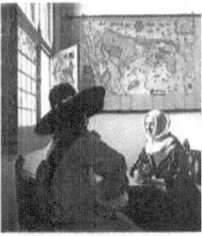

Officers in the Delft Militia
Captain Melling
Captain Lambertus Morleth
Lieutenant Balthens, Vermeer's uncle

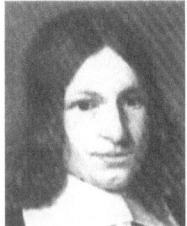

Master Painter
Pieter de Hooch
born 1629 - died 1684

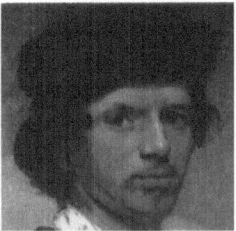

Carel Fabritius
(1622 - 1654)
(Student of Rembrandt)

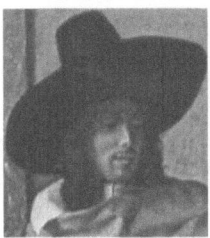

Vermeer's Patron
Pieter Claesz van Ruijven

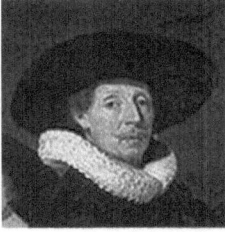

Antonie Palamedesz
1601 - 1673
Member of the
Guild of St. Luke

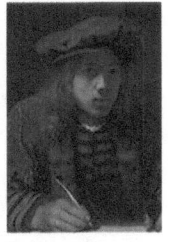

Samuel Van Hoogstraten
Member of the
Guild of St. Luke

CONTEMPORARIES OF VERMEER

A list of living artists compiled by Dirck van Bleyswijck, published in his "Description of Delft", eight years before Vermeer died, include the following residents:

Leonardt Bramer, Pieter Janz. van Asch, Adriano van Linschoten, Hans Jordaens, Cornelis de Man and Johannes Vermeer.

From: John Michael Montias
Vermeer and His Milieu: A Web of Social History
Princeton, 1989, pp. 171-172

"Ever since the powder explosion of 1654 which had caused the death of Carel Fabritius, Delft's community of artists had been shrinking. Many painters had left town, most to settle in Amsterdam, some in The Hague. Willem van Aelst, who painted still lifes, Emanuel de Witte (church interiors), and Pieter de Hoogh (genre paintings) were the most outstanding of the group that migrated to the great emporium of the north. The only painter of note to migrate to Delft in that decade was Abraham van Beyeren, who registered in the guild in 1657 and stayed there a few years before returning to The Hague in the early 1660s. Cornelis de Man returned to Delft after a long absence spent traveling in France and Italy in the 1640s and early 1650s. The older generation of Delft painters - Balthasar van der Ast, Willem van den Bundel, Jacob Pynas was dying out.

The survivors - Antony Palamedes, Leonaert Bramer, Cornelis Rietwijck were constantly called upon to become headmen of St. Luke's Guild because there were hardly any qualified younger people left to take their place. The guild had even been obliged to choose Pieter Bronckhorst as headman in 1655 and Willem Ploij in 1656.

Bronckhorst was sixty-seven years old, Ploij seventy-two. Guild members for four decades, they had pursued careers of self-effacing mediocrity. It is not so much a credit to Vermeer's precocity as a sign of the decline of Delft as an artistic center that he was elected headman at the age of thirty, in the fall of 1662. He was the youngest artist to become a guild officer since the guild had been reorganized in 1611. Newly-discovered evidence suggests that Vermeer continued to take an active part in the guild after his two-year stint as headman.

Despite its decline, Delft remained an important city of passage that many artists occasionally visited. It contained many fine collections that a local painter could easily have access to. And if he wanted more stimulation, he could always take a seat in an

inexpensive horse-towed barge and glide in comfort to The Hague, Amsterdam,
Leyden, or Rotterdam, which he would reach in less than a day. All the major towns
of Holland were connected through a dense network of canals, along which barges
traveled back and forth according to a tightly-ordained schedule. Ease of travel helped
to keep the country ideologically and artistically compact.

The artistic traffic was intense both during Delft's heyday as a ville d'art and
afterward. Many out-of-town artists left a trace of their presence when they signed as
witnesses at a local notary's office. Ter Borch...suddenly appeared in Delft in March
1653, coming from some other undetermined place of residence; Moses van
Uyttenbroek and Jan Baptista van Fornenburgh visited from The Hague, Pieter de
Grebber from Haarlem. The excellent seascape painter Simon de Vlieger departed for
Amsterdam in the late 1630s but delivered tapestry cartoons to the municipality of
Delft in 1640 and 1641. Pieter de Hooch, who had also migrated to Amsterdam in
the late 1650s, came back for at least one visit in 1663.

There must have been other visitors who had other things to do while they were in town
rather than witness deeds. It is hard to believe, for instance, that Nicolaes Maes and
Samuel van Hoogstraten, who both lived in Dordrecht in the 1650s, did not once stop
over in Delft on their way to The Hague or Amsterdam, perhaps to talk shop with
Carel Fabritius who, like them, had once been a pupil of Rembrandt or, after
Fabritius's death, to fraternize with other member of the artists' community.

Maes had anticipated De Hooch's achievements of the 1650s in rendering realistic
interior scenes with finely modulated contrasts of light and dark. Van Hoogstraten
seems to have been the first to do trompe l'oeil paintings. Along with Fabritius he also
constructed peep shows in boxes in which illusionistic scenes could be viewed in
perspective through a small opening.

Two heads ("tronien") by Van Hoogstraten were found in Vermeer's death inventory.
Vermeer must also have seen the works of Maes, some features of which became part
of the visual vocabulary of the Delft School."

THE CAMERA OBSCURA

The following excellent information is excerpted from the preeminent website on Vermeer studies, Essentialvermeer.com:

"Why have people imagined that Vermeer was a camera obscura user? There is absolutely no documentary evidence to support this idea. The only source of information is the paintings themselves. Before eyes had been accustomed to the modern photographic camera's way of seeing, in 1891 Joseph Pennell, American lithographer, etcher and friend of Whistler, was the first to suppose that Vermeer may have employed an optical device as an aid to his painting.

Curiously enough, one of the most widely read and heatedly discussed books about Vermeer in recent years, *Vermeer's Camera: Uncovering the Truth behind the* Masterpieces, by Philip Steadman, was not written by art historian. The controversial subject of this book is Vermeer's use of the camera obscura - a kind of predecessor to the modern photographic camera - as an aid to his painting.

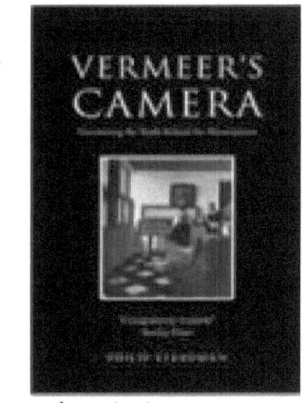

Since American photographer Joseph Pennell in 1891 first supposed that Vermeer employed the camera obscura the subject has been widely debated among art historians. However, not until Steadman's book has the topic been so thoroughly researched. Steadman, an architect by training, painstakingly develops his argument through careful study of the history of the camera obscura, an exploration of 17th-century optics, and a detailed study of the light, optics, perspective, and measurement of a series of Vermeer's paintings.

He goes to remarkable lengths to reconstruct Vermeer's studio and its furnishings, down to the angle of the light from its windows. The science is complex, but always clearly explained. Steadman's arguments are so carefully articulated and rational tested, that he has probably come as close as theoretically possible to proving that the camera obscura was in fact an integral part of the elusive Dutch master's working method.

Professor Steadman: "I was teaching perspective drawing to a group of summer school students in the 1970s, and decided to set them an exercise in reconstructing the three-dimensional scenes shown in paintings, using a method of 'reverse perspective'. We chose 17th century Dutch interiors, including some by Vermeer, because the rooms have tiled floors. From there I became interested in the question of whether

Vermeer shows the 'same' room or rooms repeatedly in his pictures. Only later did I come to realize that this question might have a bearing on his use of the camera obscura. So my route towards the research reported in Vermeer's Camera was a circuitous one. Just recently I remembered, for the first time in many years, that we had had a reproduction of 'Girl with a Pearl Earring' at home when I was a boy; so perhaps she provided some kind of long-term unconscious inspiration.

There were two significant points on which I remained dubious and undecided in the book, and offered different possibilities. The first was whether the room with the 'squares and circles' patterns of leading in the windows - which appears many times in pictures painted from the late 1650s onwards - is or is not the first floor studio used by Vermeer in Maria Thins's house on the Oude Langendijk. In the book I thought there was insufficient evidence to come to a conclusion about this. But I was wrong.

In 2002 Ab Warffemius published his very convincing reconstruction of Maria Thins's house, based on the 1675-8 pictorial map of Delft, a 19th century cadastral map giving the dimensions of the site, a drawing by the 18th century topographical artist Abraham Rademaker, and the probate inventory of the house and its contents made after Vermeer's death. (See 'Jan Vermeers huis: Een poging tot reconstructie', Delfia Batavorum: Historisch Jaarboek voor Delft 2001, pp.60-78). Warffemius obtains dimensions for Vermeer's studio that are extremely close to those which I derived – quite independently and on the basis of completely different sources, i.e. the paintings themselves – from my perspective calculations. Warffemius also shows windows and ceiling beams as in my reconstructions. (His arguments here have to do with the building's structure, and the evidence of the Rademaker view, and not just with what is shown by Vermeer.) I think all this leaves little doubt that the paintings were made in, and depict, this actual room."

By painstakingly reconstructing the three dimensional space of ten of Vermeer's interiors using the method of "inverse perspective," Steadman deduced that they were all painted in the same room. He then was able to deduce the exact measurements of the rooms themselves using the measurements of a few objects represented in Vermeer's painting which have survived till today, such as the maps which hang on the far wall and the Spanish chairs.

Based on these calculations Steadman arrives at the his key finding which he states in a reply to his critics in *Vermeer's Camera* :

Afterthoughts:

"For each of the ten paintings, it is possible to determine the theoretical perspective viewpoint: that point in the room in which Vermeer would have had to put his eye to see the precise view in question. The entire extents of his view - everything that is visible in the painting - is contained in a "visual pyramid" whose apex is at the back of the viewpoint. If the lines forming the edges of this pyramid are carried back to meet the wall of the room, the define a rectangle on that wall. For at least six paintings this rectangle is the size of Vermeer's canvas. " Thus according to Steadman, "the camera lens would have been positioned at the theoretical viewpoint of the picture for each composition, and the back of the wall served as the projection screen. The projected images of the room are the same sizes of Vermeer's canvases, because he has traced them."

Function

"The principle of the camera obscura (*in latin camera=room and obscura=dark*) is as simple as it seems magical even today. The windowless box or chamber has a small hole in one site and a white side of wall opposite the side with the hole. Light entering the camera obscura through the hole projects onto the screen wall, and (following the laws of optics) produces and upside-down and reversed image. Most camera obscuras were fitted with a lens in the hole to focus the image. In portable form, the camera obscura became popular for recording landscape and city views. Using a system of lenses and mirrors that allowed the image to appear on a translucent screen, draftsmen could trace the views to produce early versions of tourist snapshots. The rooms-sized version of the camera obscura was useful to scientists interested in the behavior of light." A few camera obscuras of this sort can still be found near popular tourist resorts.

The image of the camera obscura had two particular properties which made them quite different from reality. The image was projected upside down and the luminosity was in general rather weak. This was due to the small aperture, usually no wider than a finger, which emitted only the minimum of light. This could be remedied by a larger aperture but the image was more blurred, unless a lens was mounted in the aperture as was the case in the sixteenth-century.

History

The fundamental principle of the camera obscura was already know by the Chinese. The earliest mention of this type of device was by the philosopher Mo-Ti (5th century BC). He formally recorded the creation of an inverted image formed by light rays passing through a pinhole into a darkened room. He called this darkened room a "collecting place" or the "locked treasure room."

Aristotle (384-322 BC) understood the optical principle of the camera obscura. He viewed the crescent shape of a partially eclipsed sun projected on the ground through the holes in a sieve, and the gaps between leaves of a plane tree.

In 1038 AD, an Arab scholar named Alhazan described a working model of the camera obscura. Although Alhazan did not actually construct the device, his work influenced a medieval philosopher Roger Bacon who was interested in optics. In 1267 AD, Bacon created convincing optical illusions by using mirrors and the basic principles of the camera obscura. Later, he used a camera obscura to project an image of the sun directly upon an opposite wall. These medieval cameras were literally "dark rooms." Inside the room, one could see what was happening outside. It was virtually magic, and experience as such.

Leonardo da Vinci first suggested that the camera obscura might be of interest to the artist in 1490. The first transportable models could be used to draw from nature views of cities or panoramic landscapes. This version of the camera obscura included a tent large enough to contain the draftsman. The image was projected onto a flat surface where the draftsman had no great difficult in tracing it. Nevertheless, it appears that this type of device was used only on special occasions and generally for topographical work. Years late the Italian landscape painter Canaletto used this kind of camera obscura to create his amazingly accurate perspective views of Venice.

The camera obscura was well known in the time of Vermeer. Constantijn Huygens, a major figure of Dutch contemporary culture, who seems to have been aware of Vermeer's work and had contacts with some of the most important Dutch painters of the time, bought a camera obscura in 1662 in London and wrote: "it produces admirable effects by reflecting on a wall in a dark room. I cannot describe its beauty in words, but all painting seems dead by comparison...."

Huygens took the camera obscura back the Netherlands where is know to have recommended its use to painters. Samuel van Hoogstraten, a Dutch painter and Constantijn Huygens art theorist often associated with Vermeer's work stated: "I am certain that seeing this projections in the dark will give the vision of young painters no small light, for beside acquiring knowledge of nature, one sees here what on the whole or in general a truly natural painting ought to have. "It has been suggested - although this is wholly speculative - that Vermeer have might developed an interest in optics through a connection with the painter Carl Fabritius, who moved to Delft in about 1650; or, via Fabritius, with his friend Samuel van Hoogstraten of Dortrecht. Both men were fascinated by the tromp-l'oeil and perspective illusion."

"In Delft, vision-extending and vision-transforming instruments such as the camera obscura must have been readily available. They were the passion of Anthony van Leeuwenhoek, an industrious researcher now best known for his discovery of micro-organisms through the microscope. It is almost impossible to imagine that these exact contemporaries, both baptized in 1632 and both high achievers in their fields, would not have come across each other in the small city of Delft".

AUTOPSY OF AN ARTIST

The burial registers of the Oude Kerk (Old Church) record the death of Johannes Vermeer as December 15, 1675, less than a year after the end of the Second Anglo-Dutch war. The major actions of this war took place within the immediate vicinity of Delft, which is only about 20 miles from the site of the several major naval battles fought between Dutch and English ships, as the crow flies. Today you can drive in a car from Delft to London, England in about 6 hours (490 km or 304.47 miles).

The naval blockage, and land invasion by enemy armies, caused an economic collapse of the region that put an end to commercial prosperity in the area -- especially for artists.

Although I was a member of the Delft Militia during the war, I did not fight actively. The war definitely traumatized every citizen of the town, and the war itself indirectly affect my livelihood, although, in reality, I never earned a living with my own painting sufficient to support my ever-growing family.

I was supported primarily by Maria Thins, my mother-in-law, and two patrons, supplemented marginally by loans, and trading in works of art provided to me by other painters through the artisans Guild of St. Luke in Delft, in which I was active from an early age.

The year my death my only private patron died. According to public records, I borrowed 1,000 guilders from a banker early in 1675. I also attempted to collected all of the money owned to my mother in law. After that, I was out of money and out of options!

In a statement written to her creditors about a year after my death, my wife, Catharina Bolnes, wrote in her own words the practical circumstances of the final years of my life:

"During the ruinous war he not only was unable to sell any of his art but also, to his great detriment, was left sitting with the paintings of other masters that he was dealing in."

"As a result and owing to the great burden of his (11) children, having no means of his own, he had lapsed into such decay and decadence, which he had so taken to heart that, as if he had fallen into a frenzy, in a day or day and a half had gone from being healthy to being dead."

There are several other possible contributing factors to the "frenzy" of Vermeer's death. One of those factors is drinking alcohol, which ruins the liver, resulting in death by toxic accumulation in the blood. Vermeer was raised in an inn owned and managed by his father, and after the death of his father, continued to be run by his mother until her death. The Dutch drank beer, rather than water. Water was not safe to drink, untreated. No water sanitation system existed except for boiling.

The brewing process, which boils water, combined with the resulting of alcohol content from yeast and sugar, made it a safe liquid staple of the daily diet. Wine was consumed to a lesser degree, but Dutch beer often had an alcohol content as high as wine. It was often commented by foreigners that Holland was run by the women because the men were too drunk to do anything!

In addition, constant exposure to certain heavy metals used commonly in painting pigments cause a breakdown in nervous function, when exposure is too severe, or when exposed over a long period of years, as was the case with Vermeer, and Pieter de Hoogh. Pieter de Hoogh, in his last years, deteriorated mentally, became depressed and despondent and eventually died in an insane asylum from unknown causes. Other famous cases of "insanity", usually attributed to syphilis, were the French painters, Van Gough, and Gauguin, but could easily been affected by high levels of heavy metals.

Recent studies in the late 20th century have proven conclusively that lead and mercury are both very deadly poisons that cause the nervous system, including the brain, to short-circuit electrically, so that normal mental and physical functions are disrupted. Combined with alcohol, this can easily overload the cleansing organs of the body, especially the liver. Pigments used historically, and even today, by oil painters include:

- ∞ white lead (lead is very volatile and very poisonous when touched or breathed)
- ∞ vermilion (manufactured by heating mercury and sulfur.

Mercury is the 3rd most deadly substance to human beings in the world, even in microscopic quantities, when touched or breathed.)

These heavy metals can not be eliminated once exposed, as these metals lodge in the tissue of the muscles, organs and fat, and cannot be dislodged except through extensive detoxification therapies. The effect of exposure to heavy metals, especially mercury used in dental fillings, and childhood vaccinations, is sited in many studies as the cause of autism, a severe and irreversible mental dysfunction. The epidemic increase of autism in the United States is directly linked to the use of mercury in childhood vaccinations.

FOOTNOTES

I "...Saint Praxedis..."

"In recent years only one new painting has been seriously proposed as an addition to Vermeer's canon: Saint Praxedis, [1] (FOOTNOTE) a virtual duplicate of an original 1645 painting of the same name by the Florentine painter, Felice Ficherelli, whose nickname was il Riposo. St. Praxedis was a 2nd-century Roman Christian who, along with her sister, Pudentiana, cared for the often-severed bodies of those martyred for their faith. By the late 16th century she was especially revered by the Jesuits, an order which lived next door to Vermeer's mother-in-law, Maria Thins, along the Oude Langendijk in Delft.

While a number of scholars (are) skeptical about the attribution, (the curator of Northern Baroque painting at the USA's National Gallery of Art, Arthur Wheelock Jr.) remained resolute in his belief about its authenticity. He marshaled both direct and inferential evidence to support his claim.

First, he noted that the painting had, very unusually, two Meer signatures: at the lower left was the name "Meer," with the date "1655." At the lower right edge, there appeared the word "Meer," followed by the letter "N", the letter "R," then two lower case "O's." Wheelock claimed that both "signatures and the date are integral to the paint surface." Further he argued that the second signature could be interpreted as: "[Ver]Meer N[aar] R[ip] o [s] o" or "Vermeer after Riposo," Ficherelli's Italian nickname."

Reference: from the most excellent Vermeer website, Essentialvermeer.com:

II "... Guild of St. Luke..."

Please refer to the article, in the **APPENDIX** of this book entitled:

"The Guild of St. Luke: A Successful Education System" for details of about the guild system at work in Europe during the lifetime of Vermeer.

III "...Artemis..."

"In Greek mythology, Artemis was the daughter of Zeus and Leto, and the twin sister of Apollo. She was the Hellenic goddess of forests and hills, virginity/fertility, and the hunt and was often depicted as a huntress carrying a bow and arrows. The deer and

the cypress were sacred to her. In later Hellenistic times she even assumed the ancient role of Eileithyia in aiding childbirth.

Artemis was one of the most widely venerated of the gods and one of the oldest (Burkert 1985, 149). Her later association with the moon is a popular idea which has little foundation. She later became identified with Selene, a Titaness who was a Greek moon goddess, and she was sometimes depicted with a crescent moon above her head. She also became identified with the Roman goddess Diana and with the Etruscan goddess Artume."

Reference: Wikipedia.org

IV "... My friend and fellow artist, Carl Fabritius..."

"Carel Pietersz, Fabritius
Midden Beemster 1622 - Delft 1654

Carel Fabritius was a great painter who died young in the explosion of the powder magazine in Delft in 1654 and whose pictures are too rare to perpetuate his reputation. He became a pupil of Rembrandt at an early age and it could be argued that he was the most original painter Rembrandt ever had in his studio. Fabritius appreciated Rembrandt's analytical approach to human character and interpreted it in his own quiet way instead of just imitating the outward bravado of brushwork. Fabritius has also occupied a peculiar position in the context of the painting style in Delft in the 1650s. This is caused by the fact that the rediscoverer of Vermeer, Thoré-Bürger, who owned Fabritius's Goldfinch, saw Fabritius as a link between Rembrandt and Vermeer."

Reference:

http://www.essentialvermeer.com/dutch-painters/fabritius.html

V "...Maria Thins, Catharina's mother..."

"Maria Thins - Born in Gouda, ca. 1593 - died in Delft, December 27, 1680. was a member of the Gouda Thins' family. In 1622 she married to Reynier Bolnes, a prominent and prosperous brick maker. In 1635 the marriage deteriorated; her sister found her crying in bed after her husband had beaten her. The couple moved to another house, where previously Wouter Crabeth had lived. There Bolnes had his dinner in the front room, together with his son, while he refused to talk to her and slept in a room upstairs. At one time her daughter Cornelia was locked up by her father. In 1641

Maria Thins decided to move to Delft, where her brother lived. Her husband refused to divorce her, but in 1649 she received a considerable sum of money from him.

In 1653 her daughter Catharina married Johannes Vermeer in Schipluiden and at some time the couple moved in the rather spacious house on Oude Langendijk. Vermeer had his atelier on the front side of the second floor.

Vermeer and his wife buried a child in the Old Church in 1660. The same document states that at the same time, Vermeer and his wife were living in the house of Maria Thins on the Oude Langendijk in Delft. Although Maria Thins lived to be 87, surviving Vermeer, she was already about 67 years old in 1660 when the family moved into her house."

Reference: Wikipedia.org

VI   "... we produced 15 children together during our 22 years of marriage."

It is difficult to imagine, or comprehend, by comparison to modern, middle-class American standards and life-style, how enormously difficult it was to maintain a household in Holland during the 1600s. The daily regimen of shopping for or raising food, getting fuel for cooking and heating, pumping or carrying water, cleaning, making and mending clothes, washing bodies and clothes, and personal hygiene (doubly so for feminine hygiene) was an arduous, full-time job at the very least.

This was all accomplished <u>without</u> the miracles of our electronic civilization which provide us with air conditioning, refrigeration, electricity, easy transportation, abundant and inexpensive access to food and clothing, entertainment, and other luxuries that we have grown to take for granted. Every cleaning chore was done by manual labor with brooms, buckets, muscle and sweat! No soap or disinfectants existed. No maid service. No supermarkets. The infrequent services of a household cook or helper, were sometimes available when income allowed -- which was not usual, beyond the employment of a maid by Maria Thins.

Today, every time I go into a supermarket or department store I am <u>amazed</u> by the superabundance of consumer goods. The level of technology and prosperity, so taken for granted in 2009, was an entire universe apart from anything that could have been <u>vaguely</u> conceived in 1670!

Typically, the women banded together to share these relentless chores, and trained the children to assist them as soon as they were physically able to help. This was one of the advantages of having lots of children: that is, the older girls helped their mother and grandmother with household duties, and caring for the younger children. To that degree they produced more than they consumed, and were an asset and a blessing -- in addition to the joy of their youthful energy, enthusiasm and playful spirits!

The natural environment of Delft, although enchantingly beautiful most of the year, was rigorous, including hot, humid summers, when heavy clothing was worn according to cultural protocol. The brutal, frozen features of winter weather in the North Sea regions, which last nearly 6 months of each year, were painfully oppressive.

Compound the ardors of these elements by the birth of 15 children in 22 years, with the diapers, children's clothing, bathing, bedding, supervision, education, care during sickness, attendance at church, and the thousands of tiny demands for attention by each child for love and communication!

Fortunately, Catharina and her mother, Maria, were both diligent, hard-working, tireless, relentless, practical, clever and industrious household managers who thrived on the joys of motherhood. For my part, I have always loved all of my children.

Being a painter, or writer, or any other creative artisan requires intense concentration, attention to minute technical details, and the isolation required to muse aesthetically and philosophically. Families are a very survival mechanism for furthering the genetic line, but they are an unwelcome distraction from the creation of a private, personal universe of a spiritual being. Artists always have been, and continue to be, very jealous of solitude and the priority of creative isolation for day-dreaming.

It is ironic that artists, and preachers, are often inflicted by passion for both spiritual and carnal fulfillment. Unfortunately, the aesthetics of sex and the obsessive compulsion to experience this addictive sensation is driven by unremitting doses of testosterone! Aesthetics is an measurable electronic wave that most closely approximates the almost infinitely tiny, yet powerful, wave emitted by the spiritual energy. It is the essential spark that animates all life forms. This singular phenomenon, unmitigated by personal discipline, is a most ruinous factor in Earthly existence.

If it had not been for incessant demands on my wife to have sex there would not have been a herd of children in our house. In spite of her reluctance, I managed to covertly and overtly persuade her to relent. More often than not, sexual activity was not a leisurely, loving communication between us. It was a quick and frantic action in the dark. That is not to say that we did not share a passionate love for each other, especially when we were young.

Sexual modesty in the home was demanded by the moral codes and religious regimen of the age. Personal hygiene was not what it has become in the 20th century. There was no running water -hot or cold - no toilets, bathtubs, soap, or washing machines. Women didn't shave their bodies, nor did they parade around naked!

Fluffy feather bedding and blankets were not common in Holland either, so comfortable lovemaking was not convenient -- especially in a house full of kids who often shared the same bed with their parents for the sake of space and warmth! Sex was mostly a quiet, bedtime activity performed quickly, in the dark, and partly clothed. Most of the time it was an act of tired resignation during the dark, cold nights when exhausted sleep was far more desirable than a frisky fuck!

For men, sex is primarily a convenient way to relieve physical, hormone-driven stress, after which the nearly inevitable consequence of pregnancy, for which there seemed to be no prevention other than abstinence.

Catharina had the disadvantage of her Catholic upbringing which forbade her to deny my satisfaction. The Catholic Church, being entirely patriarchal, and utterly demeaning and dismissive of women, forbade them the experience of sexual pleasure. All the while the priests insisted on the sexual slavery of women to populate the parishes with superstitious peasants whose duty it is, they are told, to fill the ecclesiastical coffers with gold, under threat of Earthy and/or eternal pain. Factually, the Protestant churches were no different. Every sperm is precious to the Church: it means more gold!

Although my parents were Protestants, the reasons I chose to become a Catholic when I married Catharina were several. First, because I didn't really think that church organizations differed in any meaningful way. It seemed to me, that during that relatively tolerant period, it was a greater advantage to align myself with the financial stability of her mother, Maria Thins, for whom being a Catholic was a matter of great important.

Second, my middle class father and I were artisans in the Guild of St. Luke, which, although secular, was rooted in Catholic traditions. I depended on The Guild for artistic training, and we both required a membership to pursue a livelihood in Delft. Further, the Protestant churches did not endorse or support the arts, especially painting, and revolted against grandiose embellishments sponsored by the Catholic Church. Aesthetic austerity doesn't work for a painter.

During more than 20 years of marriage, our passionate devotion matured into mutual responsibility. Through our years of sharing joys and pleasures of life, as well as the tragic deaths of several children, and other family members, our bond grew more intense. This became a deeper respect, tempered with mutual dependency, and a greater acquiescence to reality.

Ultimately, the unrelenting births and demands of financial and physical support of 11 surviving children became overwhelming. When the war and financial calamity crushed the national economy, we were undone. Vermeer was finally overwhelmed and died in a fit of depression.

Catharina, as are most women, when compared to men, was a tougher, more tenacious survivor. Our lives and livelihood would been better served had I the discipline to sheath my nuptial sword within my trousers, rather than insisting that I be allowed to thrust and parry with my wife each night like a teenaged boy playing pirate. The issue from that sword is as fatal as a slashing saber!

-- The Author

VII "...camera obscura..."

"The **camera obscura** *(Latin dark chamber) is an optical device used, for example, in drawing or for entertainment. It is one of the inventions leading to photography. The principle can be demonstrated with a box with a hole in one side (the box may be room-sized, or hangar sized). Light from a scene passes through the hole and strikes a surface where it is reproduced, in color, and upside-down. The image's perspective is accurate. The image can be projected onto paper, which when traced can produce a highly accurate representation.*

Using mirrors, as in the 18th century overhead version (illustrated in the Discovery and Origins section below), it is possible to project a right-side-up image. Another more portable type is a box with an angled mirror projecting onto tracing paper placed on the glass top, the image upright as viewed from the back.

As a pinhole is made smaller, the image gets sharper, but the projected image becomes dimmer. With too small a pinhole the sharpness again becomes worse due to diffraction. Some practical camera obscurae use a lens rather than a pinhole because it allows a larger aperture, giving a usable brightness while maintaining focus.

The first mention of the principles behind the pinhole camera, a precursor to the camera obscura, belongs to Mozi (470 BC to 390 BC), a Chinese philosopher and the founder of Mohism. The Mohist tradition is unusual in Chinese thought because it is concerned with developing principles of logic. Aristotle (384 to 322 BC) understood the optical principle of the pinhole camera. He viewed the crescent shape of a partially eclipsed sun projected on the ground through the holes in a sieve, and the gaps between leaves of a plane tree.

The first camera obscura was later built by Arab scientist Abu Ali Al-Hasan Ibn al-Haitham, born in Basra (965-1039 AD), known in the West as Alhacen or Alhazen, who carried out practical experiments on optics in his Book of Optics."

Reference: Wikipedia.org

VIII "... The Guild of St. Luke..."

*"The **Guild of Saint Luke** was the most common name for a city guild for painters and other artists in early modern Europe, especially in the Low Countries. They were named in honor of the Evangelist Luke, the patron saint of artists, who was identified by John of Damascus as having painted the Virgin's portrait.*

One of the most famous such organizations was founded in Antwerp. It continued to function until 1795, although by then it had lost its monopoly and therefore most of its power. In most cities, including Antwerp, the local government had given the Guild the power to regulate defined types of trade within the city. Guild membership, as a master, was therefore required for an artist to take on apprentices or to sell paintings to the public. Similar rules existed in Delft, where only members could sell paintings in the city or have a shop. The early guilds in Antwerp and Bruges, setting a model that would be followed in other cities, even had their own showroom or market stall from which members could sell their paintings directly to the public. The guild of Saint Luke not only represented painters, sculptors, and other visual artists, but also— especially in the seventeenth century—dealers, amateurs, and even art lovers (the so-called liefhebbers). In the medieval period most members in most places were probably manuscript illuminators, where these were in the same guild as painters on wood and cloth - in many cities they were joined with the scribes or "scriveners". In traditional guild structures, house-painters and decorators were often in the same guild. However, as artists formed under their own specific guild of St. Luke, particularly in the Netherlands, distinctions were increasingly made. In general, guilds also made judgments on disputes between artists and other artists or their clients. In such ways, it controlled the economic career of an artist working in a specific city, while in different cities they were wholly independent and often competitive against each other."

Reference: Wikipedia.org

IX "...Gerard ter Borch..."

"(December 1617 – 8 December 1681). He received an excellent education from his father, also an artist, and developed his talent very early. The inscription on a study of a head proves that Ter Borch was at Amsterdam in 1632, where he studied possibly under C Duyster or P Codde. Duyster's influence can be traced in a picture bearing the date 1638, in the Ionides Bequest (Victoria and Albert Museum). In 1634 he studied under Pieter Molyn in Haarlem. A record of this Haarlem period is the Consultation (1635) at the Berlin Gallery.

In 1635 he was in London, and subsequently he traveled in Germany, France, Spain and Italy. It is certain that he was in Rome in 1641, when he painted the small portraits on copper of Jan Six and A Young Lady (Six Collection, Amsterdam). In 1648 he was at Münster during the meeting of the congress which ratified the treaty of peace between the Spaniards and the Dutch, and executed his celebrated little picture, painted upon copper, of the assembled plenipotentiaries--a work which, along with the a portrait of a Man Standing, now represents the master in the national collection in London. The picture was bought by the marques of Hertford at the Demidoff sale for 1280, and presented to the National Gallery by Sir Richard Wallace, at the suggestion of his secretary, Sir John Murray Scott.

At this time Ter Borch was invited to visit Madrid, where he received employment and the honor of knighthood from Philip IV, but, in consequence of an intrigue, it is said, he was obliged to return to the Netherlands. **He seems to have resided for a time in Haarlem;** (ONLY ABOUT 60 km FROM DELFT) *but he finally settled in* **Deventer,** (ABOUT 150 km FROM DELFT) *where he became a member of the town council, as which he appears in the portrait now in the gallery of the Hague. He died at Deventer in 1681."*

Reference: Wikipedia.org

X "... Camera Obscura..."

Please refer to the article in the APPENDIX of this book entitled: **"Camera Obscura"** for more in depth information.

XI "...Delft militia..."

"In the Netherlands, the 12th and 13th century ushered in progressive urbanization of the growing population. Civic guards or militia, as they are also called, became necessary to protect the towns because traditional private guards of the aristocratic rulers proved insufficient. Protection was required not only from foreign enemies, but from fire or the flooding as well. Popular revolts had to be occasionally put down. Hence the Dutch name for their guards was Schutter *(in German: 'Schütze', from: 'beschützen') which in the original meaning of the word is "guardian" (to guard, to protect) and not "shooter."*

In the Schuttersboek *from 1674 Johannes Vermeer is listed as member of the first squadron of the* oranje vendel *commanded by Abraham Coeckebacker. We know that the acclaimed Delft painter (a family friend of the Vermeers) Leonaert Bramer, had been a sergeant in the same company and a member of a select group known as the* Brotherhood of Knights *(broederschrappe). Two other important figures in the life of Vermeer had played a role in the Delft Civic Guard. The first was Captain Teding van Berckhout, who headed the second banner of the third quarter. Van Berckhout had once registered in his personal diary a visit to the Vermeer's studio. Although Van Berckhout's entry was very brief, it proves that the Delft artist enjoyed a certain fame since he was referred to as the "celebrated painter named Vermeer." In any case, his membership probably brought him into contact with rich collectors and potential clients.*

The second person was Anthony van de Wiel, sergeant of the first squadron in the second banner of the third quarter. Van de Wiel had been Vermeer's brother-in-law while his sister Gertruy was alive. Van de Wiel served under Van Berckhout.

We do not know when exactly Vermeer joined the Civic Guard. It appears that the captains of the Delft Civic Guard remained unaware of the painter's difficult financial situation or perhaps by necessity or deference, they chose to ignore it. Perhaps the rules set down to guide the functioning of the Civic Guard were practiced less rigidly. Nevertheless Vermeer certainly enjoyed a good reputation of an honorable citizen. He had been elected two times as the chairman of the local St. Luke's Guild, one of the most powerful organizations in Delft.

The inventory of 1676 of movable goods from Vermeer's estate (Vermeer died in 1675) lists an iron armor with a helmet and a pike in the "great hall" (groote zael). Pikes were used by the pikeniers from the infantry both for attacking foot soldiers or to defend their unit's musketeers from enemy cavalry. Pikeniers were near the bottom of the the Guard's standings. Vermeer may have been involved in watching tasks, as pikes are typical weapons for watching at gates or doors within a castle. Two pikeniers

are able to quickly block a gate or door for the first by crossing the long pikes, without shooting (and perhaps wounding the wrong person).
It is unlikely that Vermeer was involved in battles outside of Delft, perhaps he helped defend he city during the French invasion. 300 Delft Civic Guards were sent to Geertruidenberg, Heusden, Den Briel and Gorkum in 1672."

Reference: Essentialvermeer.com

XII "...painted around the time Vermeer and his wife borrowed 200 guilders from Van Ruijven."

"On Nov. 30 (1657) Vermeer and his wife were lent the sum of two hundred guilders from Pieter Claesz. van Ruijven, a wealthy Delft citizen and art collector who may have purchased in the following years more than twenty of Vermeer's works. This money may have been a kind of advance payment on the purchase of future works. Van Ruijven is now rightly considered Vermeer's patron. He was almost seven years older than Vermeer and seems to have had had a personal relation with Vermeer that went outside the usual client/artist relationship."

Reference: Essentialvermeer.com

XIII "...the Thunderclap..."

"The greatest disaster and no other struck a deeper wound or caused more destruction and damage was the explosion of the gunpowder magazine on October 12th, 1654, in the morning at half-past ten. The "Delft Thunderclap", as this disaster has become known to history, has, as is well-known, also cost the life of (the painter and friend of Vermeer) Carel Fabritius and his family.

Dirck van Bleyswijck in his description of the happenings in Delft, published in the year 1667, gives an extensive account of this accident. There must have been, according to him, "eighty or ninety thousand pounds of gunpowder stored up at the time of the explosion, and this quantity, unfortunately, exploded, with such a horrible rush and force, that the arch of heaven seemed to crack and to burst, the whole earth to split, and hell to open its jaws: in consequence of which not only the town and the whole land of Delft with all her lovely villages shock and trembled, but the whole of Holland rocked from the ghastly rumble.

The houses in towns, boroughs, villages, and hamlets lying some miles away from us, heard the horrible rumble. The sound was heard even as far as Den Helder, yes, on the island of Texel, on the North Sea and in some provinces outside Holland...

That (powder) house, which had provided stocks from the days of our Fathers, must now, alas, destroy their children. The misery and disaster which resulted from it are impossible to describe properly and in proportion to the facts; because so great was the noise, to the surprise of all who heard it far from or near this town, from which, after the clap, they saw such a frightful mixture of smoke and vapor rise, just as if the pools of hell had opened their throats to spew out their poisonous breath over the whole world to cover it and darken it.

This cloud included a great deal of rubble, chalk, stones, beams, and all sorts of flying bits, mixed with pieces of people, which later were found strewn around, outside. as well as inside the walls, making a sight which the spectators could not face without shrinking emotion and melting hearts.

How the accident really was caused has remained a mystery until now. The powder-house had been completely blown away with its foundations, without leaving a scrap or stick or brick or beam or pole behind, nothing but a pool of water measuring in depth fifteen to sixteen feet."

The results of the explosion must have been terrible, the number of victims was very large. It does not require much imagination to form a clear picture of the extent of the damage which we shall endeavor to present through Van Bleyswijck's description:

"Not only both the neighboring Arquebusiers houses but for many hundred feet round everything was razed to the ground and demolished. The great and small Arquebusiers streets, also all the newly built houses on the Lakengracht where the old vegetable-frames used to stand, as well as the whole neighborhood of the Geerweg with the Verwersdijk were knocked down on both sides of the road and reduced to heaps of rubble The huge and strong trees in the Doelen (shooting range) were mostly chopped off level with the ground, the gardens there ploughed up, so that hardly a tree or the semblance of a tree was to be found.

The numbers of houses which were completely toppled over, was estimated at far over two hundred. Besides these over three hundred houses were bereft of roofs and window panes, furthermore it was said that there was not one house to be found within the whole city, which had not suffered some damage; many were damaged inside, the furniture spoilt, all the china broken with other things too which fell out of their positions from the horrible shaking.

Both parish churches, those great imposing buildings, had not escaped but had suffered such a hard shock that they could not be used for some time, without glass, the iron stanchions (which were very thick and heavy) bent and torn out, the roofs shattered, the walls split in many places.

At the Town Hall too all the window-panes had fallen out. Above all in the north- west of the town (where the force of the explosion had been most felt) it was pitiful to see, the more as one remembered all the people who lay shattered and smothered under the fallen and overturned houses. Various accidents and disasters have from old passed over this city, but not one of them, how heavy one might rate it, is to be compared with this great unspeakable blow, because this extraordinary and never-before heard-of thunder-clap swept whole families away, even streets with people, old, young, sick, well, rich, poor."

Reference: Essentialvermeer.com

XIV "... Anthony Van Leeuwenhoek..."

"(October 24, 1632 – August 30, 1723) was a Dutch tradesman and scientist from Delft, the Netherlands. He is commonly known as "the Father of Microbiology", and considered to be the first microbiologist. He was born the son of a basket maker. At age 16, he secured an apprenticeship with a Scottish cloth merchant in Amsterdam. He is best known for his work on the improvement of the microscope and for his contributions towards the establishment of microbiology. Using his handcrafted microscopes he was the first to observe and describe single celled organisms, which he originally referred to as animalcules, and which we now refer to as microorganisms. He was also the first to record microscopic observations of muscle fibers, bacteria, spermatozoa and blood flow in capillaries (small blood vessels).

During his lifetime Van Leeuwenhoek ground over 500 optical lenses. He also created over 400 different types of microscopes, only nine of which still exist today. His microscopes were made of silver or copper metal frames holding hand-ground lenses. Those that have survived the years are able to magnify up to 275 times. It is suspected, though, that Van Leeuwenhoek possessed some microscopes that could magnify up to 500 times.

Van Leeuwenhoek was a contemporary of another famous Delft citizen, painter Johannes Vermeer, who was baptized just four days earlier. It has been suggested that he is the man portrayed in two of Vermeer's paintings of the late 1660s, The Astronomer and The Geographer. It is known that Van Leeuwenhoek acted as the executor when the painter died in 1675."

Reference: Wikipedia.org

XV "... Constantijn Huygens..."

Reference: Anthony Bailey, *A View of Delft, Vermeer Then and Now*, page 150.

XVI "...on a typically day of coastal clouds, is mildly temperate and mostly humid."

"Note: This is an abstract of an article which originally appeared in the Dutch scientific magazine on shipping history, Tijdschrift voor Zeegeschiedenis, *March 2000.*

In the View of Delft by Johannes Vermeer, one of the great masterworks of Dutch painting, the harbor or 'Kolk' of Delft and the various ships in it are given a prominent place. This article discusses the various types of ships on this painting and questions whether these ships are shown in a documentary way, adding to our knowledge of the painting.

In the detailed Dutch language article in the Tijdschrift voor Zeegeschiedenis each type of ship is discussed as to its depiction, shape, size and uses. Information is given on the tow barges as most archival documents deal with their rules and regulations from 1655 onwards. Research and literature is mentioned in notes. **The article** *discusses all of these types of ships and finally* **proposes a precise dating** *for the scene of Vermeer's painting 'View of Delft'. The dating is analyzed by this step by step method.*

Each year the active season of the herring busses was limited by law from June 1st to the end of December. Herring busses were costly investments. These ships were used optimally during that legal fishery season. These two ships are however far away from their regular harbour of Delfshaven and are clearly under repair, missing a few masts and being otherwise empty, floating extremely high on the water. This in turn indicates an early season for the total scene. Given the orientation of the scene, the full green foliage and the active maintenance works on these two ships which are moored at the Delft shipyard - getting ready before June 1st - it follows that the intended scene and/or the actual conception of this painting must be dated at an early morning in the first half of May.

Of which year? Because of conflicting evidence one cannot tell for sure whether there were bells visible in the tower of the New Church up until 1660. The delivery by the Hemony firm of the carillon of the New Church tower started in 1660 by hoisting down existing bells of the New Church tower to a shed at ground level. All bells were hoisted up again late in the summer of 1661. Vermeer clearly shows an empty bell tower in his painting. **This supports the dating in 1660-1661**, *a period being previously suggested on the basis of Vermeer's stylistic development.* **Thus we are watching a scene during an early morning in the first half of May 1660 or 1661**. *As Vermeer worked slowly and meticulously (and newer paint layers have filled "premature drying cracks" in older layers) the painting may have been finished somewhere around 1662 to 1665 when he will have delivered it to his maecenas, art collector Pieter Claesz van Ruijven and his wife Maria de Knuyt."*

Reference: Kees Kaldenbach, Art Historian

XVII "... the North Sea region, on the average, was not a pleasant place to live in winter."

" Burroughs (Weather, 1981) analyses the depiction of winter in paintings. He notes that this occurred almost entirely from 1565 to 1665, and was associated with the climatic decline from 1550 onwards. He claims (however incorrectly) that before this there were almost no depictions of winter in art, and hypotheses that the unusually harsh winter of 1565 inspired great artists to depict highly original images, and the decline in such paintings was a combination of the "theme" having been fully explored, and mild winters interrupting the flow of painting.

The famous winter paintings by Pieter Brueghel the Elder (e.g. Hunters in the Snow) all appear to have been painted in 1565. Snow also dominates many villagescapes by the Pieter Brueghel the Younger, who lived from 1564 to 1638. Burroughs states that Pieter Brueghel the Younger "slavishly copied his father's designs. The derivative nature of so much of this work makes it difficult to draw any definite conclusions about the influence of the winters between 1570 and 1600...".

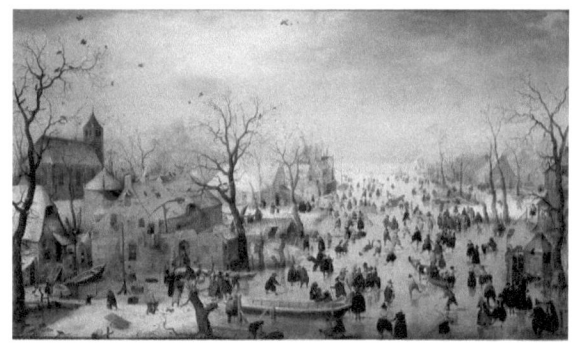

(Netherlands Winter landscape with ice skaters, c. 1608, by Hendrick Avercamp.)

Dutch painting of the theme appears to begin with Hendrick Avercamp after the winter of 1608. There is then an interruption of the theme between 1627 and 1640, with a sudden return thereafter; this hints at a milder interlude in the 1630s. The 1640s to the 1660s cover the major period of Dutch winter painting, which fits with the known proportion of cold winters then.

The Little Ice Age *brought bitterly cold winters to many parts of the world, but is most thoroughly documented in Europe and North America. It probably brought about the demise of the Norse settlements in Greenland, which had died out by the 1400s. In the mid-17th century, glaciers in the Swiss Alps advanced, gradually engulfing farms and crushing entire villages. The River Thames and the canals and* *rivers of the Netherlands often froze over during the winter, and people skated and even held frost fairs on the ice.*

The first Thames frost fair was in 1607; the last in 1814, although changes to the bridges and the addition of an embankment affected the river flow and depth, hence the possibility of freezes.

The freeze of the Golden Horn and the southern section of the Bosphorus took place in 1622. In 1658, a Swedish army marched across the Great Belt to Denmark to invade Copenhagen. The winter of 1794/1795 was particularly harsh when the French invasion army under Pichegru could march on the frozen rivers of the Netherlands, whilst the Dutch fleet was fixed in the ice in Den Helder harbour. In the winter of 1780, New York Harbor froze, allowing people to walk from Manhattan to Staten Island. Sea ice surrounding Iceland extended for miles in every direction, closing that island's harbors to shipping.

The last written records of the Norse Greenlanders are from a 1408 marriage in the church of Hvalsey — today the most well-preserved of the Norse ruins.

The severe winters affected human life in ways large and small. The population of Iceland fell by half, but this was perhaps also due to fluorosis caused by the eruption of the volcano Laki in 1783. Iceland also suffered failures of cereal crops and people moved away from a grain-based diet. The Norse colonies in Greenland starved and vanished (by the 15th century) as crops failed and livestock could not be maintained through increasingly-harsh winters. In North America, American Indians formed leagues in response to food shortages

Some confine the Little Ice Age to approximately the 16th century to the mid 19th century. It is generally agreed that there were three minima, beginning about 1650, about 1770, and 1850, each."

Reference: Wikipedia.org

XVIII   "...Cupid..."

"The Cupid (in Vermeer's painting) holds aloft a card on which appears a number one which visually echoes the engraving's caption: "a lover ought to love only one."

The same Cupid appears in other paintings by Vermeer. The Cupid is a work of Cesar van Everdingen and is very likely the Cupid described in Vermeer's death inventory of 1676. - Reference: Essentialvermeer.com

CUPID ("cupido", Latin for "desire") was a lesser god of Olympus to the Romans. In Roman mythology, **Cupid** (also called **Amor**) was the god of love, often represented as a small, winged boy, blindfolded (as "love is blind"), carrying bow and arrows. The arrows, once they struck someone's heart, made the victim fall in love. Our current image of Cupid as a winged cherub is primarily based on images from painters of the Renaissance. Though Cupid was often a boy in Roman myth, the images of winged, rosy-faced babies may be based more on a small group of winged infants who often accompanied Cupid called the AMORINI (or Amoretti; "the messengers of love"). To the Romans, Cupid was the personification of "falling in love."

A second century (A.D.) Roman named Apuleius wrote an allegorical tale of the union of love (Cupid) and the soul (Psyche), in which Cupid was a young man. But Apuleius apparently believed none of what he wrote, and meant it more as a pretty "fairy tale" than as mythological doctrine (though he may have adapted the story from earlier myths). The story of Cupid and Psyche has two main elements: the "beauty and the beast" prototype, and the "trials of Psyche", the seemingly impossible tasks imposed on Psyche by Venus as Psyche attempts to win back her love.

To the Romans Cupid was an innocent (a child), though sometimes mischievous and a "naughty boy". To the ancient Greeks however, the god Eros, (whom the Romans co-opted as Cupido) was a older, more terrible god. Eros was one of the oldest of the gods, born from Chaos and originally was the god personifying creative power and harmony (perhaps comparable with the "yang/yin" of ancient Chinese philosophy). Plato called him the first of the gods. Eros was not a child of Aphrodite(Venus), but only found with her occasionally. Among the Greeks, not only Hermaphrodite but Eros too were in sex both male and female.

Eros was no meddlesome child to the Greeks, but a powerful god to be feared and to entreat: his/her arrows burned with the fire of lust and madness as well as romance, at its worst capable of driving men and women to betrayal of their families or countries, to rape, to murder, to suicide.

This was the "terrible Aspect" of Eros, known as Anteros (not so much Eros'
brother, but another incarnation of Eros). But Eros had all of the
positive aspects of love as well. In attendance upon him/her were
Himeros (Longing) and Hymen, the "God of the Wedding Feast".
Hesiod (Greek poet, 8th cent. B.C.) called Eros "Fairest of the deathless gods."
Later, by the time of Plato (Greek philosopher, 4th cent. B.C.) Eros'
image had softened:

> *"Love - Eros - makes his home in men's hearts, but not*
> *in every heart, for where there is hardness he departs.*
> *...he cannot do wrong...For all men serve him of their*
> *own free will. And he whom Love touches not walks in darkness."*

Reference: *http://www.lyberty.com/encyc/articles/cupid.html*

XIX "Her generous fiscal support of myself, my wife and my children..."

"In a Delft register of 1674, Maria Thins was one of 1,300 or so residents of the town recorded as being wealthy enough to be taxed 1/2 percent of their assets; she paid 130 guilders in tax, indicating a net worth of 26,000 guilders -- though that valuation may have been inaccurately low. She owned land in various places and had an annual income from rents or interest of about 1,500 guilders".

Reference: Anthony Bailey, "A View of Delft: Vermeer Then and Now", page 66

XX   "... the virginal..."

"The virginal was an instrument greatly admired by the Dutch upper class during the mid-seventeenth century. The lyrical yet restrained tones that resonated from its keyboard underscored the refinement in taste that accompanied the increase of wealth and influence enjoyed by this society. Although Vermeer enjoyed economic security for most of his career, in his later years encountered serious economic difficulties due to the French invasion and subsequent crash of the art market. Thus, it is unlikely that the artist possessed such a luxury item at that time. In any case, it is generally held that Vermeer had contact with one the most illustrious art connoisseurs in the Netherlands, Constantijn Huygens, who was himself a composer of great stature. Diego Duarte, who in turn was connected to the illustrious Huygens family, was an immensely rich

Antwerp banker and possessed "a young lady playing the clavecin, with accessories, by Vermeer."

Duarte was an accomplished organist. The virginals are a kind of harpsichord. Klaassen's Muselaer virginals were built by Louis van Emmerik, after The Muselaer virginals, have the keyboard on the right, and they have a richer sound than the spinet virginals, which have the keyboard on the left. The virginals in Vermeer paintings are of the Muselaer type. "

Reference: www.essentialvermeer.com

XXI "...Albrecht Dürer..."

"Albrecht Dürer was born on May 21, 1471, third child and second son of his parents, who had between fourteen and eighteen children. His father was a successful goldsmith. Dürer exerted a huge influence on the artists of succeeding generations, especially in printmaking, the medium through which his contemporaries mostly experienced his art, as his paintings were predominately in private collections located in only a few cities. His success in spreading his reputation across Europe through prints was undoubtedly an inspiration for major artists such as Raphael, Titian, and Parmigianino, who entered into collaborations with printmakers to distribute their work beyond their local region.

Dürer has never fallen from critical favor, and there have been revivals of interest in his works Germany in the Dürer Renaissance of about 1570 to 1630, and in the early nineteenth century."

Reference: Wikipedia.org

XXII "... was influenced by Martin Luther..."

"Martin Luther (10 November, 1483 – 18 February, 1546) was a German monk, theologian, university professor, Father of Protestantism, and church reformer whose ideas influenced the Protestant Reformation and changed the course of Western civilization.

Luther's theology challenged the authority of the papacy by holding that the Bible is the only infallible source of religious authority and that all baptized Christians under Jesus are a universal priesthood. According to Luther, salvation is a free gift of God, received only by true repentance and faith in Jesus as the Messiah, a faith given by God and unmediated by the church.

At the Diet of Worms assembly over freedom of conscience in 1521, Luther's confrontation with the Holy Roman Emperor Charles V and his refusal to submit to the authority of the Emperor resulted in his being excommunicated from the Roman Catholic Church and being declared an outlaw of the state as a consequence.

His translation of the Bible into the vernacular of the people made the Scriptures more accessible to them, and had a tremendous political impact on the church and on German culture. It furthered the development of a standard version of the German language, added several principles to the art of translation, and influenced the translation of the English King James Bible. His hymns inspired the development of congregational singing within Christianity. His marriage to Katharina von Bora set a model for the practice of clerical marriage within Protestantism."

Reference: Wikipedia.org

XXIII "...through looking-glasses..."

*"**Through the Looking-Glass, and What Alice Found There** (1871) is a work of children's literature by Lewis Carroll (Charles Lutwidge Dodgson), generally categorized as literary nonsense. It is the sequel to Alice's Adventures in Wonderland (1865). Although it makes no reference to the events in the earlier book, the themes and settings of Through the Looking-Glass make it a kind of mirror image of Wonderland: the first book begins outdoors, in the warm month of May, on Alice's birthday (May 4), uses frequent changes in size as a plot device, and draws on the imagery of playing cards; the second opens indoors on a snowy, wintry night exactly six months later, on November 4 (the day before Guy Fawkes Night), uses frequent changes in time and spatial directions as a plot device, and draws on the imagery of chess. In it, there are many mirror themes, including opposites, time running backwards, and so on. Alice ponders what the world is like on the other side of a mirror (the reflected scene displayed on its surface), and to her surprise, is able to pass through to experience the alternate world. There, she discovers a book with looking-glass poetry, "Jabberwocky", which she can read only by holding it up to a mirror."*

Reference: Wikipedia.org

XXIV "... we had continual news brought to us by sailors who visited myriad exotic countries around the globe."

"In 1601, Oliver van Noort, former pirate and Rotterdam innkeeper, sailed west through the Strait of Magellan to the Moluccas, south of the Philippines, and home around Africa. He was only the fourth captain in history to sail around the world (after one Portuguese and two Englishmen).

It was always trade, rather than colonizing, that provided the prime motivation far Dutch expansion, yet a colonial empire emerged in the process. The mariners built strong points on distant shores to protect their ships and stores tram natives or marauding European ships; the strong points became forts, the forts led to further conquests. In 1605 the Dutch drove the Portuguese from the Moluccas; in 1618 they established a settlement called Batavia on Java; in 1624 they founded New Amsterdam in America; by 1630 they controlled trading on the northeast coast of Brazil and by 1660 had taken over from the Portuguese on Ceylon.

In European waters, by the middle of the 17th Century, the Dutch merchants were handling three quarters of the enormous Baltic grain trade and they virtually monopolized the Bordeaux wine trade. Even Spain relied so heavily on the cargoes carried by Dutch ships that the embargo on them in Spanish ports was relaxed. Dutch vessels had become the freight carriers of Europe.

The highest rewards carne tram the trade in spices, the most coveted product of the East Indies. Spices such as black pepper, cloves and cinnamon helped preserve and make palatable the dreary food of an age whose only other means of food preservation were pickling and salting. The lure of spices became as strong as the lure of gold; in the greedy struggle far East Indian resources in such places as Batavia and Ceylon, Dutch, Spanish, Portuguese and eventually English traders killed one another and any of the local population who stood in their way. Rather than see prices go down or leave something for a competitor, they burned down plantations, deported entire villages and turned the natives into virtual slaves.

All this was strictly a business operation. For or example, in 1644 the Board of the Dutch East India Company stated that their holdings in the Far East were not Dutch conquests but "the property of private merchants, who were entitled to sell those places to whomever they pleased, even if it were to the King of Spain." These policies paid enormous dividends to the investors in the trade.

One venture in 1599 made a 400 per cent profit, and from 1630 on, annual dividends of 30 per cent and more became normal for investors in the East India Company. (On the other side of the globe, in the West Indies, Dutch seamen also sometimes found ready-made profits: after Admiral Piet Hein's capture of a $50 million Spanish silver fleet in 1628, the West India Company paid a 75 per cent dividend.)

Later in the 17th Century, tea became a popular item in the tropical trade. The same Doctor Tulp whom Rembrandt had immortalized in his Anatomy of Dr. Nicolaas Tulp started a great fad for tea by prescribing it for all ills; he is said to have made his patients drink 50 cups of tea a day. A colleague wrote a little book, subsidized by the East India Company, extolling tea's virtues-perhaps the first-known example of the "Doctors recommend. ..." technique of advertising.

Another popular Far Eastern product was porcelain. In the first half of the 17th Century, the Dutch imported and shipped on to the rest of Europe more than three million pieces of Chinese porcelain. The interest in porcelain led to the creation of the famous Delft Blue pottery industry, which still thrives. By 1700 Delft Blue pottery makers had become so proficient that they were exporting pieces of mixed Oriental and Dutch design back to Japan.

By no means all the goods brought in from abroad were sent on to foreign markets. Many of them stayed in Holland, as contemporary paintings clearly testify. Tobacco was as popular then as now-it was first brought from the West Indies and the Americas in the 1500s-and the unsavory dens where the common man enjoyed his smoke made a favorite subject for such genre painters as Adriaen Brouwer and Adriaen van Ostade.

Other products, faithfully recorded in the art of the day, added a cosmopolitan touch of luxury to the homes of the merchants who had gambled fortunes to import them: besides porcelain there were fine silk and\ satin fabrics, rare woods, and Turkish carpets (used as rugs, wall hangings or tablecloths). All of these appeared as props in hundreds of paintings of interior scenes, particularly those of Jan Vermeer."

Reference: The World of Vermeer: 1632-167 *by Hans Koningsberger, New York, 1967*

XXV "... the slave trade between Africa and the rum producing plantations in the Americas."

"Before the 1630s, Dutch participation in the Caribbean slave trade "was sporadic, if not ambivalent." The first Dutch slaving expedition arrived in the Caribbean as early as 1606; in 1619 a Dutch ship delivered the first cargo of enslaved Africans to the British colony in Virginia. The first WIC was formed in 1621 in part to control the African slave trade, giving the Dutch "a twenty-four year monopoly over trade with America and Africa from the Tropic of Cancer to the Cape of Good Hope," with military and naval backing from the Dutch States General.

Serious Dutch involvement in the slave trade began as the Dutch attempted to wrest the valuable sugar plantations along the Brazilian coast from the Portuguese between 1624 and 1654. WIC vessels seized several Portuguese outposts on Africa's Atlantic coast in the 1630s; they scored a major coup in 1637 when they took the largest Portuguese base and slave market, Ft. Elmira. This marked the beginning of the brief Dutch dominance of the international slave trade. The large amount of capital which Dutch merchants possessed, along with their strong fleet, allowed them to penetrate Africa "on a scale not yet achieved by the English or the French."

Expeditions into the interior were initially launched by small companies organized by traders who were looking for a quick return on their investments (as opposed to Dutch forays into the East Indies, which were organized by major capitalists who could sustain higher investment risks for longer periods). Soon the first WIC was organizing these expeditions and coordinating the shipments across the Atlantic.

If the groundwork for Dutch involvement in the slave trade was already laid in Africa well before the Peace of Westphalia, the 1648 cessation of hostilities between the Netherlands and Spain expanded opportunities. Between 1640 and 1662 Spain granted no asiento contracts, relying entirely on privateers to supply its American plantations. The Dutch consolidated their role in this period. The financial transactions of slaving were complex and required a heavy capital outlay that Spain did not have; private financiers in Amsterdam eagerly stepped in to provide the necessary financial backing. The extensive WIC fleet was used to transport the human cargo."

Reference:
http://books.caribseek.com/Curacao/Commercial_History_of_Curacao/rise-of-the-dutch-slave-trade.shtml

XXVI   "...the slave trade between Africa, the Americas and Europe provided revenue to the Netherlands that was the source of prosperity I benefited from as an artist."

"The Netherlands despite being a small country, lacking in natural resources, was able in the 17th Century to become the centre for European overseas trade, including the trade in human beings. This 'Dutch Miracle' was a product of numerous innovations in navigation, manufacturing and finance, which allowed for slaves and slave produce to be transported at greater capacity and at lower cost. The first recorded trader sold 20 Africans to the colony of Virginia in North America in 1619, but the Dutch trade only really took off in response to labor shortage in the newly conquered sugar plantations of Northern Brazil in 1630. Wars with Portugal (1620-1655) left the Dutch in control of many of the slave depots on the West African coast, centered on modern Ghana, which by 1650 had dispatched 30,000 slaves to Brazil alone. After the return of the Brazilian colonies to Portugal in 1654, the Dutch traders were able to draw upon their network of forts to supply other European powers, dominating the supply to Spain until the 1690s. However the near constant warfare the Netherlands were waged in with other European nations, such as Spain, France and Britain, by Imperial Spain, did eventually sap its strength, and Dutch involvement in the trade declined in the 18th Century, and effectively ceased in 1795.

When the final abolition of the trade and institution of slavery formally occurred in 1863, Dutch agents had brought 540,000 Africans to the Americas and cast the specter of slavery east, from the Cape of Good Hope to the Indonesian archipelago.

Amsterdam ranks as a European capital of slavery. While its mills processed almost all the sugar from the Portuguese colonies, its financiers bankrolled the Danish, Swedish and Brandenburg slave trade, and in turn Scandinavian and German sailors made up half its slaving crews. As home to the world's most sophisticated banking and insurance system, it was the natural home for the expensive and potentially risky business of slaving, and for this reason alone as many as 10,000 vessels were associated with the port.

The17th Century has been widely described as the Netherlands' 'Golden Age.' The period saw the flowering of the arts and sciences. The average Dutchman was wealthier than his counterparts in any other country in the world and lived in a relatively tolerant country. This progress was achieved in part at an appalling human cost, and several of era's great advances helped tighten the noose around the African continent.

Dutch innovation transformed shipbuilding. The Netherlands had to import almost all of its wood from abroad, and to save money found ways of making fast and efficient ships from cheap materials. The Fluyt or 'fly boat' was one such design, based on low quality wood and easily pre fabricated parts, and requiring a much smaller crew than the ships of foreign competitors. This ship became a familiar site throughout Europe, Africa and the Caribbean, and its vast cargo hold and shallow draft made it ideally suited for slave voyages. The nation's talent for shipbuilding encouraged countries across the continent to either borrow Dutch designs, or simply commission fleets to be constructed in Dutch ports. Thanks to vessels like the Fluyt come 1670 the Netherlands had more ships than England, France, Germany, Portugal, Spain and Scotland put together, boasting the most 'efficient' slave ships afloat."

Reference:
http://www.antislavery.org/breakingthesilence/slave_routes/slave_route s_netherlands.shtml

XXVII "Maria (Thins) was a Catholic, who eagerly embraced the manufactured mythos of the Papal superstition machine."

"Vermeer's parents were married in 1615 in Amsterdam before Jacobus Taurinus, a famous Calvinist and Orthodox Reformed Church Minister. Although their marriage arrangement would seem to imply a commitment to the Reformed faith, neither of them was officially registered as a member of the faith which would have given them the right to participate in the sacrament of communion and an obligation to educate themselves

in the doctrinal issues as well as a public confession of faith. Thus, it seems probable that Vermeer's parents belonged to a sizable group of people called liefhebbers *(supporters), or those who for one reason or another did not comply with the strict requirements of membership or had a dislike for religious discipline.*

Although nothing is known of Vermeer's religious thoughts before his marriage, we know for certain that he was baptized on 31 October 1632 in the Reformed Church in Delft.

Vermeer's mother-in-law, Maria Thins, was a devoted Catholic and was most likely instrumental in the painter's conversion. She was also a Delft patrician with excellent family ties who had grown up in a stronghold of Dutch Catholicism, the town of Gouda. There, her family celebrated mass secretly in their home, De Trapjes *(The Little Steps.) Her sister became a nun in Louvain. Although not common, religious conversions happened. The renowned Dutch poet Joost van den Vondel converted. Maria Tesselschade, the talented daughter of Roemers Vischer and a friend of Contantijn Huygens, became a Catholic in 1642 causing much grief to Huygens who went so far as to write a poem in protest.*

Perhaps Vermeer's conversion was inevitable. The Council of Trent (1545-1563) had decreed matrimonial unions between Catholics and non-Catholics null and void. Thus, the marriage between Catharina as a Catholic and Vermeer as a non-Catholic would not have been accepted by the Catholic Church as a union in the understanding of the Catholic Church. According to the Council of Trent the Roman Catholic Church had always taught the dogma of the Holy matrimony as part of the Seven Sacraments, contrary to the Protestant Church. **The apostolic vicar to The Netherlands, Phillip Roveniusi, writing in 1648, equated the marriage of a Catholic to a nonbeliever to a pact with the devil.**

However, since Vermeer was already baptized, together with basic lessons in the Catholic faith, only a short consecrating act would have been necessary to convert to Catholicism. Each new "soul" was warmly welcomed by the Catholic Church, even in these times of repression. Since priests operated in utmost secrecy, it is not difficult to understand why notations of conversion have not survived.

Since Vermeer was not a full member of the Reformed Church as Abels states, he would have found little motivation to refuse conversion which would have caused serious problems to his new family."

Reference: EssentialVermeer.com

XXVIII "Generally, food was plentiful, and much enjoyed, during several meals each day."

"Possessing the strongest merchant marine of any European nation during the 17th century, the Netherlands had access to foodstuffs from around the world. Wine was imported from France, Italy, and Spain, and beer from Germany. India and the Spice Islands supplied spices, while the Mediterranean made a fine source of raisins, dates, figs and nuts, and Poland and Prussia provided all-important cereal grains. The Dutch rounded out their diet with the plentiful fish, butter, cheese, fresh fruits and vegetables that were produced domestically.

In addition to providing Netherlanders with a plentiful and varied selection of foodstuffs during the Golden Age, the rich trade economy was also largely responsible for the nation's notable prosperity during this period. While not all Golden Age Netherlanders lived the high-life of the wealthy burgerlijk and regent classes, the Dutch generally enjoyed a higher standard of living than their counterparts throughout the rest of early modern Europe.

In the face of such abundance, 17th-century Netherlanders generally sought moderation in their everyday eating habits. However, celebratory feasts were a phenomenon of Golden Age Dutch culture, and most Netherlanders indulged in excess at least a few times a year. For example, newborn children were often welcomed with a kindermaal celebration and its requisite round of sweet kandeel; the feast of St. Nicholas, New Year's Day, and Twelfth Night were similarly recognized with specialty foods. Lesser events—including a child's beginning school or apprenticeship, the purchase of a new house, or a loved one's departure on a long journey or his return home—were also acknowledged with feasts. Many Dutch burghers even celebrated jokmaalen, a feast of inversion during which masters and mistresses waited on their servants."

Dutch Meal Patterns

In earlier centuries, most Netherlanders ate only two meals per day, the first of which consisted of two dishes and was served around eleven o'clock in the morning and the second of which was served just before bedtime, around nine o'clock. Towards the end of the Middle Ages, a third meal—breakfast—became increasingly common; as resources grew especially plentiful during the prosperous Golden Age, yet a fourth meal could be added to the daily regimen.

During the 17th century, the wealthy middle and upper-middle classes had access to a surprising variety of foodstuffs. A typical day's menu follows.

Breakfast generally consisted of bread topped with butter or finely shredded cheese; as one Englishman noted of his Dutch-origin neighbors in New Netherland, "they pretend [grating it to the consistency of coarse flour] adds to the good taste of cheese."

Beer was generally drunk at breakfast—as well as during the other meals of the day—although buttermilk and whey were popular breakfast drinks on farms.

Midday supper was the heartiest meal of the day and typically consisted of two or three dishes. The first was often a hutspot—a meat stew with vegetables—while the second was usually fish or meat cooked with currants or prunes. Fruit and cooked vegetables or koecken (cake) or pasteyen (spiced meat pie) might round out the meal.

Two to three hours after the midday meal, affluent Netherlanders enjoyed a small mid-afternoon meal of bread with butter or cheese. The final meal of the day, eaten just before retiring to bed, consisted of leftovers from the midday meal or of another serving of bread with butter or cheese.

Among the poor and working classes, meals were less plentiful. Most Netherlanders sustained themselves on only two meals per day, the first of which was eaten at noon and generally consisted of two dishes. The first of these dishes likely consisted of peas and beans, while the second would have been one of the following: salted or smoked meat, sausage with groats and raisins, bacon with carrots or cabbage, salt cod, herring, or dried cod. The evening meal was one of several varieties of porridge. Both meals were served with bread.

Bread: The Mainstay of the Dutch Diet

Though northern Netherlands soil proved too wet for large-scale wheat farming, participation in the Baltic grain trade allowed the nation ample access to this staple crop. By the 17th century, the Dutch virtually controlled wheat and rye production in Poland, East Prussia, Swedish Pomerania and Livonia (Schama 168).

Silos in the Dutch cities of Amsterdam, Rotterdam and Middelburg stored large grain surpluses, thereby safeguarding against price fluctuation and bread shortage. As a result of these and other government-enforced measures, the Dutch enjoyed greater food stability than their counterparts throughout much of 17th-century Europe.

At least two meals per day in a typical Dutch household included sliced bread, usually topped with butter or cheese. The more affluent enjoyed herenbrood—"white" bread made from wheat flour—on a regular basis, while the less prosperous typically depended on semelbrood, "black," rye-kernel bread, for their daily starch. During times of extreme food scarcity, some peasants turned to bread made from ground chestnut meal.

Butter and Cheese: Celebrated Products of the Netherlands

Though unsuitable for wheat farming, northern Netherlands soil lent itself to cattle grazing, and the nation would eventually become famous for its dairy products. Butter and cheese appeared frequently in the Dutch diet, especially as dressing for sliced bread

(For additional information about milk in the Dutch diet, see "Beer: the common beverage" below).

Cooking with butter—rather than with lard—was another significant symbol of affluence. When the Reformation swept through Europe during the sixteenth century, the use of butter acquired religious implications as well.

Rose writes: The Catholic obligation to fast [which, during the sixteenth century, consisted of avoiding meat, dairy, and eggs during about 150 days of each year] was difficult and expensive, causing some medievalists to believe this could be one of the reasons for the success of the Reformation. It is worth noting that most olive-oil producing countries remained Catholic and most butter-producing countries became Protestant (Rose 19, Rose 16).

Cheese, by contrast, acted as "the great leveler, the universal enjoyment of which dissolved rank within national community" (163). The Netherlands had begun to produce several varieties of cheese, made from both cows' and sheep's milk, by the fourteenth and fifteenth centuries. Edam and Gouda, named for the towns in which they originated, are still popular varieties of cheese today.

Fruit and Vegetables: Local, Exotic—and Newly Invented

Orchards located in close proximity to towns produced apples, pears, plums, and nuts, allowing Dutch burghers easy access to seasonal fresh fruit. Dried fruit—especially raisins, prunes, and figs—were even more common to the Dutch diet than their fresh counterparts. Used to flavor meat dishes as well as pies and cakes, fruit of one sort or another was a necessary ingredient of such standard Dutch recipes as pea and prune soup—and of such delicacies as minced ox tongue with green applesauce.

Despite its strong ties to Dutch culinary tradition, fruit carried some negative cultural associations during the 17th century. In 1655, for example, blue plums and black cherries were blamed for a particularly severe outbreak of the plague—presumably because of their close resemblance to buboes—and were temporarily banned from sale in Holland. Though it had been successfully cultivated in the gardens of at least two Dutch noblemen, pineapple retained its dangerously exotic associations, and was also proscribed: at least one doctor warned of its tendency to cause "gastric ailments from the Orient."

By the sixteenth century, the Netherlands had become known throughout Europe for its vegetable production, and vegetables appeared in the Dutch diet perhaps even more frequently than fruit. Golden Age horticultural innovations led to the introduction of cauliflower and the variety of short, orange Horn carrot commonly enjoyed in the United States today, while improvements in cultivation methods brought about increased yields of these and other vegetables.

In light of these facts, it is unsurprising that one 17th-century traveler referred to the Netherlands as a "nation of salad eaters." As early as 1556, Geeraert Vorselman published Een Nyeuwen Coock Boeck, *the first known Dutch-language cookbook to include salad and vegetable recipes. Served at the beginning of meals, salads were typically dressed with oil and vinegar or melted butter and vinegar. Kool slaa, the forerunner of present-day coleslaw, was commonly enjoyed.*

Pancakes and Olie-koecken: Favorite Confections of a Sweet-Toothed Culture

The Dutch incorporated honey cake, gingerbread, marzipan, cinnamon bark, and other confections into their daily eating patterns, while treats such as waffles, pancakes, and olie-koecken (deep fried balls of dough) were generally reserved for celebrations.

By the 1640s, over fifty sugar refineries operated in Amsterdam, and as Brazilian sugar arrived in the Netherlands in large enough quantities that families of even middling wealth could afford it, the traditional Dutch taste for sweets could be further indulged with caramelized sauces and sugar dustings added to waffles and pancakes.

Excess of any kind was frowned upon by religious leaders, and one minister expressed particular concern about the popularity of sweets:

Sweetness and excess is today grown so great that were they not ashamed to do so, men would found an Academy to which they would send all cooks and pasty bakers [pastry cooks] to teach them how to excel in the preparation of sauces, spices, cakes and confections, so that they should taste delicious.

Beer: The Common Beverage

Recommended for children and adults alike, beer was the most popular beverage among members of 17th-century Dutch society. Since beer was boiled during preparation, it was safer to drink than plain water—which only the "common sort" deigned to sip from the notoriously polluted Amsterdam canal and other potentially tainted waterways. As early as the fourteenth century, breweries were thriving in Haarlem and Amersfoort, and most Netherlanders engaged in additional brewing at home.

In the countryside, buttermilk and whey were acceptable alternatives to beer, especially at breakfast, but whole milk was largely distrusted; one Dutch physician of the period recommended that a drink of milk be followed with a rinse of wine or honey in order to prevent tooth decay. Among those who could afford them, sweet wines from the Mediterranean countries were also popular, and young white wines from France and Germany—mixed with honey and spices to counteract their natural tartness—made a fine end to a large meal.

Tea: A Drink to Cure All Ills

Though "teatime" would eventually become a convention of the Netherlands, tea was initially too expensive for all but the wealthiest members of Dutch society to drink. Gradually introduced to the Netherlands by way of travelers and colonists returning from the East, the beverage was not available in significant quantities until the 1660s—at which time its price per pound dropped from a steep 100 guilders to less than ten guilders.

Though many foodstuffs met criticism from moralist physicians of the period, tea was touted as wholly healthful. Dr. Johannes van Helmont prescribed tea to restore body fluids lost to sweating while a Dr. Tulp endorsed it as a remedy for cramps and sluggishness. A particularly enthusiastic supporter of the beverage recommended eight to ten cups per day in order to maintain minimum health—and fifty to two hundred cups for increased benefits.

Towards the end of the 17th century, the third meal of the day became associated with the tea ritual and was shifted to late afternoon. Though women's coffee houses had begun to operate by the beginning of the eighteenth century, most 17th-century Netherlanders associated the tea ritual with women, while coffee—generally purchased and consumed in public coffeehouses—held masculine connotations.

Reference:
http://www.albanyinstitute.org/Education/archive/dutch/dutch.foodways.htm

XXIX "... false jewel is then varnished to emulate the luminosity of a pearl."

"Imitation pearls have a range of uses in several industries - Toys, Buttons, Fashion and Clothing, Artificial jewellery and many others. These pearls are used to make junk jewellery as well. Imitation pearls are fairly popular since they can be dyed into any color and are can be created in a variety of shapes from perfect spheres to ovals in any size. Called by several names like Faux pearls, Venetian pearls, Turkish Rose Pearls, semi-cultured pearls, Majorca pearls, Bohemian pearls, Organic pearls - the list of names for imitation pearls is long.

Imitation pearls are not gemstones and are manufactured manually or by machines. The process is rather simple. First, the desired shapes of beads in ceramic, glass or plastic are manufactured- sometimes even organic objects like shells are used. These are then coated and colored to recreate the look of real pearls. Several processes exist in the coating and coloring of imitation pearls. The coating used on imitation pearls (called pearl essence or essence d'orient) was discovered by a Frenchman named Jacquin.

He found that fish scales emitted a pearly substance in water - he extracted this substance and mixed it with other chemicals to create the essence d'orient. This product is normally used to coat the beads to give them a pearly appearance. Hollow glass beads are coated inside with pearlessence and then filled with wax. Plastic beads are coated on the outside with this substance. These coated glass and plastic beads are then dipped in various solutions to give them a high luster and gloss.

The Majorca imitation pearls are renowned for their high quality and offer guarantees against chipping, discoloration etc. The technology behind manufacturing of these pearls is a closely guarded secret. Hand and machine made special nuclei are coated several times with high quality essence d'orient or other chemicals, polished, given a protective coating again and finally treated under ultraviolet radiation to give them a luster and radiance comparable to cultured pearls. Although Majorca pearls are imitation, with good care, they can last for a long time."

Reference:

http://www.jewelinfo4u.com/Imitation_Pearls.aspx

XXX "... Lysistrata..."

Lysistrata is an ancient Greek comedy, written in 411 BC by Aristophanes. The title character devises a plan to end the war Athens is embroiled in by convincing all the women of Greece to refrain from sex with their husbands until they come to a peace agreement. Lysistrata and her band of followers take over the Acropolis to cut off funding for the war and eventually succeed in getting the opposing armies to declare peace. This play offered social commentary on the current state of Athens as it struggled with Sparta for control of Greece in the Peloponnesian War.

Led by the titular character, Lysistrata, the story's female characters barricade the public funds building and withhold sex from their husbands to end the Peloponnesian War and secure peace. In doing so, Lysistrata engages the support of women from Sparta, Boeotia, and Corinth - both sides of the war. All of the other women are first against Lysistrata's suggestion to withhold sex. Finally, they agree to swear an oath of allegiance by drinking wine from a phallic shaped flask (the traditional implement, an upturned shield, would have been a symbol of actions opposed to the aims of the women). This action is ironic and therefore comical, because Greek men believed women had no self-restraint, a lack displayed in their alleged fondness for wine as well as for sex.

The men attempt to fight the women but the women refuse to back down, and angrily tell how they were forced for so long to stay silent and listen to the stupid decisions of men. They explain that they will take over the financial affairs of the city as they handled the finances of their homes, and also explain the injustice the war does to the women: that men will have no problem finding wives but women will never get husbands if they are too old.

Like the men, the women begin to miss sex and attempt to sneak home to their husbands. Lysistrata has them stay strong and they return to the public funds building. After several days, the men begin to experience physical pain from lack of sex. They quickly settle peace negotiations between the countries. Lysistrata declares the sex feud over and allows the women to return home with their husbands."

Reference: Wikipedia.org

XXXI "...Lacemaker..."

"Lace-making is an ancient craft. True lace was not made until the late 15th and early 16th centuries. A true lace is created when a thread is looped, twisted or braided to other threads independently from a backing fabric.

Lace is an openwork fabric, patterned with open holes in the work, made by machine or by hand. The holes can be formed via removal of threads or cloth from a previously woven fabric, but more often open spaces are created as part of the lace fabric. Originally linen, silk, gold, or silver threads were used.

References to lace are made in the Bible in the Book of Exodus (Exodus 28:28, King James Version). Lace was used by clergy of the early Catholic Church as part of vestments in religious ceremonies, but did not come into widespread use until the 16th century. The popularity of lace increased rapidly and the cottage industry of lace making spread throughout Europe to most European countries. Countries like Finland (city of Rauma), Slovenia (city of Idrija), Belgium, Hungary, Ireland, Malta, Russia, Spain, Turkey and others all have their own unique artistic heritage expressed through lace."

Reference: Wikipedia.org

XXXII "... pigments used in my paintings..."

"The pasty substance know as paint consists primarily of two components: pigment and binder. Pigment is the actual coloring substance and usually is of mineral or organic origin. Some pigments, such as the all important lead white, were artificially produced as well (the Dutch were renowned for their lead-white which was fabricated with the so-called Dutch stack process). The pigment, after being separated from impurities and thoroughly cleansed usually presents itself in powdered form although

some are organic extracts. These dyes must first be fixed on a more solid, but at the same time transparent, substance such as alum or clay before they are bound with oil.

The binder is an unctuous natural drying oil. Poppy, linseed and walnut were preferred. Each oil has its own characteristics.

Painters could acquire their materials from shops specialized in artist's materials, apothecaries, sailors from abroad and even quack doctors. It should be noted that "it was quite common for painters to buy equipment outside the cities where they worked. If we examine the accounts of Crijn Hendrikszoon Volmarijn, the major dealer in painter's materials known from Dutch sources of this period, who was active in Rotterdam in the first half of the seventeenth-century , we find that he had a large number of clients from Delft." Materials could also be easily found in Utrecht and Amsterdam were great number of artists lived. However, "in the city of Delft there seems to been an accumulation of specialized knowledge of the nature, composition and application of pigments and other substances used in painting. In addition to the painters themselves, there was also a group of apothecaries and artisans (largely involved in producing Delftware) who were experienced in the production of pigments."

A deep transparent blue originally obtained from the plants cultivated in India. It was used in Europe from very early times as a dyestuff.

For example, the pigments used in "The Pearl Earring" are as follow:

1. *white lead* **(lead is very volatile and very poisonous when touched or breathed)**
2. *yellow ochre*
3. *vermilion* **(manufactured by heating mercury and sulfur. Mercury is the 3rd most deadly substance to human beings in the world, even in very tiny quantities, when touched or breathed.)**
4. *red madder*
5. *red ochre*
6. *brown ochre (raw umber?)*
7. *charcoal black*
8. *bone black*
9. *ultramarine (natural lapis lazuli)*
10. *indigo*
11. *weld"*

Reference: Essentialvermeer.com

XXXIII "...Peiter De Hoogh..."

"De Hooch was born in Rotterdam to Hendrick Hendricksz de Hooch, a bricklayer, and Annetge Pieters, a midwife. He was the eldest of five children and outlived all of his siblings. He studied art in Haarlem under the landscape painter, Nicolaes Berchem. Beginning in 1650, he worked as a painter and servant for a linen-merchant and art collector named Justus de la Grange. His service for the merchant required him to accompany him on his travels to The Hague, Leiden, and Delft, to which he eventually moved. It is likely that de Hooch handed over most of his works to la Grange during this period in exchange for board and other benefits, as this was a common commercial arrangement for painters at the time, and a later inventory recorded that la Grange possessed eleven of his paintings.

De Hooch was married in Delft in 1654 to Jannetje van der Burch, by whom he fathered seven children. While in Delft, de Hooch is also believed to have learned from the painters Carel Fabritius and Nicolaes Maes, who were both early members of the Delft School. He became a member of the painters' guild of Saint Luke in 1655, and had moved to Amsterdam by 1661.

The early work of de Hooch, like most young painters of his time, was mostly composed of scenes of soldiers in stables and taverns, though he used these to develop great skill in light, color, and perspective rather than to explore an interest in the subject matter. After starting his family in the mid-1650s, he switched his focus to domestic scenes and family portraits. His work showed astute observation of the mundane details of everyday life while also functioning as well-ordered morality tales. These paintings often exhibited a sophisticated and delicate treatment of light similar to those of Vermeer, who lived in Delft at the same time as de Hooch.

Though he began to paint for wealthier patrons in Amsterdam, he lived in the poorest areas of the city. Around this time, de Hooch's painting style became coarser and darker in color, and his simple domestic scenes were replaced by highly-decorated images set in palatial halls and country villas. Most scholars believe that de Hooch's work after around 1670 became more stylized and deteriorated in quality. It has been surmised that this was in part due to deteriorating health; de Hooch died in 1684 in an Amsterdam insane asylum, though how he came to be there is unrecorded."

Reference: Wikipedia.org

XXXIV "... our lives all of us were greatly disrupted..."

The Dutch saying from 1672 is a very accurate description of this moment in history, which is repeating itself in 2008 in the United States as I write this book:

It's people, "redeloos" (without reason), its government "radeloos" (witless) and the country itself "reddeloos" (beyond rescue).

Apparently, the very same "merchants of chaos" who caused political, economic and social devastation in Holland, as well as the rest of the world throughout history, are rampaging just as they did 330 years ago. Therefore, through the "camera obscura" of historical perspective, it should not be difficult to predict the future, as the greed and murderous activity of the self-anointed aristocracy repeats again and again, like a broken record, ad infinitum.

Vermeer might have continued to survive and feed his family long enough to see them mature and live out the extent of his own natural life. However, when the unforeseen disaster of war and economic collapse occurred, he did not have the job skills to change vocations. He did not have the desire to give up his art for the greater good of his family, and attempt to seek a livelihood in another trade. And, so, he perished in a fit of depression on a dismal December day.

If one assumes the view that spiritual beings return to inhabit new bodies, life after life, it must necessarily follow that history must repeat itself, unless something has been done to alter the behavior of people during the intervening ages.

The only proven deterrents to such destruction are education, self-awareness, social responsibility, policies based on ethical equanimity and moral discipline sufficient to curb or prevent the overt and covert destruction of one's self, fellows and environment we share with our fellow citizens of Earth.

After all, we are the beings who made our history, live in the present and mold the world for our own future selves. We are the beings who will inhabit the bodies of our own grandchildren, and great grandchildren, and so forth. Our own actions today paint the landscape we will inhabit in all of our tomorrows -- if we don't do something to change this interminable condition.

XXXV ...tulip bulbs..."

"...prices for bulbs of the newly-introduced tulip reached extraordinarily high levels and then suddenly collapsed. At the peak of tulip mania in February 1637, tulip contracts sold for more than 20 times the annual income of a skilled craftsman. It is generally

considered the first recorded speculative bubble. The term "tulip mania" is often used metaphorically to refer to any large economic bubble.

The event was popularized in 1841 by the book Extraordinary Popular Delusions and the Madness of Crowds, written by British journalist Charles Mackay. According to Mackay, at one point 12 acres (5 ha) of land were offered for a Semper Augustus bulb. Mackay claims that many such investors were ruined by the fall in prices, and Dutch commerce suffered a severe shock. Although Mackay's book is a classic that is widely reprinted today, his account is contested. Modern scholars believe that the mania was not as extraordinary as Mackay described; some suggesting that no economically meaningful bubble occurred..."

Reference: Wikipedia.org

END

**For more information about this book or other books
by Lawrence R. Spencer**

visit

http://www.lulu.com/pan

www.ingramcontent.com/pod-product-compliance
Lightning Source LLC
Chambersburg PA
CBHW030935180526
45163CB00002B/571